INVESTING IN
WHEAT, SOYBEANS, CORN

Wm Grandmill

Published by Windsor Books
P.O. Box 280
Brightwaters, N.Y. 11718

Manufactured in the United States of America

ISBN 0-930233-38-7

INVESTING IN WHEAT, SOYBEANS, CORN

TABLE OF CONTENTS

PART I

A NEW APPROACH TO TRADING WHEAT, SOYBEANS, and CORN

THE PURPOSE OF THIS BOOK

There were probably many times during your commodity trading days when you wished you had a reliable friend to whom you could turn for advice. There were also probably many times when you asked your broker such questions as, "Would this be the time to sell soybeans?" or "Do you think that March wheat is a buy?" But your broker must be cautious. If he gives you the wrong advice, he might lose you as a customer. So what do you get? You get an ambiguous answer – an answer which can be interpreted either way. Such an answer leaves you uncertain and frustrated. "Is there no one who can give a straight answer?", you ask. What you are looking for is an advisor who will say straight out that it is a good move to buy March wheat or that you should sell November soybeans or that you should stay out of the market. Such advice, if obtainable, would be worthwhile. It is to the point: it has direction: it is advice which you could act upon: there is nothing ambiguous about it. But from where is such advice forthcoming? Who or what advisor can give such an unbiased, definite answer?

This book is designed to be such an advisor. The Forecasting Graphs are designed to tell you whether you should **buy** or **sell**, or stay out of the market. As you see by the title, the book cover says, "Self Help Series – Be Your Own Advisor". That's what this book does – it helps you to become your own advisor. Now you can get instructions which do not leave you uncertain about your future course of action. The Forecasting Graphs will tell you whether to buy or sell or to stand aside.

The keys to forecasting the future price of grains in this book, are the new Forecasting Graphs, or Forecasting Charts as they are sometimes called. They were produced specifically for this book. The charts are based on the world's supply and demand for wheat, soybeans, and corn, the only reliable indicator of prices. All varieties of weather and economic conditions are incorporated into the graphs. The grain data of the past 15 years was used, and during that time there was a good variety of droughts, bumper crops, recessions, and good times. All of these conditions are in the graphs.

Another thing. There is no technical trading in this book, such as moving averages, RSI, etc. Technical trading would require you to spend about 20 minutes a day updating your charts and records. It is doubtful that you will spend 20 minutes a month by using this book. And it is a good thing, too, because most people using this book are working people who wish to relax after work, rather than spend every night on their charts.

This book will introduce you to a method of trading which is relaxed, stress free, safe and profitable. The unique Forecasting Graphs will enable you to estimate the price of wheat, soybeans, and corn months in advance, and whether you should buy or sell when the right time comes. Now you can be your own advisor.

LONG TERM TRADING VS TECHNICAL TRADING

In this book, long term trading means taking a commodity position and holding it for two to eight months. To do long term trading, one must be able to look ahead and have a forecast of what the future price of the commodity will be at a certain date in the future. Usually only the supply and demand of the grain will help you to determine the future price. In other words, long term trading is based on the fundamentals of the grain.

Technical trading, in most cases, has no interest in supply and demand, no interest in any of the underlying fundamentals of the commodity. Instead, technical trading is based on the behavior of prices and price patterns. The perfect technician is one who prefers to deal only with prices. He doesn't want any news at all. He is not interested that there is a drought in the grain growing areas. He doesn't want to know that the flow of oil from the Middle East has been disrupted. Instead he wants only a steady input of prices which he will use in one or more of the dozens of mathematical systems, such a as moving average, RSI, etc.

Which of the two trading types is the better one? There is no sure answer because the two proponents will stoutly defend his own method. The real answer may lie in the personality of the commodity trader. If you are the type of person who likes action, excitement, some danger, then technical trading is for you. It will also require you to spend time each day staying in touch with your broker and spend more time in the evening updating your charts and records.

If you are the kind of person who prefers tranquility, no tension, peaceful sleeps, and a good profit, then long term fundamental trading is for you. Also, it you are a working person who cannot get to the phone several times a day to call your broker, then you are better off in long term trading. Obviously this author prefers long term trading – that's what this book is about. It is also my opinion that the profits are greater and more certain in long term rather than in technical trading – particularly by using my new Forecasting Graphs and the year round trading method outlined in this book. Then there's the matter of safety, but more about that topic in the next chapter.

A STOP PRICE IS NOT A TRADER'S BEST PROTECTION

We can remember the days when we first ventured into commodity trading. Remember when you bought your first long position? Likely your broker suggested that you protect your self against undue loss by placing a **stop price** just below your entry price. "This way ", he would say, "You won't lose much money if prices go against you. It's like insurance". What a wonderful idea! Unfortunately the price dipped enough to touch your stop, and then rebounded. Bad luck! But there you are, out of the market, and facing one of the many crisis decisions which you will be making over the coming months. What to do, you wonder. Should you buy in again now or wait for the price to fall a bit – but, on the other hand, prices might keep rising and you will have missed your chance, and on it goes... We have all experienced those indecisive times when we have been stopped out of a position.

Stop prices cause more anxiety and problems than most people realize, not to mention a loss of money every time your stop price is touched. It doesn't take many activated stop prices before your working capital is reduced to almost zero. The grain prices, especially soybeans, are fluctuating all day long. So if you placed a stop price at about 10¢ to 15¢ from your entry price, then there is a likelihood that the stop will be touched off quickly. Then an idea! Why not place a stop price a long way from the entry price! Let's use wheat as the example. Suppose our trader thinks this way, "I am going to place a stop price at 40¢ below my entry price of my long wheat position – this way, I will be beyond the reach of those irritating price fluctuations. In fact, it will take a real genuine trend reversal to touch my stop, and I think that event is unlikely because I believe that the long term trend is up." Good thinking! This trader has really made a major improvement in his trading methods. He put $2000 (40¢) into his account and tells his broker to place a stop price at 40¢ below his entry price on his long wheat position. He intends to ride out any price fluctuations and temporary price reversals. He will now wait for prices to rise, with none of those anxious moments when he used a close-up stop price. In truth, what this trader has done is to begin long term trading tactics. He has made the right move but it can be made even better, as you will see soon.

TRADING GRAIN WITHOUT USING A STOP PRICE

This chapter will put forth the suggestion that you should not use a stop price at all when trading wheat, corn, and soybeans. Instead, you should back up your grain position with enough extra money so that you can ride out any unexpected price reversal, or you can use an option (more about options later).

If you are convinced that you should take a long wheat position, for example, (and this is the purpose of the Forecasting Graphs in this book, which is to tell you whether you should be buying wheat or whether you should be selling wheat) then you should have the courage to stick with your long position through temporary price declines – and they happen in every trade. This is done by depositing into your commodity account sufficient extra money to protect your trade. How much is "sufficient extra money"? It will be explained later on how to determine the amount needed.

This book promotes stress-free profitable trading and that is what you get when you trade long term, without using a stop price. The profits are good. When you make a wheat investment, for example, on a year round basis (by investment is meant the amount of extra backup money which you put into your commodity account to protect your grain position) you should think of the wheat investment in the same perspective as an investment in a good stock – that is, you put up a considerable amount of money to buy the stock, you are in it for the long term, and you expect that prices will go against you sometimes but you expect a profit in the long term. The big difference between investing in wheat and investing in a good stock, is that the grain investment is much more profitable, and yet it can be just as safe as a stock in the DJIA.

Once again, stop orders cause more harm than good, in this author's opinion. Extra back up money or an option is a superior method of trading. **But, is there a place for at all for a stop price?** Yes, there is a place – and that is for protecting a profit in an uncertain market. **Here's an example:** Suppose the December Forecasting Chart indicated that Dec wheat would reach $4.20. And suppose that by the end of October,

Dec. wheat reached that objective of $4.20. But you think that there is still some strength left in the market. Therefore, instead of liquidating your long position, you place a stop order with your broker to sell Dec. wheat at $4.10, in this example. This way, if there is still some upward price strength remaining, you will benefit from it. On the other hand, if prices weaken you will be stopped out at $4.10 with a profit. This is a good example of the proper use for a stop price.

INVESTMENT IN GRAIN

You saw the title of this book, "Investing In Wheat, Soybeans, Corn". At first glance you may have thought that the word "Investing" is just a fancy word for "Trading In Wheat, Soybeans Corn". No, it is not. The true meaning of "investing" is meant here - a sum of money invested for a long period of time. ***In this book the period of time is 1 year, and the sum invested is the amount of backup capital or the cost of an option if you choose to use an option.***

Think about this. Suppose you bought a good stock from the Dow 30 at $40 per share. You pay out $4000 for 100 shares, and you sit back and wait - figuring that the share price should double over the next few years. You know that prices do not rise in a straight line, and there will be times of temporary price reversals. But such a thought does not worry you because you are in this for the long term. You are confident that prices will rise eventually.

Let's say that at the end of 4 years the share price had doubled and you took your 100% profit. You would be justified in congratulating yourself because you would likely have beaten the Dow's rise by a wide margin.

But how would your $4000 have fared in a grain investment? You would likely have done much better. Using wheat as an example, based on the wheat prices of the past 15 years and based on the use of the Wheat forecasting Graphs in this book, you would have earned about 100% ***every year.***

But what about safety? Surely a Dow 30 stock is much safer and the profit more certain than trading in wheat - everyone knows that commodities are notorious for their losses. The answer is: it's not necessarily so. Over the years several of the Dow 30 stocks have lost money and some have been dropped from that select group. And as far as the grain commodities are concerned, the new Forecasting Graphs in this book are the tools which will give you a trading edge. These new unique Forecasting Graphs will change your whole attitude to trading in wheat, soybeans, and corn. Later you will learn how the Forecasting Graphs were made and how to use them.

SUPPLY AND DEMAND DETERMINE
LONG TERM PRICES

The SUPPLY of grain is more important than the DEMAND, in determining grain prices. Why? Because the global demand is constant - the 5 billion people on this

4

planet consume a constant average amount of grain and the total demand only rises because the world population is increasing.

The grain supply, on the other hand, is critical to prices. Suppose there was a world wide drought and the world grain supply was cut in half. What would happen? Well, the constant world demand for grain would still be there because people and livestock still have to eat but there would not be enough grain available for all. Consequently, grain would have to be rationed. How is rationing done? For grains, it is done by raising prices, and continuing to raise them until the demand slackens off and a balance has been reached between demand and supply. In this fictitious example, prices would have to go very high indeed. In real life, a 10% decrease in world supply is enough to send wheat prices, for example, to near $5. To sum up: even though supply and demand work together, the one to watch closely is the supply because supply will affect prices more than demand will affect prices.

The grain supply affects prices only over the long term, not for the short term. For example, if you were in the corn market, expecting to make a quick profit over the next 10 days, then the corn supply would not affect the outcome at all. but if you were in the market for 6 months, then the corn supply would be the dominating factor.

One of the principles of this book is: **the supply of a particular grain will determine its price over the long term.**

HOW TO EXPRESS A GRAIN'S SUPPLY

In this book, wheat, soybeans and corn are all referred to as "grains". But in the true sense of the word, soybeans are not a grain. Because soybeans are traded in Chicago along with the other grains, this book has taken the liberty of referring to all of them as "the grain trade".

There are 3 ways to express the amount of grain available: (1) **crop production**, which is the size of the crop at harvest (2) **total supply,** which consists of the crop size plus the amount of grain which was left over from the previous crop year (3) **the carryover**, which is the amount of grain left over at the end of the current crop year after all the sales have been made.

Of the 3 ways listed above, **the carryover** is the most important indicator of prices. Why is it the most important indicator? Because it can tell you in an instant whether a particular grain's supply is scarce or plentiful. A scarce supply means higher prices ahead: a plentiful supply means low or moderate prices ahead. To use an extreme example, if wheat's carryover was 0 bushels, prices would rise through the roof. But if the carryover was 2500 million bu., then a farmer would lose money because the price which he would get for his wheat would not be enough to pay the costs of growing it.

Now that we have narrowed down **the carryover as being the main price determinant,** we can still further refine the carryover number to make it more meaningful. Here is what is meant. Suppose one learned that the wheat carryover was 500 million bu. for the current crop year. If a trader who had not traded wheat before saw that number of 500 m. bu., he would not know if that was a lot of wheat left over, or whether it was a small amount. But if someone told this new wheat trader that the U.S. usually sells and uses about 2000 million bu. every year, then he could conclude that the 500 m.b. represented a tight supply remaining - which means that prices could be higher than average later in the year.

By comparing the **carryover** to the **total use** (which is the amount of the particular grain which is used as food, feed, seed plus the amount of the grain which is exported) one can get a good idea whether the carryover represents a tight supply or a surplus. And this comparison is best done by using percent; by showing **the carryover as a percentage of the total use.** Using the wheat example in the paragraph above, the carryover was 500 m. bu. and the total use was 2000 m. bu. To get the % number: 500 divided by 2000 multiplied by 100 = 25%, the carryover is 25% of the total use. This represents a tight supply because the average wheat carryover for the past 15 years was about 48%. Therefore a 25% carryover would indicate that above average prices were ahead.

A % carryover number also tells us how long the carryover would last in case of a crop failure. Thus, the 25% carryover from the wheat example in the last paragraph indicates that there is only a 3 months supply of wheat on hand (25% of 12 months = 3 months). That's not much wheat on hand. The largest wheat carryover since 1972 was 97% which represented a big surplus - and wheat prices fell to as low as $2.60 that crop year. The tightest wheat carryover was 17% in the crop year 73/74 and prices came close to $6 then. **From this information you can see that the size of the carryover gives a hint of future prices**. If 97% carryover for wheat, in the examples above, represented the lowest price and if the 17% wheat carryover represented the highest price, then theoretically the percentage gradations between the two would also represent gradations in prices between the lowest and the highest prices.

THE CONCEPT OF *THE RIGHT PRICE*

Most things for sale have a **"right price"**. Any supermarket shopper knows when the price of an item is too high, and so will not buy it. Also the shopper knows when an item's price is lower than usual and so it represents a bargain to be snapped up. The same idea applies to the price of grain - foreign buyers know when the price is right. If one exporting country is asking too much for its grain, then the buyer will turn to a different exporter for the grain. **Then what, in the international grain trade, determines what an importing country is willing to pay?** What single factor is the most important in determining the international price? The answer is: **the total supply available of that particular grain.** An importing country is willing to pay more for a particular grain when it becomes evident that the harvest is below normal and that the grain will become scarce. If the U.S. soybean harvest, for example, was below average, foreign buyers would try to buy the soybeans early in order to beat the higher prices which will inevitably follow. That's why prices peak early in a tight market - one buyer is trying to get his full share before a competitor does the same. Thus the highest price for May soybeans would likely occur in October in a tight soybean market, as importers rush to buy at harvest time. The reverse is true in a plentiful market which has a large carryover. In this case, importers would be in no hurry to buy and would wait as exporters gradually lowered prices to attract buyers. From this you can see that prices will rise in a time of low % carryover until the price matches the demand. In other words, the *right price* is reached when the supply, price, and demand balance out.

You will remember from the wheat example a page or so back, that a 17% carryover meant a tight supply of wheat which pushed prices to near $6 and that a 97% carryover meant a big surplus which brought prices down to near $2.60. What this book attempts to do is to correlate the size of the carryover % with a certain price level. A careful study of the relationship between the carryover % for each grain and its price was done, going all the way back to the crop year 1973/74, with the objective of finding the *right price* for each % carryover, for each grain, for each contract month. Then this information had to be presented in an easy-to-use form.

THE FORECASTING GRAPHS AND HOW THEY WERE MADE

For years this author believed that one should be able to get a good long-term estimate of future grain prices in the upcoming crop year by using the carryover % as a price indicator. Everyone knows that prices rise when the grain is scarce and that prices fall when there is a grain surplus. Therefore, between those two extremes there must be some sort of price gradation.

It may be hard to understand how one can arrive at the *right price* for soybeans, for example, when soybean prices are bouncing all over the place in the summer, fed by weather rumors. But when the soybean harvest begins, weather is not a worry any longer so those wild speculative price moves gradually die down and soybeans will settle near the *right price* as determined by the size of the estimated carryover %. Soybeans are rated as one of the most speculative of all commodities and prone to rumors of all kinds. Soybeans are particularly difficult to trade from June to the end of August because of the threat of adverse weather. False rumors shake the market every week and prices react accordingly. But this author believes that this book has made some sense of soybean trading and maybe this wild market has finally been tamed.

The Forecasting Graphs are based on actual prices of each of wheat, corn, and soybeans all the way back to 1973. Why stop at 1973? Because in that year an event occurred which changed the pricing structure for grains worldwide, for all time. A world wide grain shortage occurred caused mainly by dry weather abroad. Up until 1973 grain prices dawdled along at a steady pace. Soybean s traded usually about $3 to $3.50 per bushel, for example. Corn was about $1.50 per bu. During early 1973, the U.S. market ambled along seemingly unaware of the situation abroad. And then in the summer the hordes descended upon the United States, the breadbasket of the world, and bought every grain they could get their hands on. Suddenly there was a scarcity of grain in the U.S. Russia entered the U.S. market for the first time and bought its grain before the prices went through the roof - thus revealing for the first time that Russia was unable to feed itself. Prices soared. Just to show how rapid was the price rise - on Jan 1st 1973 soybeans were priced at about $3.50 and by July 1973 the price was getting near $12, a record which has not been touched since then. This, *a new pricing era began in 1973* and we have never hone back since then to the old days. Therefore the research did not use data from before 1973 because it would have been unrealistically low and would have distorted the calculations.

Starting with the crop year 1973/74, all the carryover % were compared to the prices of wheat, soybeans, and corn - for each of their contract months. The objective was to find the **right price** for each of the grains, for each contract month. It was discovered, as you probably already knew, that the "right price" is not an exact number. For example, a 50% carryover for wheat might, at various times and in different crop years, give a "right price" for Dec. wheat on Dec. 1st as a set of prices ranging from say $3.61 to $3.80. Therefore an average would be taken so that there would be only one "right price" for Dec wheat with a 50% carryover. In this example the "right price" was $3.70 which you can see on the Dec. wheat Forecasting Graph. Because the Forecasting Graphs are made from averages they are not 100% precise. But they are accurate enough for our purposes. The forecasting Graphs point out the direction of the market - they tell you whether you should buy or sell, as you will later learn.

Here is an interesting example. Everyone knows that wheat prices are lowest at harvest time and highest in the winter. Agreed? So to make money, all one has to do is to buy March wheat in July or August and sell it on March 1st for a handsome profit. Right? Alas, it doesn't work out that way in real life. A trader who followed that method would have been wrong more than half of the time. The Forecasting Graphs tell a different story. A test of that 15 year period by using the Forecasting Graphs revealed the following: by using the graphs, a trader would have **bought** wheat for only 6 of those 15 years, he would have **sold** wheat for 8 of those 15 years, and he would have been advised to stay out of the market for 1 of those years becarse there was not enough profit to make the trade worthwhile. Then a **further analysis** was done of those 8 years when the graphs recommended **to sell wheat** in July or August - to see whether it was the right decision. The analysis revealed that those 8 years would have made an average profit of 56¢ ($2800) within a 6 or 7 month period. The Forecasting Graphs point the direction to go - to buy or to sell.

THE USDA CROP REPORTS

The USDA issues a monthly crop report **which is vital to the successful use of this book.** The monthly crop reports will contain such information as: the estimated planted acres, the estimated yield, crop size, exports, and the carryover for the crop year coming up. The reports are issued about the 11th of each month. Be sure to get this report from your broker or direct from the USDA.

As each month progresses through the growing season, the crop report becomes increasingly more accurate. For example, the April crop report is lacking in accuracy because the corn and soybeans have not been planted yet, so you might get only the planting intentions. But the May report has the estimated planted acres and maybe an estimated yield. By the time the August report comes out, there is plenty of reasonably accurate information to work on. **You can put the Forecasting Graphs to good use from the May report** right on through the rest of the year.

Going back to the April report. It was mentioned that there is little information about corn or soybeans in it. However, wheat is an exception because the winter wheat was planted in the previous fall, and by April there is positive information on winter wheat which you can use with the wheat Forecasting Graphs. Winter wheat dominates the U.S. wheat market because about 70% of all wheat grown in the U.S. is winter wheat. Therefore by using the information in the April and May crop reports in conjunction with the wheat Forecasting Graphs, you can get a good estimate of the prices for July wheat and December wheat, and act according to the graphs.

A few words here in praise of the USDA. This is without doubt the best source of agricultural information in the world. No other organization comes close. Because of their good work, we have the best information at hand, and it is constantly being updated. But best of all is the way that information is disseminated so that everyone has an equal opportunity to get it immediately. The crop report is issued after the market closes for the day, usually about the 10th, 11th, or 12th of each month. Get it from you broker or you can get it directly from the USDA.

WHERE TO GET THE GRAIN DATA

This is the best book for Wheat. The USDA publishes two books which will give you the information you need. One is called **"WHEAT - Situation and Outlook Report"** which is published 4 times a year. It is only $10 a year which is a bargain. The contents include data on wheat supplies both in the United States and all other grain exporters and importers in the world. In other words you get the U.S. supply and demand as well as the World supply and demand. The U.S. data is in great detail. **Eveything you need to trade wheat is in this publication.**

To subscribe to **"Wheat - Situation and Outlook Report"** you may phone a toll free number which is 1-800-999-6779. Or you can write to: U.S. Dept. of Agriculture, 1301 New York Ave. N.W., Washington, D.C. 20005-4788.

This is the book for Corn and Soybeans (It also has U.S. and World wheat data but in much less detail then the wheat book mentioned above, but it is useful data.) This publication is titled **"World Agricultural Supply and Demand Estimates"**. It has both the U.S. and the World supply and demand for corn, soybeans, wheat, oats. This publication is mailed to you every month. The price is $18 per year which is a bargain. **Everything you need to trade corn and soybeans (and wheat and oats) is in this book.**

To subscribe to **"World Agricultural Supply and Demand"** you may send your check to: Superintendent of Documents, U.S. Government Printing Office, Washington, D.C. 20402 - 9372. Make the check payable to the Superintendent of Documents ($18 to a U.S. address, $22.50 foreign).

If you have a computer. The World Agricultural Supply and Demand Estimates, as well as the monthly reports and other USDA reports can be accessed electronically on the day of release. For details, phone (202) 447-5505.

Use your broker. If you pay a full service commission, then you are entitled to get information from your broker to facilitate a trade. If you broker does not have it, ask him to get it from the head office of the brokerage house which will have a research department with all the grain data on file.

USING OPTIONS

You will recall that one of the basic principles of **"Investing In Wheat, Soybeans and Corn"** is that one should avoid using a stop price (except to protect a profit already earned). Instead, one should back up his long or short future's position with sufficient money to ride out any temporary price reversal. *Or, instead of using backup money, one could use an option.* That's what this chapter is about - using options.

The use of options is particularly applicable to soybean trading because soybeans are the most erratic of the 3 grains described in this book. Just to give you an idea of how volatile soybean trading is, the following will illustrate it: when experienced commodity traders get together over a cup of coffee, inevitably the conversation gets around to the wild markets which they have traded in the past. A few commodities will be mentioned frequently in that group, but likely the commodity most frequently mentioned is soybeans. Soybeans are considered to be one of the most speculative of all commodities. What makes the soybean market so volatile? Because it is prone to rumors of all kinds, especially weather rumors. Weather rumors run rampant during the 3 month period of June, July and August - many of them false. But false or not, the rumors send soybean prices up and down by about 20¢ to 30¢ every week almost, causing havoc by setting off stop prices along the way.

But that wild soybean market has been tamed! The Soybean Forecasting Graphs, assisted by backup capital or an option, have done the job as you will see when you read the section on **"Investing in Soybeans"**.

Don't hesitate to use options. They are simple and easy to do. Even if you have never taken an option position, you will find it easy after you read the information below titled "Option Trading Basics". Also, the options used in this book are the simple, straight forward type: which are, *buying a call and buying a put.* Nothing could be easier! You will be further assisted by *Grandmill's new option graph* - one of which is included with each of the 3 grains, wheat, soybeans, and corn.

OPTION TRADING BASICS

Compared to futures, how are options different?

Even though you may be new to option trading, it is likely that you are experienced in trading futures. Now you want to try your hand in options because you are seeking more security and safety than you had in futures trading. You have heard that options are safer – none of those unpleasant limit moves against you which you experienced in futures when things went wrong. You heard correctly. There are no limit up or limit down price moves in options. You are in a safer form of trading.

The reason why I expected you to have traded in futures already, is that options are the next logical step after futures. Option prices, you see, are based on the price of the underlying future e.g. the price (premium) of a November soybean call would depend on the price on Nov. soybeans. That means that the future's price is the basis of the option's price. In other words, the future's price is the most important factor in option trading. All option prices are dependent upon the futures' prices. But it is safer to be in options than in futures as you will see later.

When you traded futures, you gave your broker an order to **buy** a contract when you expected prices to rise, and you gave him an order to **sell** a future's contract when you expected prices to fall. You use the same words in options: "buy or sell". The word "buy" has almost the same meaning in options as it has in futures, but the word "sell" has a different connotation. This difference will be explained later. But, first, let's become familiar with option terminology.

Two kinds of options

There are 2 distinct kinds of options: a **call** option and a **put** option. They are opposites, like up and down. Think of the call as belonging to the "up", and the put as belonging to the "down".

Know the trend

You should never take an option or a future's position without some hint or reason why prices will move in the direction you desire. Otherwise, you are guessing and there is no place for guessing in either option or futures trading. What, then, should a new trader do, to find the price trend?

The answer, of course, is to use the Forecasting Graphs. The graphs will tell you whether the price of the grain is likely to rise or to fall. Once you know the price trend, then you can buy your option after you consult the option graph. This new option graph is designed to tell you whether an option is worthwhile taking.

Buying a call

You "buy a call" when you believe that the underlying future's price is rising or is about to rise. If the Forecasting Graph indicates that the future's price will rise in the months ahead, and if the option graph indicates that the option is worth taking, then you phone your broker to buy an at-the-money call (an at-the-money call is a call which is as close to the underlying future's price as you can get – for example, if Nov. soybeans are at $6, then you would buy a $6 Nov. soybean call).

11

Buying a put

You "buy a put" when you believe that the underlying future's price is falling or about to fall. If the Forecasting Graph indicates that the future's price will fall in the months ahead, and if the option graph indicates that the option is worth taking, then you phone your broker to buy an at-the-money put.

Remember, in this book, there are only 2 kinds of options to buy. You either buy a call or you buy a put. You buy a call to profit from rising prices. But all this will be carefully explained again in the sections which deal with each grain individually.

When you traded futures you were required to deposit margin money into your acocunt. But that is not the case with options. No margin money is needed when you buy a call or buy a put. It is like buying an article at the market – you pay the price for it and it is yours – end of transaction.

Therefore, when you buy a call, for example, you pay the price, and the call is yours. No more money is required – not even if prices go against you. In future's, remember, you sometimes were asked by your broker to deposit more money into your account if prices went against you. But not when you buy a call or buy a put – you pay the price for it and it is yours.

In other words, the most money you can lose when you buy a call or a put is the premium (option price) which you paid for it. You will never be asked for more. By the way, in this book the words "option price" and "option premium" and "option value" have the same meaning. Sometimes one is used, sometimes another.

PART II

INVESTING IN
WHEAT

WHEAT PRICES HAVE ECONOMIC LIMITS

There is a price level below which wheat prices will not fall. Think about that statement. It says that there is a floor price, a rock-bottom price for wheat which will not be penetrated.

At this date (1989) the bottom limit is $2.30. About nine years age, the bottom limit was $2.10. About 9 years from now the bottom limit will be about $2.60.

Where do these limits come from? From past wheat history. Even with huge wheat surpluses around the world, and even with a couple of recessions, wheat prices still did not penetrate those floor prices mentioned above. For example, between 1985 and 1987, the United States had its greatest wheat surplus ever with a 97% carryover (almost a full year's supply of wheat left over at the end of the crop year), but even that enormous burden did not push prices below $2.40 per bu. So this book is saying that the floor price at this time is $2.30, a bit below what actually occurred just to be on the safe side.

Wheat touched its 9 year cyclic low of $2.40 at the end of the harvest time in 1986. In about 9 years, about 1995, another cyclic low is due. But it will be a higher low, probably about $2.60 or $2.70. Why will it be higher than in 1986? Because of inflation and increased farming costs. The cost of producing a bushel of wheat will be greater in 1995.

The numbers in the paragraphs above were reality – the way it happened. But let's look at it from an economic point of view. First, it costs over $3 to grow a bushel of wheat, and much higher in some areas. No farmer wants to lose money. So when prices fall to $2.80, for example, a farmer will withdraw into the protection of one or more of the many government programs available to him – like the loan program So the wheat which goes into a government program is off the market for several months, usually. In theory this will cause a scarcity of "free wheat" (wheat not under a govt. program) and prices will stabilize and maybe rise.

Another thing. The size of the carryover determines how low prices will fall at harvest. Our largest carryover to date was 97%, resulting in a low of $2.40. At the other extreme, a carryover of 25% is bullish and the lowest price for that crop year would likely be about $3.50. So now we have named two things which influence the low price of wheat – the growing costs, and the size of the carryover.

How can we use this information to our benefit? Here is a practical example. Let's say that the U.S. carryover is 50% (which, by the way, is about the average U.S.

carryover for the last 15 years). Let's also say that the Dec. wheat price at harvest time is $2.90. This is a great chance to go long Dec. wheat.

But first, let's put up enough money to protect our long position all the way down to $2.30, the floor price, the price below which the wheat price is not likely to fall. Therefore, $2.90 - $2.30 = 60¢. If we deposit 60¢ ($3000) with our broker, in addition to the required margin, then we can sit back and wait for a profit. There is no way the price will come close to $2.30 with a 50% carryover. It would take a 100% U.S. carryover to get close to $2.30. It is a safe, stress-free investment. According to the Dec. Forecasting Graph, the Dec. Wheat price on Dec. 1st should be about $3.68 for this particular example. This wheat trade is as safe as good stock. No stop price was used.

Look upon the $3000 backup money in this example as the investment – just as you would look upon the cost of 100 shares in a good stock as the investment. The term for investment in wheat is one year, from harvest to harvest. A wheat investment gives a much better return on your money than a stock does.

At this point you may say, "OK, I'm convinced. I can see that **buying** wheat is safe if I use sufficient backup capital. But what about **selling** wheat? If I sell wheat and if the price keeps on rising, then it seems to me that there is no ceiling price to stop the rise. It looks as if the sky's the limit".

Good point! There is truth in that statement and that problem must be faced head-on because this book's year round investment plan entails both buying and selling.

First, there is an economic barrier to rising prices but it is not as clear cut as it is for falling prices which use the $2.30 price level. Here is an example. The average U.S. carryover for the past 15 years has been about 50% which had an average high December wheat price of close to $3.70. Let's use an average year in our example. The question is, "Why should the wheat price stop rising near $3.70 – why doesn't it keep in going up and, past $6, past $7, past $20?" The answer is; no one will pay $6 for a bushel of wheat with so much for sale around the world (a 50% carryover shows there is a fair size surplus of wheat on the market). In fact the consumers of the world figured that $3.70 was as high as they would go, in this example.

In the example above, it was supply which determined how high the wheat price would go. And supply is best illustrated by using the carryover as%. To give you a better perspective, a 90% carryover would bring a high price of about $3.40 – whereas a 20% carryover would suggest a high price of about $4.80 because a 20% carryover indicated that wheat is in short supply. You can see now that there are limits to how high the price of wheat might go, and the limits are determined by supply and demand. To sum up, the top price limits are determined by the size of the carryover % which in turn reflects the amount of wheat available on the world market.

HOW TO FIND THE AMOUNT OF BACKUP CAPITAL

How much money is needed as backup capital so that one can trade wheat safely without using a stop price? It is easy to calculate if one is **buying** wheat because one can use enough money to protect the long wheat trade all the way down to the $2.30 level. But usually that much money is not needed – often less money will do the job.

Below are the reduced versions of two charts. The full size charts are at the back of the book. One graph is used when you are **buying** wheat, and the other graph is used when you are **selling** wheat.

Note: the title says, The **Maximum Amount** Of Backup Capital Needed. That means that the answer which you get from the chart will likely cover any worst case situation which may arise. You will understand what is meant when you see how the charts were made. Here is how they were constructed.

Using the past 15 years of wheat prices, simulated wheat positions were taken to determine how much backup capital was needed to trade safely without using a stop price. Both buying and selling were done at various price levels – and at various carryover %. The results were brought together in the form of two easy to read graphs – one to use when buying wheat and one to use when selling wheat. Only the worst numbers were used in the graphs – by that is meant that if, for example, three similar wheat buys were made at $3.40, all at 60% carryover, and if the needed backup capital amounts were $2000, $2500, $3000 – then the $3000 amount would be the number used for the graph. This way, you will find the estimated **maximum amount** of backup capital when you use the charts.

Below, you see the graph which you will use when **buying wheat.** Look at the graph. On the left side is the amount of the of the U.S. carryover % for the crop year which you are in. Along the bottom line are the various wheat prices at the time when you take the long position. **Example:** Let's say that you intend to take a Dec. wheat position. By consulting the Forecasting Graphs, you find that this is the time to **buy** Dec. wheat. Let's also say that the carryover % is 46% for the present crop year. You look in the newspaper at yesterday's closing wheat prices and you see that Dec. wheat closed at $3.20. How much maximum backup capital will you need to trade safely, in addition to the required margin? (1) look along the bottom row to locate $3.20. (2) move vertically upward until you intercept the 46% line. (3) look at the slanting lines and you will see that you are right on the $1000 line. (4) the answer of $1000 means that a backup of $1000 would have been sufficient for any one of the past 15 years used in the data, at a carryover of 46%, when you bought wheat at $3.20 **as indicated by the Forecasting Graphs.** Soon you will be learning about the Forecasting Graphs.

BUYING WHEAT

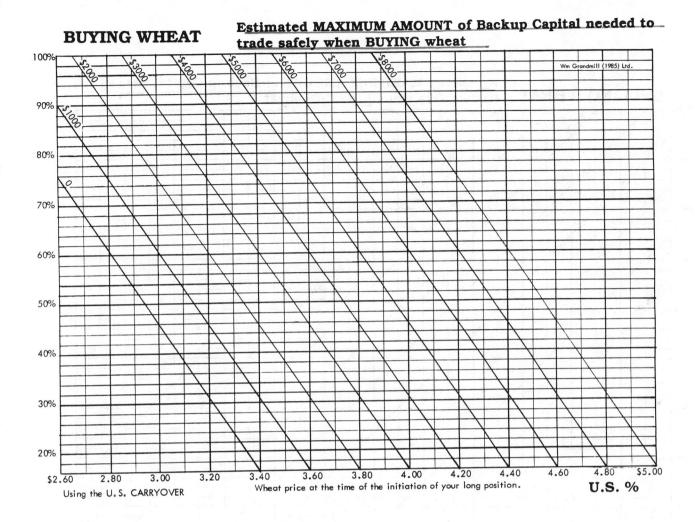

Using the U.S. CARRYOVER   Wheat price at the time of the initiation of your long position.   **U.S. %**

Below, is the chart for **selling wheat.** **Example:** you wish to take a May position. You consult the May Forecasting Graph (which you will soon learn how to use) and it tells you to **sell** May wheat (the graph tells you whether to buy or sell). Here are the steps in the operation and follow the steps in the chart above. (1) Let's say that the U.S. carryover for the current crop year is 40%. (2) You look in your morning newspaper and see that May wheat closed yesterday at $4.00. (3) Look along the bottom row of the chart above to locate $4.00, and then go vertically up to intersect the 40% line. (4) Look at the slanting lines and you will see that you are at the $3500 point. (5) This means that $3500 was the **maximum** amount of backup money needed in any one of the past 15 years, when selling wheat at $4.00 and at $40%.

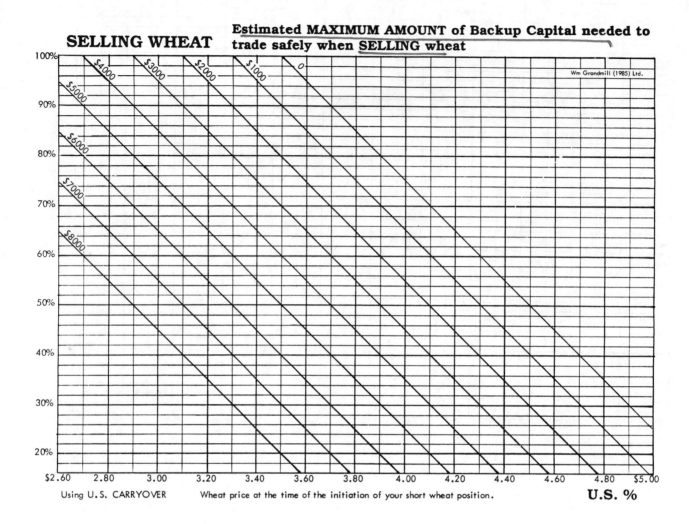

SELLING WHEAT **Estimated MAXIMUM AMOUNT of Backup Capital needed to trade safely when SELLING wheat**

Using U.S. CARRYOVER   Wheat price at the time of the initiation of your short wheat position.   **U.S. %**

Wm Grandmill (1985) Ltd.

Here is one for you to do – it has an important point to it. *Do this:* find the amount of backup capital needed sell May wheat if the U.S. carryover is 20% and May's present price is $3.50. Did you get an answer? Some surprise, isn't it! $8000! You will say, "No way would I put up that much money." And quite right, too. But this particular example would never happen because the Forecasting Graph would have told you to buy May wheat, not to sell it. Second, a 20% carryover is very bullish and prices would rise, not fall. This example was deliberately chosen to bring out the point that the Forecasting Graphs will indicate where the profits are, whether to buy or sell.

There are 6 charts at the back of the book, a buy chart and a sell chart for each of the 3 kinds of carryovers: the U.S. carryover, the World carryover, the Combination carryover. All will be explained soon.

ANOTHER WAY OF FINDING THE AMOUNT OF BACKUP CAPITAL NEEDED

Here is a different approach to finding the amount backup money needed to invest safely without using a stop price. The graphs are on the following pages.

These graphs will likely indicate more money for the backup than the graphs on the previous pages had indicated. You may think that the graphs overstate the amount of money needed to trade safely. No, such is not the case. The graphs are based on prices as they actually occurred.It is likely true that the backup graphs indicate more money than you have used in the past. **But *keep this fact in mind: this is an investment, not a speculation.*** Therefore, look upon it as an investment. It is designed to be as safe as a Blue Chip stock. You probably wouldn't hesitate to put up $4000 for 100 shares of a Blue Chip stock. The same principle applies here. The main difference being that a grain investment will give you a better percentage return on your money.

Be safe by using the amount indicated by the graphs. What if one type of graph indicates a larger amount of backup than the other type? This book suggests that you use the larger amount. Err on the side of safety. You may be concerned that you will have a large amount of money lying idle in your commodity account as a result of using a large amount of backup. It's not really being idle because it will be earning a good percentage return over a year's time. One other alternative is to do this: (1) use both types of graphs to find the largest amount of money needed (2) put half of the estimated backup amount into your commodity account and put the other half into a liquid financial instrument such as a T-bill. This way, if you need money quickly, it is no problem getting the money into your commodity account.

The following wheat backup graphs were made using only the lowest of all the low prices and only the highest of all the highest prices, as the prices occurred since 1973. For example, if the lows for a 40% carryover $2.80, $2.70, $2.90, $2.65, then $2.65 would be the number used to make the graph. But you may say,"If the price fell to $2.65 before, it can do it again." Agreed- but you also have margin money in your account - so you are protected beyond the lowest of the low prices. Look the following graphs over. You will see example of their use on the graphs.

SUMMARY

This section has attempted to impress upon you the ease and profitability of long term, stress free, wheat investing. It is similar to trading a good stock in that it is long term and safe. The main difference between the two is that wheat investing is more profitable.

This book also makes the point that a stop price order is a source of anxiety and often it is a money losing tactic. Instead, this book recommends that sufficient backup capital be used instead of a stop price. If a wheat position is worth taking in the first place, then it is worth protecting with extra capital.

HOW MUCH BACKUP MONEY IS NEEDED TO INVEST IN WHEAT?

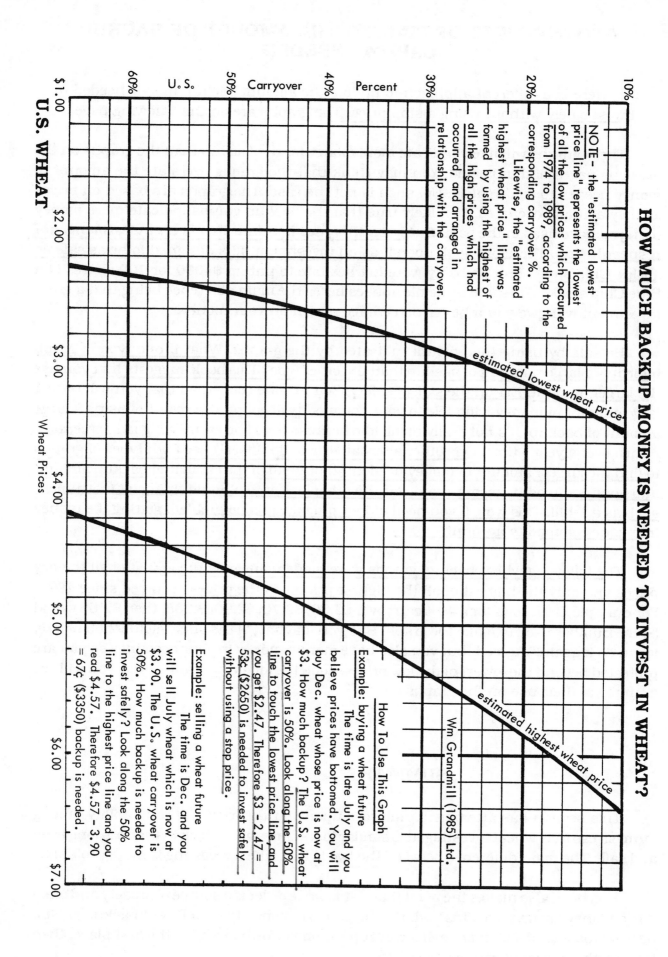

U.S. WHEAT

NOTE - the "estimated lowest price line" represents the lowest of all the low prices which occurred from 1974 to 1989, according to the corresponding carryover %.

Likewise, the "estimated highest wheat price" line was formed by using the highest of all the high prices which had occurred, and arranged in relationship with the carryover.

estimated lowest wheat price

estimated highest wheat price

Wm Grandmill (1985) Ltd.

How To Use This Graph

Example: buying a wheat future

The time is late July and you believe prices have bottomed. You will buy Dec. wheat whose price is now at $3. How much backup? The U.S. wheat carryover is 50%. Look along the 50% line to touch the lowest price line, and you get $2.47. Therefore $3 - 2.47 = 53¢ ($2650) is needed to invest safely without using a stop price.

Example: selling a wheat future

The time is Dec. and you will sell July wheat which is now at $3.90. The U.S. wheat carryover is 50%. How much backup is needed to invest safely? Look along the 50% line to the highest price line and you read $4.57. Therefore $4.57 - 3.90 = 67¢ ($3350) backup is needed.

21

HOW MUCH BACKUP MONEY IS NEEDED TO INVEST IN WHEAT?

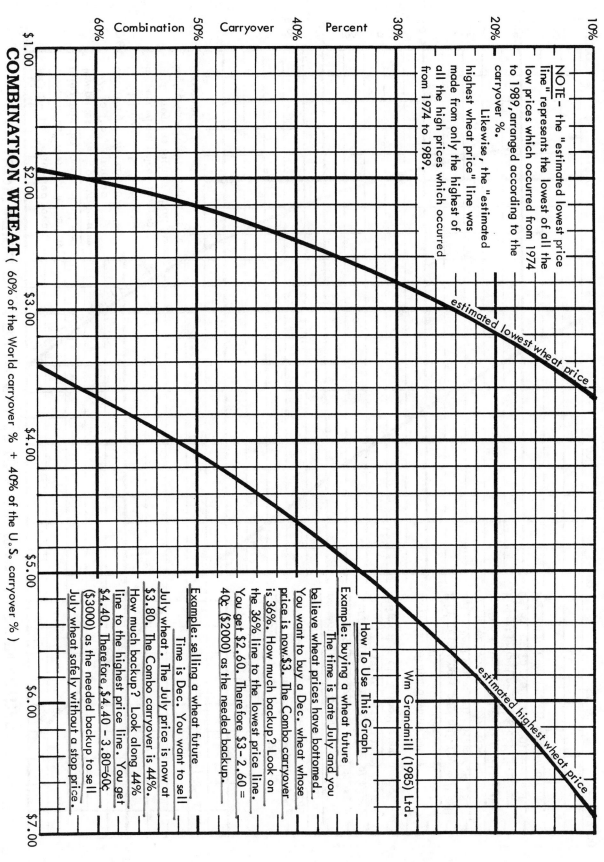

NOTE- the "estimated lowest price line" represents the lowest of all the low prices which occurred from 1974 to 1989, arranged according to the carryover %.

Likewise, the "estimated highest wheat price" line was made from only the highest of all the high prices which occurred from 1974 to 1989.

estimated lowest wheat price

estimated highest wheat price

How To Use This Graph

Wm Grandmill (1985) Ltd.

Example: buying a wheat future
The time is Late July and you believe wheat prices have bottomed. You want to buy a Dec. wheat whose price is now $3. The Combo carryover is 36%. How much backup? Look on the 36% line to the lowest price line. You get $2.60. Therefore $3 - 2.60 = 40¢ ($2000) as the needed backup.

Example: selling a wheat future
Time is Dec. You want to sell July wheat. The July price is now at $3.80. The Combo carryover is 44%. How much backup? Look along 44% line to the highest price line. You get $4.40. Therefore, $4.40 - 3.80=60¢ ($3000) as the needed backup to sell July wheat safely without a stop price.

COMBINATION WHEAT (60% of the World carryover % + 40% of the U.S. carryover %)

Combination Carryover Percent

10%
20%
30%
40%
50%
60%

$1.00
$2.00
$3.00
$4.00
$5.00
$6.00
$7.00

HOW MUCH BACKUP MONEY IS NEEDED TO INVEST IN WHEAT?

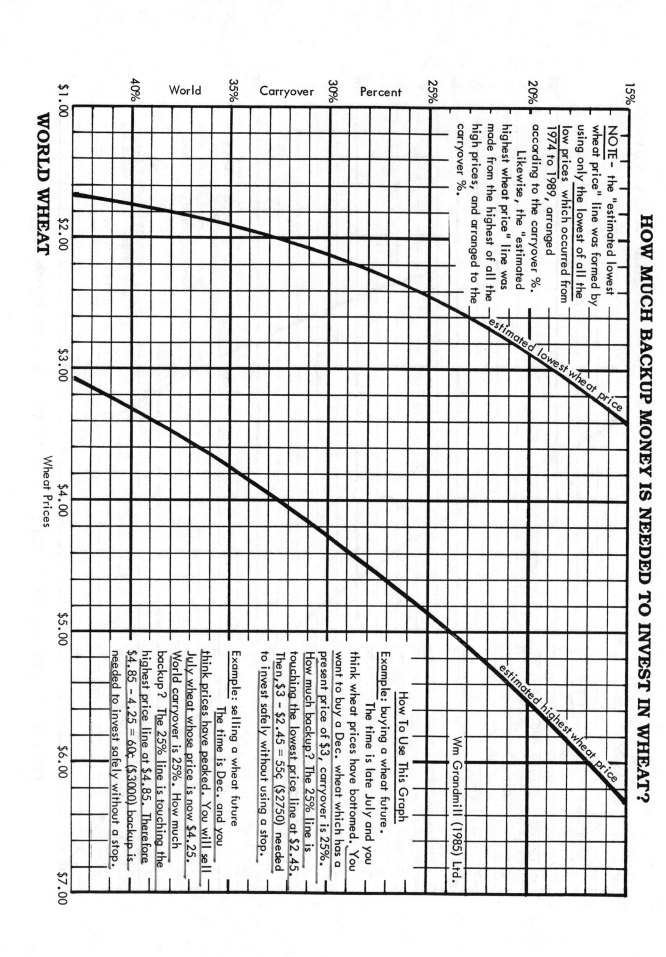

WORLD WHEAT

Wheat Prices

World Carryover Percent

NOTE - the "estimated lowest wheat price" line was formed by using only the lowest of all the low prices which occurred from 1974 to 1989, arranged according to the carryover %.

Likewise, the "estimated highest wheat price" line was made from the highest of all the high prices, and arranged to the carryover %.

estimated lowest wheat price

estimated highest wheat price

Wm Grandmill (1985) Ltd.

How To Use This Graph

Example: buying a wheat future.
The time is late July and you think wheat prices have bottomed. You want to buy a Dec. wheat which has a present price of $3. carryover is 25%. How much backup? The 25% line is touching the lowest price line at $2.45. Then, $3 - $2.45 = 55¢ ($2750) needed to invest safely without using a stop.

Example: selling a wheat future
The time is Dec. and you think prices have peaked. You will sell July wheat whose price is now $4.25. World carryover is 25%. How much backup? The 25% line is touching the highest price line at $4.85. Therefore $4.85 - 4.25 = 60¢ ($3000) backup is needed to invest safely without using a stop.

23

THE USDA AS A SOURCE OF INFORMATION

The United States Dept. of Agriculture is a source of much valuable information to both wheat traders and to farmers. It compiles the best wheat data in the world, both on the global wheat supply and on the domestic supply. One of the things which is of particular importance for the users of this book is USDA's monthly crop report which is released about the 11th of each month. What's in it? Important information which you need to use this book to the best advantage, such as the estimated planted acres of wheat, harvested acres, production, total use and the estimated wheat carryover at the end of the crop year. Each monthly crop report increases in value as the year progresses. In April we get the estimated planted acres, in May the estimated crop production is added, in June we get more information such as the estimated total use and the carryover for the crop year coming up. Also, as each month passes, the information in the monthly report becomes more accurate as more data comes in from the crop areas.

THE U.S. WHEAT CARRYOVER

All information in the USDA's monthly crop report is useful but two items in it are especially useful to the people who use this book. The two items are: the size of the total use for wheat and the size of the wheat carryover. The wheat investment plan as outlined in this book is dependent upon those two pieces of information mentioned above. Why? Because the size of the carryover indicates whether wheat prices will be high or low in the coming crop year. For example, if you knew in May that the wheat carryover would be 350 million bushels (which means that supplies are tight) then you could expect wheat prices to be over $5 in the winter. On the other hand, if you knew in May that the wheat carryover for the new crop year coming up would be 2000 million bu., then you could expect wheat prices to fluctuate between $2.50 and $3.00 per bu. because such a large carryover indicates that there will be a huge wheat surplus at the end of the next crop year. *In other words, the size of the carryover is an indicator of the future price of wheat.*

There is a better way to indicate the size of the carryover. If the carryover is an indicator of the future wheat price, then one should try to make that indicator as accurate as possible so that the future price of wheat can be forecast more accurately, which in turn, adds to the profitability.

A more accurate portrayal of the size of the wheat carryover is accomplished by expressing the carryover as a percentage number. For example, a 100% carryover would indicate that there is enough surplus wheat on hand after the crop year ends, to take care of all our needs and all the exports for another whole year even if another grain of wheat was never harvested. That's a very bearish carryover and it would force what prices down to around the $2.50 to $2.75 level. At the other extreme, let's say that the estimated carryover for the crop year coming up was 20%. That's a tight supply because it indicates that there is only about 10 week supply of wheat left over at the end of the crop year. (52 weeks x 20% = 10.4) and prices would likely rise to between $4 and $5. *To sum up:* carryover expressed as percent is a more accurate indicator of the future wheat price. The carryover as % is used extensively throughout this book.

But how is the % carryover calculated? There is a standard format in the grain industry to show production, total use, carryover, etc. Below, you can see the last several years of U.S. wheat data outlined in the standard format.

U.S. WHEAT SUPPLY crop year	82/83	83/84	84/85	85/86	* = estimated 86/87	87/88	88/89 *
Beginning stocks	1164	1515	1399	1424	1905	1821	1261*
Production (all data in mil. bu.)	2812	2424	2603	2438	2113	2124	1833*
Total supply	3976	3939	4002	3862	4018	3945	3094*
Domestic use	959	1111	1154	1030	1193	1092	1060*
Exports	1502	1429	1424	927	1004	1592	1500*
Total use	2461	2540	2578	1957	2197	2684	2560 *
Carryover	1515	1399	1424	1905	1821	1261	534*
Carryover as % of total use	62%	55%	55%	97%	83%	47%	21%*

Looking at the chart above you can see that the carryover is expressed in 2 ways - once in millions of bushels and once **as the % of the total use.** It is the % of the total use which is important for this book because all the Forecasting Graphs and charts use the % figure to estimated the future price of wheat. But how is the % number calculated?

You need only 2 lines from the format above to calculate the carryover %. You need only the **total use** line and the **carryover** line. Then you do the following calculation: **"carryover" divided by the "total use" x 100 = the carryover as %. Example:** look above at the crop year 82/83. The carryover % will be calculated by using the equation above: 1515 divided by 2461 x 100 = 62%. That's all there is to it. The 62% figure above means that there is enough wheat carryover to last for 62% of a year.

From now on in this book, the carryover percent in the format above **will be referred to as the "U.S. Carryover %** because it is calculated entirely from the U.S. wheat crop. Later you will learn that there is a **World Carryover %** because it is calculated from the world wheat data. There is a page at the back of this book with the standard format on it where you can keep a record of wheat fundamentals for the future crop years. Keep it up to date each year. You will find this information very useful.

WORLD WHEAT CARRYOVER

Here is something to think about: the world wheat supply has more influence on wheat prices at the Chicago and Kansas City exchanges than does the U.S. wheat supply. It may be hard to believe but that particular point was researched for this book. The research was done to answer the question, "Which carryover % has been the more accurate in helping to forecast U.S. wheat prices -the U.S. Carryover % or the World Carryover %? The research came out in favor of the World Carryover % as being the more accurate of the two -not by much but by enough to influence profits. How can this be? Well, wheat is universally grown -every country needs wheat for its bread. Even Saudi Arabia grows enough to support itself and to export a bit. The United States grows only about 11% of the world's wheat -but she exports 38% of all world exports. Now you can see that with so much wheat grown elsewhere in the wold, the world wheat supply is certain to influence U.S. prices.

Knowing the above, it is in the best interests of all wheat traders to become familiar with the world wheat fundamentals such as the world production, total use and the world carryover. There is a page at the back of this book where you can keep a record of the world wheat data. I will tell you later where to get the information for world wheat.

When we talk about World Wheat we use new words such as hectare, metric tonne, kilogram, etc. For your information, 1 hectare = 2.47 acres, 1 metric tonne = 2204.6 pounds, 1 metric tonne = 36.74 bushels of wheat. Yield is expressed in tonnes per hectare.

The World Carryover % is calculated by using the same equation as was used for the U.S. Carryover %, which was "carryover divided by total use x 100 = carryover %". There are some changes in terminology when discussing world wheat -such as "total use" is called "consumption", and the carryover and the consumption are both use "million metric tonnes" instead of "million bushels". Example to find the World Carryover % when the consumption is 540 m.m.t. and the carryover is 120 m.m.t.; 120 divided by 540 x 100 = 22%.

The Forecasting Graphs in the back of the book are the graphs which will forecast the price of wheat for any contract month. There are graphs which use the U.S. Carryover % and there are also graphs which use the World Carryover %. This brings up a dilemma. The World wheat supply exerts more influence on Chicago and K.C. prices than does the U.S. what supply. So, if one wanted to find the estimated price of Dec. wheat months ahead of time, for example, he could use the World wheat % graph, and use the U.S. wheat graph and take the average. But an average is really not the best solution because the world wheat exerts the greater influence. So research was done to find the proportion of influence on U.S. wheat prices which was exerted by the world supply and by the U.S. supply. The result of the research was to form a new carryover called the "Combined Carryover %" or the "Combination Carryover %" -both terms are used in this book. The **Combined Carryover %** is made up of: ***60% of the World Carryover % plus 40% of the U.S. Carryover %.*** This has turned out to be an ideal compromise in tests done by using the wheat data of the past 15 years. There were good profits resulting from the use of the Combination Carryover % -and profits are the proof of its value. Therefore, there is a set of Forecasting Graphs which are used with the Combination Carryover % in the back of the book.

COMBINATION CARRYOVER %

As mentioned above, the Combination Carryover % consists of 60% of the World Carryover % plus 40% of the U.S. Carryover -thus giving a slight edge to world wheat supply. It takes only a minute to calculate the Combination Carryover %. **Example:** You have already calculated the world % and the U.S. %, so let's say that you already had a figure of 30% for the world carryover and you had 70% for the U.S. wheat carryover - therefore, to find the Combination %, do this: (30 x .60) + (70 x .40) = 18 + 28 = 46% as the Combination Carryover %. *Here is another example,* using the actual percent carryovers for the crop year 87/88. In that year the world carryover was 27%. Using the formula above, the calculation: (27 x .60) + (47 x .40) =16.2 + 18.8 = 35% as the Combination Carryover %. There is a page in the back of the book where you can keep a record of all the carryover percents. You will learn how to use the Forecasting Graphs in the next section and in that section you will be told to look upon the Combination Carryover % as your main advisor graph.

WHERE TO GET THE WHEAT DATA

The USDA is the best source of information. USDA puts out two publications which have the information you need. One is called **"WHEAT - Situation and Outlook"** which is published 4 times a year. It is only $10 per year, which is a bargain. The contents include data on both the wheat supplies in the United States and the world wheat supply and demand data. *Everything that you need is in this publication.*

To subscribe, you can phone a toll free number, which is 1-800-999-6779. Or you can write to: U.S. Dept of Agriculture, 1301 New York Ave. Washington, D.C. 20005-4788.

The other USDA publication which will be useful for this book is called, "World Agricultural Supply and Demand Estimated". This book contains world data on all grains such as wheat, corn, soybeans, rice, etc. The price is $18 per year. To subscribe, you can write to USDA World Agricultural Outlook, Washington, D.C. 20250-3800. Or you can phone (202) 783-3238.

If you have a computer, the world supply and demand figures can be accessed electronically on the day the data is released. Many other reports, including the monthly crop report can also be obtained this way. For details, phone (202) 447-5505.

HOW TO USE THE FORECASTING GRAPHS

WHETHER TO BUY OR SELL

Sometimes it is very clear as to the direction of wheat prices and sometimes it is not. That is one of the risks in wheat trading -making the wrong decision by buying when one should be selling. Well, help is at hand because <u>one of the functions of the Forecasting Graph is to tell you whether you should be buying or whether you should be selling wheat.</u>

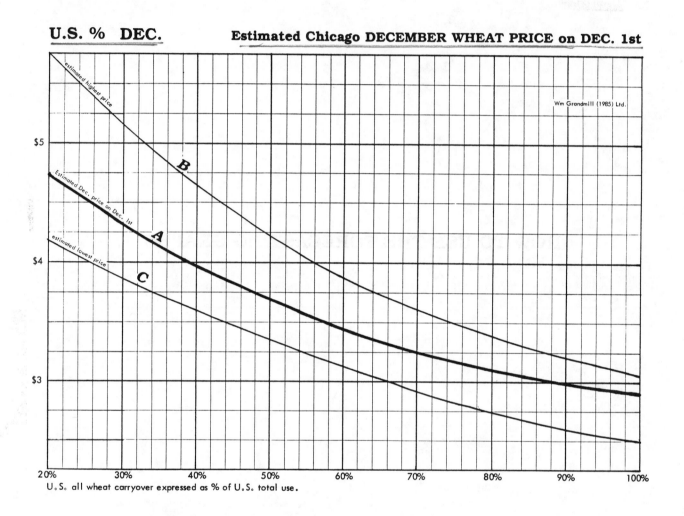

U.S. % DEC.   **Estimated Chicago DECEMBER WHEAT PRICE on DEC. 1st**

Wm Grandmill (1985) Ltd.

$5

$4

$3

20%   30%   40%   50%   60%   70%   80%   90%   100%

U.S. all wheat carryover expressed as % of U.S. total use.

Above is the December Forecasting Graph which will forecast the price of Dec. wheat as it is likely to be on Dec. 1st. Note that it doesn't forecast the prices between the time that you take the Dec. wheat position and Dec. 1st, but it forecasts only the likely price on the date of Dec. 1st. Have you got that distinction? To repeat, the Dec. Forecasting Graph forecasts only the estimated price of Dec. wheat for the date of Dec. 1st, which is the end of the contract months as far as trading purposes are concerned.

Between the time when you **take a position** in Dec. wheat and the **liquidation** of it on Dec. 1st, there are **always** price fluctuations of varying degrees. Look above at the graph again (a full sized version is at the back of the book). Note that it is using the U.S. carryover % for this example. This heavy middle line, marked A, is the line which forecasts the estimated price on Dec. 1st. The top line, marked B, depicts the highest price level that a fluctuation of Dec. prices is likely to reach. The bottom line, marked C, depicts the estimated lowest level to which the Dec. price will fluctuate. In other words, lined B and C represent the **extreme** fluctuations of Dec. wheat prices. Most often the fluctuation are much less. **Lines A, B, and C have been determined by analyzing Dec. wheat prices over the past 15 years.**

Example, using the graph above. Let's say that the date is July 15th and you are considering taking a Dec. wheat position. Let's also say the U.S. carryover % for the new crop year which had begun on June 1st is 70%. Follow this on the graph above. Locate 70% on the bottom line and go vertically up to the heavy center line marked A, and you get the estimated Dec. price on Dec. 1st to be $3.25 Now look at line B and you see that the **maximum** Dec. price fluctuation upward is about $3.72. Look at line C to get the **maximum** fluctuation downward, and you see the Dec. price of $2.87. Don't forget, lines B and C represent the **maximum extreme price fluctuations.**

Look again at lines B and C in the Dec. graph above. Note how much line B swerves upward at the 20% carryover. Note how much less line C swerves upward at the 20% carryover. Why? Well, at 20% carryover the wheat supplies are tight and traders are bullish so prices tend to be pushed higher by ardent buyers than is justified by the supply of wheat -only to have prices sink back to the true level by Dec 1st. Look at the 100% carryover and you can see that line C gets most of the action as compared to line B. That's because traders are very bearish because 100% carryover suggests there is a huge wheat surplus on hand.

Now you can see why backup money is needed to support your wheat position -because of price fluctuations. Also you can see that stop prices would be touched off by the price fluctuations.

A complete example using the Dec. graph above. The date is July 15th. You are considering taking a Dec. wheat position. (Remember, at this point you don't know whether you will be buying or selling Dec. wheat.) **(step 1)** You look in your morning newspaper and see that Dec. wheat closed yesterday at $2.80. **(step 2)** You look in your data book and note that the estimated U.S. carryover for the new crop year which began on June 1st is 70%. You will likely have got the % number from USDA's July crop report or you may have calculated it yourself from the data you have gathered so far. **(step 3)** Using the 70% column on the Dec. Forecasting Graph, you get $3.25 as the estimated price for Dec. wheat on Dec. 1st. **(step 4)** Considering the facts – Dec, wheat is now $2.80 and it is estimated to rise to $3.25 on Dec. 1 – that means that you should **buy** Dec. wheat. Also, the estimated profit should be about 45¢ ($2250). (Commissions are not considered in the calculations in this book because commissions vary from about $125 to $20, depending on whether you are dealing with a full-service brokerage house or a discount broker.) **(step 5)** Now it is time to find out how much backup money is needed for the long wheat position. (Follow this chart at the back of the book) You are **buying wheat** and you are using the U.S. % carryover. Looking at the appropriate chart, you locate $2.80 on the bottom line ($2.80 was the purchase price when you took the long position), go vertically to the 70% line and you get about $700 as the extra money needed to trade safely. You will deposit $700 into your commodity account. *(step 6)* That's it. That's all there is to it. *(step 7)* By the way, it is always a good plan to have a minimum of $1000 in your commodity account as backup capital because it is not uncommon for prices to make a 15¢ foray against you as a result of some false rumor in the market. These rumors float through the market, prices rising or falling by about 15¢, and then settling back to the original price a couple of days later -leaving thousands of traders stopped out. So, even if the backup chart says that no extra money is needed, it is wise to have $1000 as backup in your account.

In the example above you bought Dec. wheat because the present price was less than the price expected on Dec. 1st, as indicated by the graph. But suppose the situation was reversed. Suppose the present price was *larger* than the price indicated by the graph for Dec. 1st. Then you would be *selling* Dec. wheat instead of buying it as in the examples above. *Example:* follow this on the Dec. Forecasting Graph a couple of pages back. The date is July 15th and you are considering a Dec. wheat position. *(step 1)* You look in the morning newspaper and see that Dec. wheat closed yesterday at $3.60. *(step 2)* As you did before, use the 70% column of the Dec. Forecasting Graph and you get $3.25 as the est. price of Dec. wheat on Dec. 1st. *(step 3)* Therefore, you should *sell* Dec. wheat because the price is now $3.60 and it will decline to an est. $3.25 on Dec.. 1st. *(step 4)* The last step is to find how much backup money is needed to trade safely. Because you are selling wheat this time, then you must use the chart which indicates "Selling Wheat" and using the U.S.%. On the proper chart, locate $3.60 on the bottom line, then go up to the 70% column, and you get $2500 as the maximum estimated required backup money needed.

Another example showing that sometimes you should stay out of the market. Using the same Dec. Forecasting Graph and using the same carryover of 70%. *(step 1)* You look in the morning paper and see that Dec. wheat closed yesterday at $3.35. *(step 2)* Using the same graph as in the other examples, you get $3.25 as the estimated Dec. wheat price on Dec 1st. *(step 3)* It's decision time! It looks as if there is only 10¢ ($500) to be made by going short -and you can never be sure of it because it could turn out to be 0¢. What to do? Stay out! It's not worth the risk. *(step 4) Where does one draw the line* between taking a position and staying out of the market? Well, you should weigh the following in your mind: (a) The amount of backup capital needed versus the estimated profit. For example, if you needed 60¢ ($3000) as backup money to earn a profit of only 10¢ ($500) then it is not worth the risk. It is cutting it too fine. (b) Another thing to consider is the price trend at the time you wish to take the position. For example, if the Forecasting Graph indicated that you should go short and that there would only be a 10¢ profit then it is not worth it *unless* the trend is very bearish. Then it might be worthwhile because a bearish trend might push the prices lower than you had estimated. So, in the final analysis, the decision of whether to get out of the market or not, is up to you -but don't start taking chances because this book stressed safety. *(step 5) Research was done* on this particular point on the past 15 years of wheat price data -to see where the cutoff point should be, when you should get out of the market if the potential profit is too small. It was found that a 12¢ potential profit would make a good cutoff point. Thus, if the estimated profit was going to be 12¢ or less, stay out of the market. *(step 6)* If the profit from wheat is too small, then use Grandmill's Self Help paragraphs on corn or soybeans. One of them will have more profit then another. *(step 7)* Use the 12¢ rule.. It is better to have a rule and to stick to it. Not having a rule leads to indecision and stress. Of course, if the estimated profit is 50¢, for example, then there is no doubt of the course you should take.

HOW TO MAKE AN EXTRA PROFIT

Look at the Dec. Forecasting Graph a few pages back. See the lines representing the highest and the lowest price fluctuations. It is possible to take advantage of these price fluctuations and here's how to do it.

Example:

(1)   Suppose the Dec. Forecasting Graph indicated that you should **buy** Dec. wheat and that the price objective on Dec. 1st would be $3.25.

(2)   You call your broker and instruct him to buy Dec wheat at the market price.

(3)   Later your broker calls you to confirm that you are now long Dec. wheat he names the entry price.

(4)   Now is the time to make the move for the extra profit. Call your broker back and place an **open order** to **sell** Dec. wheat at $3.45, that's at 20¢ above the price objective of $3.25 which the Forecasting Graphs had indicated.

(5)   What's the strategy? As you know, the Dec. price will fluctuate as is shown by the two lines marked B and C on the Forecasting Graph. These lines represent the extremes which the wheat price has fluctuated. Because of these fluctuations, it is possible that the Dec. price, in this example, could rise higher than the objective price, then your open order may catch it at $3.45. If you are able to liquidate your long position at a price which is 20¢ above your objective price, then you have gained an extra 20¢ ($1000) profit.

(6)   How often is one successful in capturing this extra 20¢ profit? About 1/3 of the time. Research has shown that one trade out of 3 will have its open order filled at an extra profit of 20¢. This is certainly worthwhile and it doesn't cost anything to place an open order.

(7)   Place your open order for either buying or selling. The example above was for buying wheat. If you are **selling** wheat, then place your open order to **buy** the wheat at 20¢ **under** the price objective which you get from the Forecasting Graph. **For example**, if you were selling July wheat and the Forecasting Graph indicated that the July price on July 1st was estimated at $2.90, then place an open order to **buy** July wheat at $2.70. If you are successful you will have got out of the market at at better price, 20¢ better.

(8) You have to be careful how you place your order. Why? Because there are two kinds of orders like this. One is called a **day order** which is in effect or only the one day of trading. The other kind is called an **open order** which stays in force until you cancel it or until the contract month expires. And if you don't indicate which kind you want to use, then it is automatically assumed that it is a day order.

(9) **Follow this routine.** (a) Place your original buy or sell order with your broker. (b) Wait for the broker to confirm your position and he will tell you the price at which your position was purchased. (c) Only after that transaction is completed should you give him your open order and make sure that he knows it is an **open** order . (d) Check back with your broker a week later to see if your open order is still in effect, and that there was no mixup. (e) Why all these precautions? To prevent mistakes and misunderstandings. One important rule is to never give your broker two different wheat orders with two different prices at the same time -keep them completely separate. Another thing, it is important to have a routine and to follow it.

Practice Time! It is your turn to get some practice using the Forecasting Graphs. Below is a March Forecasting Graph using the U.S. carryover %. There are some problems to solve by using the Forecasting Graph. The answers are below so that you can check your responses.

U.S. %   MARCH   **Estimated Chicago MARCH WHEAT PRICE on MARCH 1st**

estimated highest price

Wm Grandmill (1985) Ltd.

$5

Estimated March price on Mar. 1st

$4

estimated lowest price

$3

20%   30%   40%   50%   60%   70%   80%   90%   100%

U.S. all wheat carryover expressed as % of U.S. total use.

33

1. The carryover is 54% and the March wheat price closed yesterday at $4.00.

    (a) Should you buy **or** sell March wheat?

    (b) What is the estimated profit?

    (c) You will place an open order to catch a possible 20¢ profit. Will your open order be to "buy March wheat" **or** to "sell March wheat" and at what price?

2. The carryover is 80% and the March price at the moment is $2.93. Should you buy or sell or what?

3. The carryover is 28%. You are looking at the quote screen on your computer and you see that March wheat is $3.84.

    (a) Should you "buy March" or "sell March" or "stay out of the market"?

    (b) What is the estimated profit?

    (c) What is the maximum amount of backup money needed?

    (d) You will place an open order to try to catch an extra 20¢ profit. Will the order be "buy March wheat" or "sell March wheat" and at what price?

Answers. 1(a) sell (b) about 50¢ ($2500) (c) buy March wheat at $3.30. 2. stay out of the market 3. (a) buy (b) about 51¢ (c) did you use the "Buying" chart with U.S.%? ans. $3000 maximum. (d) sell March wheat at $4.55

YEAR ROUND INVESTING

Now that you have learned how to use the Forecasting Graphs, it is time to get to the main purpose of this book – which is to give you a year round safe, profitable investment plan for wheat.

The year round investment plan will be of two types: (1) an easy one to do for those people who want the least complicated plan possible – as long as it is safe and profitable. This plan will be called "The Automatic Year Round Wheat Investment Plan", (2) the other plan will have opportunities for individualism for those people who like to use their own ideas on such things as timing, the open order price objective, the amount of backup money to use, etc.

The year round program is exactly that - a term of one year, from harvest to harvest. There are two parts or phases to it of about 6 months each. In one phase you will buy or sell Dec. wheat and in other phase you will buy or sell July wheat -or variations of it. To repeat, it is year round investing done in 2 phases, and the profit earned is calculated after the year is completed. Below is the least complicated, but profitable method.

AUTOMATIC YEAR ROUND WHEAT INVESTMENT PLAN

This plan consists of 2 phases: (1) the first phase is to buy or sell Dec. wheat on July 15th. (2) the second phase is to buy or sell July wheat on Dec. 1st. Each phase is described below.

Phase 1 – to buy or to sell Dec. wheat on July 15th. Remember, at this point you don't know whether you will be buying or selling Dec. wheat until you consult the Dec. Forecasting Graph. The graph will indicate which to do.

Also remember that there are 3 Dec. Forecasting Graphs at the back of the book -one each for the world carryover, the combined carryover, and the U.S. carryover. The U.S. carryover is more familiar to you **but the world carryover is more influential on the Chicago and K.C. prices.** But the best one is the Combination Carryover% which is a good compromise between the U.S. and the world carryover. The Combination Carryover consists of 60% of the world carryover plus 40% of the U.S. carryover.

Consult all 3 kinds of Forecasting Graphs when looking for the estimated price objective on Dec. 1st or on July 1st - **but look upon the Combination Carryover graph as the main advisor.** The World Carryover graph will give you a different answer from the U.S. Carryover graph. Why? Because the United States could be having a drought, for example which would produce tight wheat supplies and a low % number. Whereas, abroad, there could be lots of rain and a large production which would have a not so low% number. For example, a 20% **world carryover** represents a **moderately tight** wheat carryover, whereas in the **U.S. carryover** it represents a very tight wheat carryover. But the **Combination carryover** brings the other two kinds together in a good workable relationship.

Why do we take the Dec. wheat position an July 15th? For 2 good reasons. **First,** the date of July 15th is right after the USDA crop report on July 12th. This is a very important report -and the most accurate to date. From it you will receive the latest revised wheat data such as the latest production figures, the estimated total use **and the estimated carryover** for the new crop year. It is the new carryover and the carryover % number which you need most of all to use December's Forecasting Graph. You will get all those numbers from the July crop report.

The second reason why July 15th is a good date to buy or sell Dec. wheat is the fact that it is in the midst of the harvest season. July 15th was selected only after a lot of testing was done. Here is what was tested. Simulated Dec. wheat positions were taken, using the starting dates of June 15th,.July 1st, July 15th, Aug. 1st, Aug. 15th. Of them all, July 15th produced the best profit and needed the least amount of backup capital.

Starting the Automatic Wheat Investment Plan. About July 15th, using the new carryover % for the new crop year, consult the Dec. Forecasting Graph to find whether you should buy or sell Dec. wheat. Take the Dec. position. Find out how much Backup capital you will need. Place your open order for the extra 20¢ profit. Plan on holding the Dec. position until Dec. 1st.

What to do on Dec 1st. Liquidate the Dec. position (unless, of course, your open order was successful, which would have already taken you out of the Dec position). It is time now to take the July position. Note the latest July wheat price. Consult the July Forecasting Graph to find whether you should buy or sell July wheat, and what the price objective is on July 1st. You will have USDA's latest carryover estimate from the October or November crop reports (keep all data updated). Use the new carryover % on all 3 of July's Forecasting Graphs, but rely more heavily on the Combination Carryover graph. Take the July position. Find out how much backup capital is needed. Place your open order. Sit back and relax.

When you liquidate your July wheat position on July 1st, you will have completed the round trip. But what can you expect to happen during that full year of trading? What has happened in the past years? Again, simulated year round trading was done in each of the past 15 years, using the Forecasting Graphs. Here are the results of those 15 years of tests.

Test Statistics. A simulated Dec. wheat position was taken about July 15th (sometimes the 15th was on a weekend). The Dec. Forecasting Graph was consulted, and it was the graph which used the Combination Carryover %. An open order was placed.

What happened? the following occurred in the 15 year test:

1. bought Dec. wheat in 6 of those years.
2. sold Dec. wheat in 8 of those years.
3. stayed out of the market in 1 of those years.
4. the open order was successful in 6 of those years.
5. the largest backup capital needed for the whole 15 years was $2100.
6. the average profit was 32¢ ($1600) to Dec. 1st.
7. every year made a profit except one, and it lost 37¢. But the other half, phase 2, of the year made up the loss by earning 157¢ (the July posi – tion). It was the case that if one phase lost money, the other phase had an above average profit.

Test statistics for the other half of the year round investment. A July wheat position was taken on Dec. 1st, using the Combination Carryover % on the July Forecasting Graph.

What happened? The following occurred in the 15 years tested:

1. bought July wheat in 7 of those years.
2. sold July wheat in 8 of those years.
3. the open order was successful in 7 of those years.
4. the largest backup capital needed in any one year was $1200.
5. the average profit was 45¢ ($2250) from Dec. 1st to July 1st.
6. 13 of the years were profitable, 2 were losers. Of the 2 losing years, one lost 30¢ but the previous phase (the Dec. position) had earned a profit of 64¢ -so the year round profit for this particular year was 34¢ which was the smallest year round profit for any of the 15 years. The other losing July position lost 10¢, but its previous phase (the Dec. position) had earned 52¢ so that at the end of the year round investment, this particular year had a profit of 42¢ ($2100).

To sum up: The average profits for the 2 phases were 32¢ ($1600) and 45¢ ($2250). Adding them together for the whole year round profit of $1600 + $2250 = $3850 as an average. All years made a profit. It is surprising how little backup money was needed. The worst case required $2100. The credit goes to the Forecasting Graphs which have clear decisions on whether to buy or sell. This was the Automatic Investment Plan (called "Automatic" because the positions were taken automatically on certain dates).

INNOVATIONS

This chapter is for innovative traders; those people who want to change a system. For example, some people may wish to take a different month than Dec. wheat. Others might wish to take the July position at some other date than Dec. 1st. They want to experiment. This chapter will provide helpful material for that purpose. What you do with the material or how you use it, is up to you. One of the first materials provided are charts which show when the highest and lowest prices for December and July occurred.. this will provide a good starting point for any changes you may wish to try. There are 6 of these charts at the back of the book Below are some reduced versions.

When do the highest and the lowest prices occur? Above is a chart showing when December's highest prices occurred in each of the past 15 years. At first glance it looks

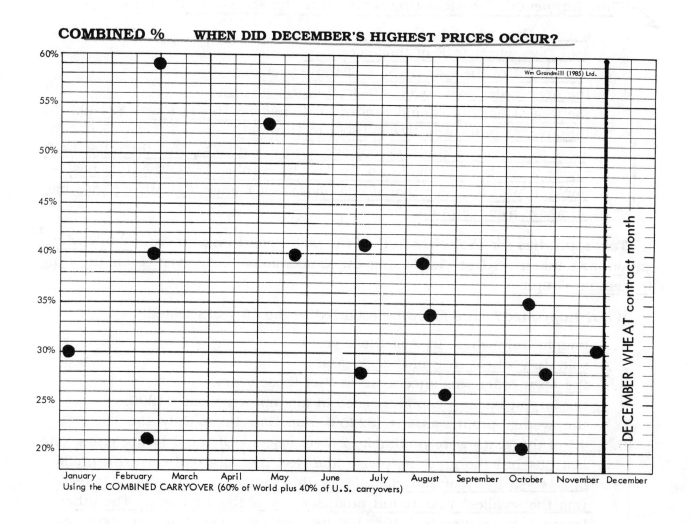

COMBINED %   WHEN DID DECEMBER'S HIGHEST PRICES OCCUR?

Using the COMBINED CARRYOVER (60% of World plus 40% of U.S. carryovers)

like a random pattern. But, do this. Cover up the 3 dots in the lower left corner. Now you can see a pattern -it flows down from the upper left corner and fans out as it approaches the bottom right corner. *What does it tell you?* It tells you that as the carryover supplies get tighter (as shown by low% numbers), then the date of the highest Dec. price moves closer toward the late fall months of October and Nov. *How does this information help you?* Here's an example: suppose you went long Dec. wheat on July 15th, and the carryover is 20%. Then you should be prepared to liquidate the Dec. position about the end of October. Also, if your objective price was reached, you could then place a stop price at 10¢ below the objective price and let your position alone, hoping that prices will continue to rise. Also, your open order could be touched off in late October. There is lots more information in the chart above.

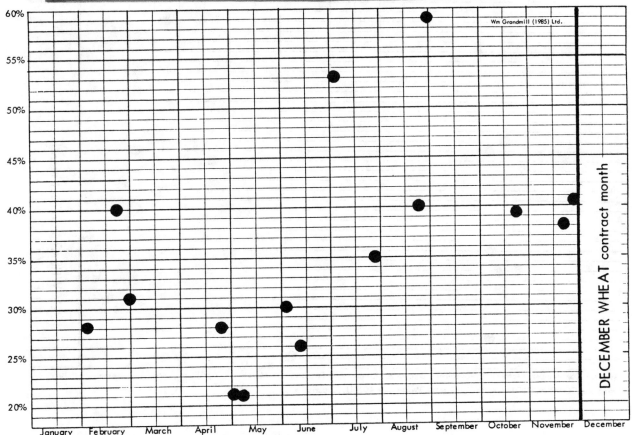

COMBINED %   WHEN DID DECEMBER'S LOWEST PRICES OCCUR?

Using the COMBINED CARRYOVER (60% of World plus 40% of U.S. carryovers)

Above is a chart which shows when December's lowest prices occurred in each of the past 15 years Again it looks like a random pattern but there is hidden information in it. Here's one. If the Combination Carryover is 30% or less, then December's lowest price is likely to occur in the first half of the year, narrowing to May as the % carryover number becomes less. *How can it help you?* If the carryover was 20%, for example, you should consult the Dec. Forecasting Graph in May and be ready to take a Dec. position. If this was the lowest price, then you will likely be going long Dec. wheat for a good profit. These charts do not give definite answers, but rather they give hints, ball park time areas, suggestions.

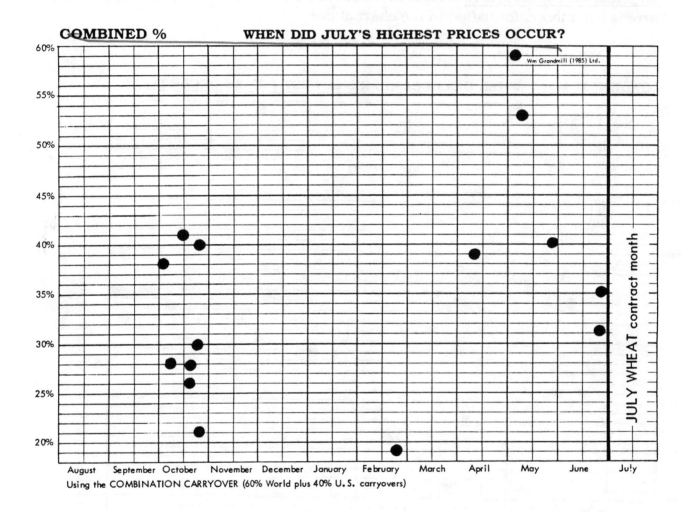

COMBINED %   **WHEN DID JULY'S HIGHEST PRICES OCCUR?**

Wm Grandmill (1985) Ltd.

JULY WHEAT contract month

Using the COMBINATION CARRYOVER (60% World plus 40% U.S. carryovers)

Above is a chart showing when July's highest prices occurred in the past 15 years. *How can the chart help you?* It appears that when the Combination Carryover is 30% or less, then the highest July price seems to occur in October. In fact, this pattern was so prominent that a *a test was done to see how profitable it would be if the July position was taken "automatically" on October 21st,* instead of on Dec 1st as was done in the Automatic Investment Plan. The July Forecasting Graph which used the Combination Carryover % was the graph consulted. Here are the results of the test on each of the past 15 years:

1.	July wheat was bought in 4 of the 15 years.
2.	July wheat was sold in 9 of the 15 years.
3.	One should stay out of the market in 2 of the 15 years.
4.	All years made a profit -no losing July positions.
5.	The maximum backup capital needed for the entire 15 years was only $1200.
6.	The average profit was 57¢ (the av. profit, you will remember, when July was taken on Dec. 1st was 45¢ -so this is a big improvement).

To sum up: There are likely many other ways to be innovative, and as you become used to the Forecasting Graphs, you will find other ways -but don't take risks.

USING A WHEAT OPTION

There are times when you will find it more appropriate to use an option for your wheat trade instead of using backup capital. Here is a reasonable example which might prompt you to use an option.

Suppose the time is July and you are intending to buy a Dec. wheat future. You check the backup graph and it indicates that the **maximum amount** of backup capital is $3000. Also you will have to deposit a margin of $1000. Altogether you will have $4000 in your commodity account to trade the long Dec. wheat position.

Then you look at the wheat option prices. You see that an at-the-money Dec. wheat call has a premium of 22¢ ($1100). Now you have a decision to make. Should you put $4000 into your account for the future's trade, knowing that you will retain that $4000 when the future's trade is successful? Or should you spend the much smaller amount of $1100, knowing that you will **not** retain it at the end because it is a cost? You profit will be less with an option than with a future, but then your money committed is less. Also, with an option, you don't care if prices go against you temporarily because you are not required to put in more money when prices go against you – as long as the price will be where you expect it at the expiration.

These are the thoughts with which you will be faced – and only you can make the decision of whether to go with the future's trade or to go with the option trade. A trader's personality may enter the decision process – an option provides a very relaxed form of trading – it's like being in a protected shelter while outside the price storms are raging. This book will not make the decision for you but it has a few guidelines which will help you to decide whether to use an option or a future's position.

OPTION TRADING BASICS

Compared to futures, how are options different?
Even though you may be new to option trading, it is likely that you are experienced in trading futures. Now you want to try your hand in options because you are seeking more

security and safety than you had in futures trading. You have heard that options are safer – none of those unpleasant limit moves against you which you experienced in futures when things went wrong. You heard correctly. There are no limit up or limit down price moves in options. You are in a safer form of trading.

The reason why I expected you to have traded in futures already, is that options are the next logical step after futures. Option prices, you see, are based on the price of the underlying future e.g. the price (premium) of a November soybean call would depend on the price on Nov. soybeans. That means that the future's price is the basis of the option's price. In other words, the future's price is the most important factor in option trading. All option prices are dependent upon the futures' prices. But it is safer to be in options than in futures as you will see later.

When you traded futures, you gave your broker an order to **buy** a contract when you expected prices to rise, and you gave him an order to **sell** a future's contract when you expected prices to fall. You use the same words in options: "buy or sell". The word "buy" has almost the same meaning in options as it has in futures, but the word "sell" has a different connotation. This difference will be explained later. But, first, let's become familiar with option terminology.

Two kinds of options
There are 2 distinct kinds of options: a **call** option and a **put** option. They are opposites, like up and down. Think of the call as belonging to the "up", and the put as belonging to the "down".

Know the trend
You should never take an option or a future's position without some hint or reason why prices will move in the direction you desire. Otherwise, you are guessing and there is no place for guessing in either option or futures trading. What, then, should a new trader do, to find the price trend?

The answer, of course, is to use the Forecasting Graphs. The graphs will tell you whether the price of the grain is likely to rise or to fall. Once you know the price trend, then you can buy your option after you consult the option graph. This new option graph is designed to tell you whether an option is worthwhile taking.

Buying a call
You "buy a call" when you believe that the underlying future's price is rising or is about to rise. If the Forecasting Graph indicates that the future's price will rise in the months ahead, and if the option graph indicates that the option is worth taking, then you phone your broker to buy an at-the-money call (an at-the-money call is a call which is as close to the underlying future's price as you can get – for example, if Nov. soybeans are at $6, then you would buy a $6 Nov. soybean call).

Buying a put
You "buy a put" when you believe that the underlying future's price is falling or about to fall. If the Forecasting Graph indicates that the future's price will fall in the months ahead, and if the option graph indicates that the option is worth taking, then you phone your broker to buy an at-the-money put.

41

Remember, in this book, there are only 2 kinds of options to buy. You either buy a call or you buy a put. You buy a call to profit from rising prices. But all this will be carefully explained again in the sections which deal with each grain individually.

When you traded futures you were required to deposit margin money into your aocunt. But that is not the case with options. No margin money s needed when you buy a call or buy a put. It is like buying an article at the market – you pay the price for it and it is yours – end of transaction.

Therefore, when you buy a call, for example, you pay the price, and the call is yours. No more money is required – not even if prices go against you. In future's, remember, you sometimes were asked by your brokler to deposit more money into your account if prices went against you. But not when you buy a call or buy a put – you pay the price for it and it is yours.

In other words, the most money you can lose when you buy a call or a put is the premium (option price) which you paid for it. You will never be asked for more. By the way, in this book the words "option price" and "option premium" and "option value" have the same meaning. Sometimes one is used, sometimes another.

GUIDELINES FOR WHEAT OPTIONS

1.   ___*If the amount of backup capital plus the margin total a large amount of money, then one should go for the option.*___ In the example above where $4000 was to be the total amount put into your commodity account, then an option is feasible. ***Consider this:*** the profit from an option is less than from a future, but in the example above, ___**one could take 2 or 3 option positions**___ for less than the $4000 needed for the future. This way, the profit from 2 or 3 options would exceed the profit from a future. But don't discount using backup capital completely. For example, if one needed only $2000 or less as backup money, then he should use it rather than using an option because, in this example, the cost of an option will likely equal more than a half of the backup money – so there would be a good saving by not using the option.

2.   ___**Do not take a wheat option unless the option graph indicates that you can earn 100% net profit or more.**___

     Why the 100%? Because you need a margin of safety with options. ***Here's what is meant.*** Suppose you bought a $4 Dec. at-the-money wheat call for 20¢. Let's say that the wheat price fluctuated in the weeks ahead and finished up at $4 on the expiration date, no gain or loss. What are the results for an option? For a future? ***Answer:*** you would lose everything if you used an option – you wouldn't lose a penny if you used a future. How could an option call or put lose everything? Because, in this example, there is a 20¢ cost – and therefore the Dec. wheat would have to rise to $4.20 just to break even on the option – and would have to go higher than $4.20 to show any kind of a profit. That's why, by aiming for a 100% profit, you are giving yourself a margin of safety.

3. ***Another consideration is volatility.*** If the wheat future's price is acting erratically by rising and falling from rumors or other causes, then an option position would give greater peace of mind because an option's profit and security are not affected by the in-between action, but only by the price at the far end.

HOW TO USE THE OPTION GRAPH

Below is a reduced version of the wheat option graph. A full size graph is located near the back of the wheat section. The graph is simple to use. Take a look at it, and note that the option's at-the-money price is on the left side of the graph. On the bottom line is the price difference between the current future's price found in the morning newspaper and the price from the Forecasting Graph. The oblique lines indicate the net profit %. (The costs of the option trade are already incorporated into the oblique lines, so the result is a net profit) The best way to illustrate the graph is to do a couple of examples. Follow them on the graph.

Example 1: The date is July 15th and the winter wheat harvest is winding down. This may be the time to buy a Dec. wheat option – the Dec. Forecasting Graph will indicate whether one should buy a call or buy a put.

(1) A look at the morning paper shows that Dec. wheat closed yesterday at $3.20.

(2) The estimated carryover for the new crop year is 47%.

(3) Using the Dec. wheat Forecastin Graph, one gets $3.80 as the estimated Dec. price on Dec. 1st.

(4) This means that there is a price difference of 60¢ between the current and the Forecast price (3.80 - $3.20=60¢) which you locate on the bottom line of the option graph.

(5) Because the price is forecast to rise, then one would ***buy a call.***

(6) Another look in the morning newspaper (or a call to one's broker) indicates that a Dec. $3.20 wheat call at-the-money, has a premium of 22¢. Locate 22¢ on the left side of the graph.

(7) It is now time to use the option graph to see whether the call will earn 100% which is the minumum one should try for with a wheat option.

NOTE: This graph has a 3¢ ($150) cost built into it ($100 for commissions and $50 for poor order fills which happen often).

Therefore, the answer which you get from the graph will represent a net profit.

It is assumed that you will be holding the option until its expiration.

(vertical axis labels, top to bottom) current wheat option premium, at the money — 60¢, 50¢, 40¢, 30¢, 20¢, 10¢, 0¢

(curve labels) 0% net profit, 100% net profit, 200% net profit, 300% net profit

Wm. Grandmill (1985) Ltd.

(horizontal axis) 0¢, 25¢, 50¢, 75¢, $1.00, $1.25, $1.50

The bottom line shows the amount of price difference between the price from the Forecasting Graph, and the price of wheat at the time when you buy the wheat option, in order to achieve the desired % of net profit.

HOW TO USE THE WHEAT OPTION GRAPH

Example A: The date is Aug. 12th, just after the USDA crop report. You are considering Dec. wheat. Using the Forecasting Graphs, you get an est. price of $4.60 on Dec. 1st. Current price is $4.00, a difference of 60¢ from the est. future price of $4.60. You will buy a Dec. call. A $4.00 Dec. call costs 20¢. How much profit to expect? Locate 60¢ on the bottom line, go up to the 20¢ horizontal line, and you read 185% as the likely % return.

Example B: Date is December, and you want to buy a May put. The Forecasting Graphs est. May wheat will be $4. A May put costs 24¢. At what price must May wheat be to earn a 100% return on your wheat option? Do this: trace along the 24¢ line to the 100% line, go down to bottom line and read 51¢ difference. So, $4 + 51¢ = $4.51 the May price at which you will buy the put, to earn 100%.

(8) Use the 22¢ option premium on the left of the graph, and use the 60¢ price difference on the bottom line.

(9) Note that the 60¢ vertical line intersect the 22¢ horizontal line at about 155% net profit.

(10) This call option is definitely worth taking.

Example 2: This example is the reverse of the one above. In this example you are thinking of buying a May put because wheat prices are weakening, as they often do in the winter and spring.

(1) Looking at the May wheat Forecasting Graph, you get an estimated $3.50 as the price on May 1st.

(2) Looking in the morning newspaper, you see that May wheat closed yesterday at $3.60 – so there is not enough difference between the two prices to warrant buying a put.

(3) The big question now is this: at what price must May wheat be so that you can earn 100% on the put?

(4) You look at the option prices and see that the current $3.60 at-the-money May price is 20¢.

(5) On the option graph, look horizontally along the 20¢ line until it intersects the 100% net profit diagonal line.

(6) Then move straight down to the bottom line and read 43¢.

(7) That means that you will need a 43¢ price difference from what the May future will be on May 1st, $3.50.

(8) In other words, you will have to wait for the current May price to rise to $3.93 before it would be wise to buy a May put. ($3.50 + 43¢ = $3.93).

(9) The option premium changes as time passes so it will be necessary to redo the process from time to time.

(10) What happens if the May price never rises to $3.93? Then use a wheat future, or try soybeans or a corn option or future.

HOW YOU CAN GET A HEAD START ON
USDA'S CROP ESTIMATE

As you have read on a previous page, the April USDA crop report is usually the first crop report which will give you data which you can use for the upcoming crop year, which begins on June 1st. The USDA April report has the estimated **planted acres**. By using the "planted acres" number, and by using Grandmill's new tables which were designed specifically for this book, you will be able to estimate the new crop size and the new carryover %, which, in turn, will tell you if the wheat prices are likely to be higher or lower next year – all this you can do and find out before mid April. For example, suppose by mid April that you found that the new carryover would be 20% – that's very bullish. Then one should buy Dec. wheat now, and not wait for the harvest low because there is not likely to be a low at harvest time. By the time mid May has passed, you would see that the professional traders will have taken their positions because wheat prices will be creeping upward.

The above is an example of how one can get a head start on price movements. Of course, if the new carryover is of medium size, e.g. 45%, then nothing much will occur to next year's prices, and there will likely be a harvest low price. So, in this example, you would not gain an edge.

Another thing. Likely at this time of year, April, you will have a July wheat position. Therefore, foreknowledge of future price behavior is an advantage to you. For example, if you were short July wheat, and if you had calculated that the new carryover was estimated at 20%, for example, then July prices will start to rise soon – so it would be wise to liquidate your short July position. This is but one example of how to use this information.

But how do you calculate the new carryover %? That will be shown to you soon. But, first, a few words of explanation are necessary. The size of the wheat crop which is harvested from June to August, depends upon two things (1) the soil moisture (2) the number of harvested acres.

About soil moisture, first. As you know, winter wheat is planted in the fall. In the U. S., winter wheat is the predominant crop, comprising over 75% of all the wheat harvested here. Therefore, the winter wheat crop size is the crop which determines the size of the future wheat prices. So it is in our interest to judge the amount of moisture in the soil, as best we can. There are 3 distinct phases or seasons to consider when estimating soil moisture. They are (1) **the Fall:** Sept., Oct., Nov. (2) **the Winter:** Dec., Jan., Feb., (3) **the Spring:** March, April, May. The size of the wheat yield depends on the rain and snow which falls during each of the 3 time phases. You will learn soon how to estimate the future crop yield, based on the soil's moisture.

Planted Acres and Harvested Acres. USDA usually publishes its estimated **planted acres** in its April crop report which is given to the public about April 11th, + or - 2 or 3 days. But the **harvested acres** are something else. The harvested acres are always fewer than the planted acres because, for some reason or another, a farmer will plow up some of his wheat acres and plant something else, usually soybeans. Naturally, USDA cannot give you the number of **harvested acres** in its April report because harvest is still months away. But we need to know, so some way should be devised which will help us to get a good estimate of the amount of harvested acres.

   How To Estimate The Number Of Harvested Acres. A search through the wheat data of the past 15 years was done to try to find a clue as to why the farmers of America would decide to plow under X acres of winter wheat. The determinant factor was **price.** Here is the rationale behind that discovery. When wheat prices are high, e.g. $4.30, then a farmer will want to sell every grain of wheat he can grow because at that high price range wheat farming is profitable. But when wheat prices are low, e.g. $2.60, then wheat farming is not profitable, and it is often to the farmer's best interest to plow up some wheat and plant soybeans, for example.   So price is the dominant factor. The price in the spring will help the farmer decide whether or not another crop will pay better.

   But price can be expressed two ways: by dollars such as $3.80, or by % carryover such as a U. S. carryover of 40%. Thus, when the U.S. carryover is 90%, for example, then there is a big surplus of wheat, which means low wheat prices during the crop year. At the other extreme, if the U.S. carryover is 20 %, then supplies are tight and prices will be over $4.00 for most of the crop year. This book will use the % carryover as an indication of whether wheat prices will be high or low or medium. But the trick is to discover how many acres are plowed under as a result of X% carryover. In other words it works like this: let's suppose that the date is about the end of March and the U.S. carryover % is 37%. By researching the data of the past 15 years concerning planted and harvested acres, it averaged out that a 37% carryover would result in a cut back of planted acres of 11% – in other words, only 89% of planted acres were estimated to be harvested. Below are Grandmill's tables, correlating the U.S. % carryover with the harvested acres.

Tables To Find The Estimated Harvested Acres

	U.S. carryover		
If the present carryover is 80% + ,	multiply the planted acres by		84%
" " " 70-80%	"	"	" 85%
" " " 60-70%	"	"	" 86%
" " " 50-60%	"	"	" 87%
" " " 40-50%	"	"	" 88%
" " " 30-40%	"	"	" 89%
" " " 20-30%	"	"	" 90%
" " " less than 20%	"	"	" 92%

   Look at the table above. See the top line where it says that if the U.S. carryover % is 80% or more, then only about 84% of the planted acres are likely to be harvested. An 80% carryover means low prices because of the surplus, so a farmer will cut back his harvested acres by about 16%. Whereas a less than 20% carryover indicates tight supplies and high prices, so the planted acres are cut back by only 8%. These percentages were arrived at from past wheat history.

   Example: The date is April 12th and USDA has issued its crop report after the markets closed for the day. For this example, let's say that USDA gave 72 million acres as its estimate of planted acres of wheat. (1) You look in your note book and see that the U.S.% carryover for the crop year in which you are in at the moment, is 43%. (2) Looking in the table above, 43% is in the 40-50% line which says that you should multiply the planted acres by 88%. (3) the calculations: 72 x .88 = 63.36 million acres are likely to be harvested in the coming summer. (4) The next step you will learn soon, is to find the estimated wheat yield, in bushels per acre. Then, by multiplying the estimated harvested acres by the yield, we will get the estimated crop size for the new crop year coming up. The new crop year begins on June 1st.

How To Find The Estimated Crop Yield. The key to wheat yield is soil moisture. If moisture is lacking, then the yield will be low. The best situation is to have average rainfall the year around – that's what nature likes best. Even excessive rainfall is not as good for the crops as normal rainfall.

Usually beginning in March or April, USDA will issue a report on the growing condition of the winter wheat crop at that time. The USDA often uses such words as, "excellent, good, fair, poor". These descriptive words could change from month to month because of a lack of rain during the month, and for other reasons. So you must check the report every month, right to harvest. Because USDA's descriptive words describe the condition of the wheat crop, there must be a correlation between those words and the wheat yield. By using this rationale, and by using the data of the past 15 years, a table was made correlating USDA's crop description with the estimated wheat yield.

USDA's Crop Condition And Yield Estimations.

Excellent = 40 bu. per acre	Poor = 32 bu. per acre
Good = 38 bu. per acre	Very poor = 29 bu. per acre
Fair = 35 bu. per acre	

Example: If, after the April crop report, you had calculated the **harvested** acres will be 63.36 million acres, and if USDA said that the crop was in "fair" condition, then by using the table above you can see that the word "fair" means about 35 bu. per acre – so by multiplying 63.36 x 35 = 2217.6m. bu. which is a bit below an average year's production figure.

Where Do You Get The Crop Report? The USDA crop report is issued within an hour after the grain markets close for the day, usually about the 11th of each month + or - 2 or 3 days. It comes over the wire right into your broker's office within an hour after the market has closed. Get it then, that very day from your broker because by tomorrow or the next day, this will be old news and likely chucked into the waste basket to make room for recent grain news. You could also make arrangements beforehand by asking your broker to write down the figures for you. But, whatever, get the information! Every dedicated grain trader gets that report – and, if you have read this section this far, then you must be a dedicated trader.

If your broker says that he doesn't have the report, ask him to phone the brokerage house HQ in New York or Chicago and ask the grain analyst for the information. Remember, if you are paying a full service commission, then you are entitled to this information and service. But, *where else* can you get the crop report? The next day's Wall Street Journal will have it, and other financial newspapers. Also, if you subscribe to a weekly grain newsletter, then it should be in the letter. Get it!

A Complete Example Of Finding The Estimated Crop Size For The Upcoming Crop

(1) Let's say that USDA issued a crop report on April 10th wherein it said that it estimated that about 80 million acres of wheat would be planted, and the winter wheat was in "fair" condition so far.

(2) You look in your note book and see that the U.S. carryover for the present crop year is 55%. You look the table a page or so back, and you see that to get the **harvested** acres, you will multiply the **planted** acres by 87%. So 80 x .87 = 69.6 million acres estimated will be harvested.

(3) The crop is in "fair" condition. Therefore, you look at the yield table a page back, and you see that a "fair" condition means about 35 bu. per acre as the yield. By multiplying the harvested acres x yield, you get 69.6 x 35 = 2436 million bushels as the estimated crop size at the coming harvest in June to August.

(4) Let's say that in the next crop report, the May report, USDA says that the crop condition is now in a "fair to good" condition. Looking back at the yield table, "fair to good" would be average of fair and good. In this example it would be (35 + 38) divided by 2 = 36.5 bu. per acre. Multiplying the harvested acres by the yield, you get 69.6 x 36.5 = 2540.4 million bu. as the estimated crop production for the coming harvest. This example was done to impress upon you that a crop report can change from month to month because of more rain or no rain during the ensuing month.

(5) The next step would be to take the process through to where you would find the carryover %. But let's put it on hold for the moment because there is an alternative method for estimating the new crop size which would be good for you to know. It involves you more into the process, and it could also be more accurate.

AN ALTERNATIVE METHOD FOR ESTIMATING THE SIZE OF THE NEW CROP

As mentioned above, the size of the new crop and its carryover at the end of the crop year, depends on 2 things: (1) the amount of planted acres of wheat (2) the amount of moisture in the soil. You get the number of **planted acres** from USDA in its April crop report. But here is a method which you can use to determine the estimated **yield**.

All you have to do here is to think back to last fall and winter, and try to remember whether there was no rain or sufficient rain during Sept., Oct., Nov. Then think of the moisture conditions in the winter months: Dec., Jan., Feb., and try to remember if the wheat fields had no snow or rain (likely snow in the North and rain in the South), or if there was sufficient moisture. Then think of the amount of rain in March and April. (It is assumed that you would be doing this about mid April, soon after you had received the USDA estimated number of planted acres of wheat.) Then you will repeat the process after the May report.

Below you see the 3 times or phases for estimating the moisture. From each of the 3 time phases, pick out the phrase which best describes the moisture situation for that time. One phrase from each of the 3 time areas. Add together the numbers at the end of each phrase: the least you can get is 0, and the largest total will be 15.

FALL: Sep. Oct. Nov.	**WINTER: Dec. Jan. Feb.**	**SPRING: Mar. Apr. May**
no rain at all 0	no snow or rain at all 0	no rain 0-3 (0 if fall & winter dry, 3 if there was rain)
only slight rain 2	only slight snow, rain 2	slight rain 2-3
below av. rain 3	below av. snow, rain 3	below av. rain 4
average rain 5	average snow or rain 5	average rain 5
excessive rain 4	excessive snow, rain 4	excessive rain 4

Select one phrase from each of the 3 seasons above, add the numbers, and apply the total to the table below. This will give you the estimated wheat yield in estimated bushels per acre. **Remember,** on a previous page, you learned how to estimate the number of the **harvested acres** from the number of **planted acres** which USDA had published in the April crop report (you did it by applying the current % carryover to a table).

So far as you know the estimated harvested acres, and you have a total number from the moisture table above. Now do this. Apply the moisture number which you got from the table above, to the table below, and you will find the corresponding estimated crop yield.

MOISTURE TOTAL	**MOISTURE TOTAL**	**MOISTURE TOTAL**
0=25 bu. per acre	5=30 bu. per acre	10=35 bu. per acre
1=26 " "	6=31 " "	11=36 " "
2=27 " "	7=32 " "	12=37 " "
3=28 " "	8=33 " "	13=38 " "
4=29 " "	9=34 " "	14=39 " "
		15=40 " "

DO THIS: multiply the harvested acres x the estimated yield = the estimated new wheat crop. **Example:** if the harvested acres were 70 million, and if the moisture total was 13 which gives an est. yield of 38 bu. per acre: then 70 x 38 = an est. crop of 2660 m. bu.

THEN DO THIS: add the new crop size found above, to the current carryover, and you now have the *estimated total wheat supply* for the coming crop year. Is this new total supply larger or smaller than the current total? If smaller prices will likely be higher next crop year; if larger, then prices will likely be less than present year.

     A Complete Example. Let's say that a USDA crop report on April 13th said that an estimated 78 million acres would be planted. **But there was no mention of the crop condition.** But that's no problem because you can now figure it out for yourself by using the moisture total from the 3 seasons, thus getting the estimated yield.

Step 1 - **to find the estimated harvested acres.** You look in your note book and see that the U.S. carryover is 35% at this time. Then you look in the "Table to find the estimated harvested acres" a few pages back, looking in the 35% row, and you see that you just multiply the planted acres by 89%, to get the harvested acres. So, 78 x .89 = 69.42 million estimated harvested acres.

Step 2 - to find the moisture number for the fall, winter, and spring weather. For this example, let's say that there was average rain in the fall: There was slight snow in the winter: there was below average rain in the spring. By adding the number values at the end of each descriptive phrase, you get 5 + 2 + 4 = 11 as the "moisture total".

Step 3 - **to find the yield by using the moisture total.** By looking in the Moisture Table and by using 11 from step 2 above, you get an astimated wheat yield of 36 bu. per acre.

Step 4 - **to find the estimated crop production.** Multiply the estimated harvested acres by the estimated yield, to get the estimated crop size. You get: 69.42 (from step 1 above) x 36 (from step 3 above) = 2499.12 million bu. as the estimated crop production or crop size as it is sometimes called. But there is still more work to do because you need the % carryover for the upcoming crop year so that you will be able to use the Forecasting Graphs, e.g. the Dec. Forecasting Graph. That's what is coming up next.

Step 5 - **to find the total wheat supply.** Add the carryover from the crop year which you are in (you will likely be doing the calculation in April or May) to the estimated production number which you have calculated for the upcoming crop, and you will now have the **Total supply** of wheat which will be available for sale and use in the upcoming crop year. **Example:** we will use the production number in step 4 above. Let's say that the present carryover is 1000 mil. bu. Then 1000 + 2499.12 = 3499.12 is the Total Supply.

HOW TO USE THE NEW FORECASTING GRAPHS

These new graphs approach the forecasted price from a different angle than the other Forecasting Graphs. These new graphs use the Total Wheat Supply for the new crop year and the Total Use from the previous crop year.

Here is the theory behind the new graphs. If the Total Wheat Supply for the new crop year is sufficient to meet the needs of the United Stated and the exports, then wheat prices will be moderate in the months ahead. But if the Total Supply is too small to meet the home consumption and foreign sales, then there will be a scarcity of wheat and prices will shoot up to $6 or more. ***In other words,*** is there enough supply to meet the demand? That's the basis of the new forecasting Graphs. It is based on wheat fundamentals.

Where do we get the Total Wheat Supply? By adding the last year's crop carryover to the estimated new crop size (which we figured out from the April grain report, or got from USDA).

Where do we get the Total Use (Demand)? By looking at the supply and demand numbers for the previous crop year – and selecting the number which represents the Total Use (home use and foreign sales).

What do we do then? Then we compare the new Total Wheat Supply with the Total Use from the previous crop year. One of the best ways to compare two numbers is to make a percentage from them. That's what is done here. ***Here is the equation for it:*** the new estimated Total Supply ÷ the last crop year's Total Use x 100=%. ***Here is an example.***

1. The date is April 15th, just after the April crop report was issued. We have just used the information from the report to calculate the estimated new crop size for the crop which will be harvested in the summer.

2. For this example, let's say that we calculated the new crop size to be 2400 mil. bu.

3. Let's also say that the carryover from the previous crop year is 600 mil. bu.

4. Therefore, the Total Supply is: 600+2400=3000 million bushels.

5. Now we need that last crop year's Total Use. For this example, let's say it was 2000 m. bu.

6. We will make a percentage: 3000 ÷ 2000 x 100=150%.

7. The 150% means that the supply is 50% larger than the likely demand or use. That means that there is plenty of wheat on hand which means that moderate prices are ahead.

Now what do we do? We will get our ***first preview*** of the estimated wheat prices on July 1st and Dec.1st. by using the 150% from the example above, on the new Forecasting Graphs below. Turn to the July graph. Locate the 150% on the left side of the graph.

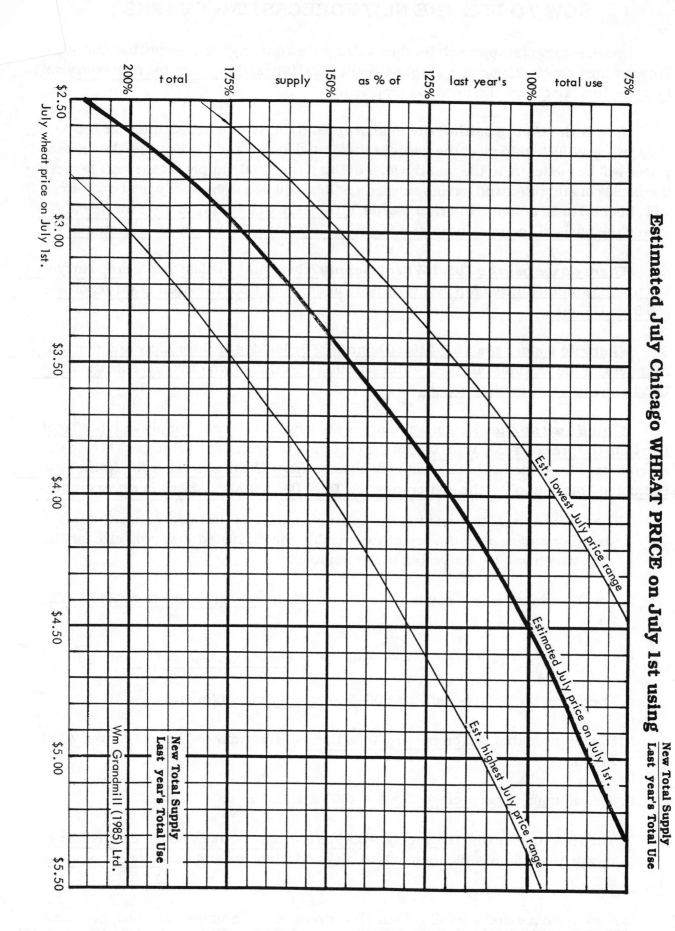

Estimated July Chicago WHEAT PRICE on July 1st using New Total Supply / Last year's Total Use

Estimated Dec. Chicago WHEAT PRICE on Dec. 1st using New Total Supply / Last year's Total Use

Est. lowest Dec. price range

Estimated Dec. price on Dec. 1st

Est. highest Dec price range

New Total Supply
Last year's Total Use

Wm Grandmill (1985) Ltd.

December wheat price on Dec. 1st.

total supply as % of last year's total use

Move to the right horizintally until you touch the heavy black line. Go straight down to the bottom line where you will read $3.40 as the estimated July wheat price on July 1st.

Then what? This may be the time to take a July wheat position.Let's say that July wheat is $4 at this date, April 15th. It would be worthwhile to sell a July wheat future, or to buy an at-the-money July $4 put option.

To sum up. The calculation which you do to find the Total Wheat Supply, and the use of the two new Forecasting Graphs, will give you a head start over the average wheat trader who will likely be waiting for the May crop report so that he can get the estimated crop size from USDA. Once the wheat trade realizes that prices will decline toward summer, then the July price will start down. Therefore the sooner that you get the July price estimate, the better.

Another Example: This time, we will use actual crop year data.

Crop Year	1983/84	84/85
Beginning Stocks	1515	1399
Production (crop size)	2424	2603
Total Supply	3939	4002
Domestic Use	1111	
Exports	1429	
Total Use	2540	
Carryover	1399	

1. The date is April 15th, 1984. We use USDA's information from the April crop report to calculate the estimated crop size for the new crop year coming up. Let's say that we get 2603 million bu. (actually this number of 2603 is the final figure, so the estimate we would make on April 15th would not be as accurate – we would have a good approximate number). Follow this in the supply and demand statistics.

2. Note that the Total Supply is 4002 mil. bu. for 84/85 which was the sum of the carryover from the previous crop year plus the crop size estimate.

3. Note that the Total Use for the previous crop year of 83/84 is 2540 mil. bu.

4. We need the % number. New Total Supply ÷ last year's Total Use: 4002 ÷ 2540 x 100=158%

5. Using 158% on the left sides of the graphs, we get an estimated July 1st price of $3.23 and an estimated Dec. 1st price of $3.38. (that year, the price on July 1st was $3.18 and the Dec. 1st price was $3.52, in real prices).

WHEAT PRICES TO THE END OF THE CENTURY

A NEW WHEAT PRICE ERA HAS BEGUN

So far this book has dealt with the wheat situation as it has been up to 1988/89, concentrating particularly on the U.S. market. But what is ahead for the next 10 years? In order to get an understanding of the wheat trade, we must broaden our outlook so that we see the global picture. The United States produces only about 11% of all the world's wheat but it exports about 1/3 of all exported wheat. This means that the amount of wheat grown abroad has a great effect on wheat prices in the United States.

Something unusual has occurred in the past two years in the world wheat trade. For the last 2 consecutive years, world wheat **consumption** has exceeded world wheat **production** by a large amount. This is significant news and it could herald a new era for wheat prices.

But first some history on our last leap forward. A new price plateau was begun in 1973/74 when the Russians swooped down on the U.S. wheat market and bought up nearly all the available wheat at bargain prices, creating a wheat shortage which sent prices almost straight up. Prior to 1973, wheat prices had been dawdling along between $2 and $2.50. Then, after the clean-out in 73-74, wheat prices rose to $5.75 and by doing so, it had raised wheat prices to a new plateau which lasted until 88/89 -but by 1986 and 1987 the momentum had slowed to a standstill so that a low of $2.40 was reached in those years and it had been several years since wheat had gone above $4.

Once again in the 88/89 crop year, we are operating between the $4 and the $5 levels because of a severe drought in 1988. The market took on a new life and trading volume increased. But will it last? Let's take a look at some world wheat statistics.

Below is a graph comparing the world wheat production with world consumption. Look at it and you will see that production exceeded consumption up to the crop year 86/87. Then in 87/88 the production dropped by about 30 million metric tonnes (1.1 Billion bushels). Then came the drought of 88/89 and there was a further drop in world wheat production of 35 mil. m. tonnes (1.286 billion bu.). But the rate of consumption continued to increase in those two years, with the result that wheat consumption has outstripped world production by a large amount. This is a serious event and it signals a new price level.

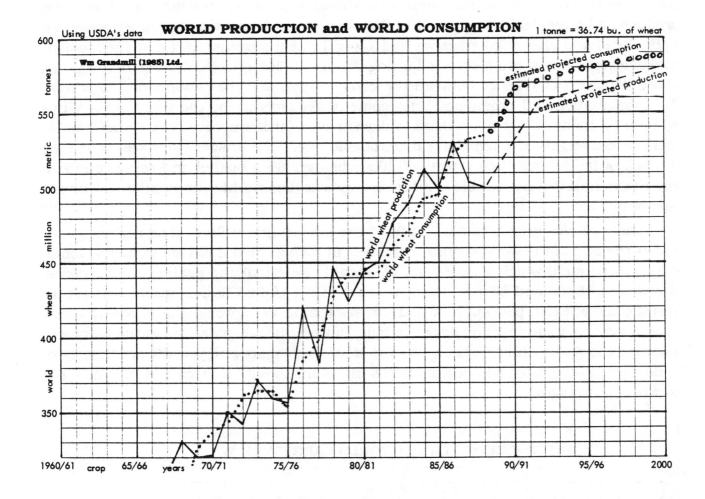

WORLD PRODUCTION and WORLD CONSUMPTION

Using USDA's data   1 tonne = 36.74 bu. of wheat

Wm Grandmill (1985) Ltd.

Will world wheat consumption exceed world wheat production in the foresee-able future? The answer appears to be "Yes" -and it's not surprising because we have been told for years that the exponential growth in the world population was creating a strain on the food supply. More and more countries are now unable to feed themselves, particularly in Africa. But the most ominous sign of the times might be in China. Just a few years ago China exported a small quantity of wheat. Now it is a buyer of wheat and will likely have to purchase wheat every year from now on. One statistic said that about 60,000 babies were born in China **every day** on average. Fortunately China has promoted free enterprise farming so the local markets will have vegetables and fruit but wheat is a different category. There are a billion people in China, and growing. The amount of arable land is shrinking in relation to the population growth.

Look again at the graph above. You will see an estimated **projection** of what the author believes will be the approximate rate of growth for both the production and consumption. It is not accurate but it is not guesswork either. The projected consumption line is based on the population growth and the wheat price. The projected production line is based on the likelihood that there are not many extra hectares available in the world for wheat planting, and on the likelihood that there will be a small increase in the wheat yield over the next 10 years.

We had a "Green Revolution" in the 60's and 70's wherein new crop strains for grain and rice were produced. These new strains were more resistant to disease and produced a better yield. As a result of that step forward, the wheat production moved right ahead and after a few years we had a world wheat surplus. But now the momentum is gone and now production is lagging the population growth. Therefore the graph above depicts a divergence between the consumption and the production. **But note** the consumption and production lines come closer together by the year 2000. Why? Wouldn't it be more logical for them to diverge even farther apart? What would cause them to converge? The reply is a materialistic one. The answer, you see, is **money** -or lack of it. By this time wheat will likely be over $6 a bushel and some countries and individuals will not be able to afford to buy wheat so world consumption will be cut back a bit.

Look at the graph below. Look at the bottom graph first. The bottom graph shows the size of the world's wheat carryover in million metric tonnes (A metric tonne = 2204.6 pounds, which = 36.74 bu. of wheat.) Note that the peak of the carryover size was in 85/86 and 86/87. In those years in the United States, wheat reached its lowest price of $2.40 per bu. Now you can see that it was a world glut of wheat which caused exports to decline and prices to fall. But see the steep decline in the carryover following the peak! And look back over the chart to compare and you will see that there is no comparable drop previously. That's an ominous sign that we are in a new era of wheat shortages.

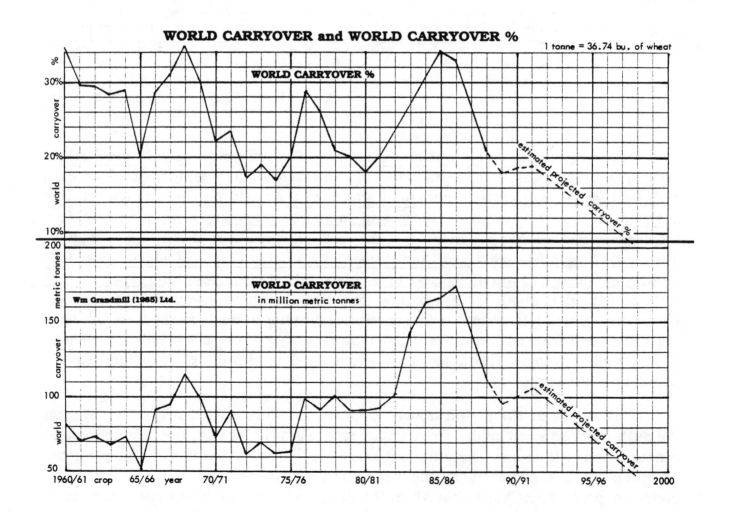

WORLD CARRYOVER and WORLD CARRYOVER %

Look at the projection into the future of the world wheat carryover. Note that the next 3 years are fairly flat -that means that wheat prices will likely fluctuate between $4 and $5 for those years. Then because consumption outstrips production, we will likely see another decline in carryover which will push prices above $5, and likely above $6 per bu.

Look at the carryover % graph above. Here you can see what world carryover % was since 1960. And you can also see where the projected carryover is headed. New percent lows will be registered in the years ahead, bringing higher wheat prices.

Below is a graph constructed specifically for this section of the book. A larger version is at the back of the book. This graph shows how a lower U.S. carryover % will affect U.S. wheat prices. The U.S. carryover will likely fall to 15% in the next 10 years, and maybe lower. See what sort of prices we can expect with a 15% carryover. The graphs were not constructed from past data because these high prices have not happened yet. Instead, the Forecasting Graphs were projected ahead to reflect new low carryover percents.

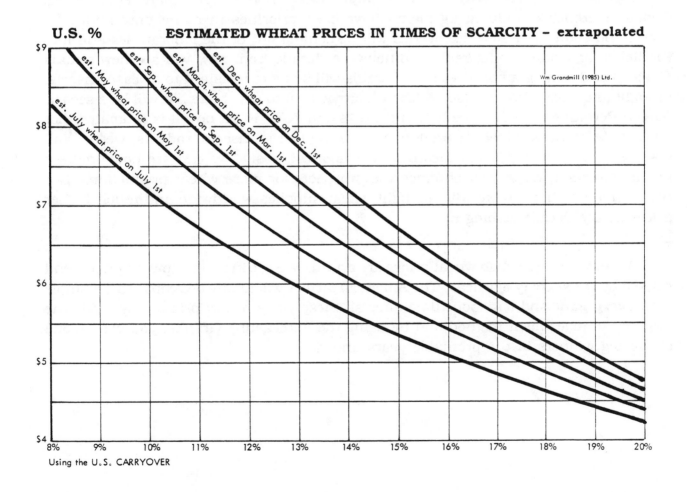

U.S. %   **ESTIMATED WHEAT PRICES IN TIMES OF SCARCITY – extrapolated**

Wm Grandmill (1985) Ltd.

Using the U.S. CARRYOVER

Is there any hope of reversing this trend to a scarcity of wheat? Yes, there is hope. There are two likely possibilities which could influence the trend from scarcity to sufficiency. Note the word "sufficiency", because it is doubtful that we will see large surpluses again. But there are two possibilities of increasing production about 10 years from now.

First, there is Russia. As you know, Russia is a good customer of the United States, buying a good quantity of wheat every year. But all that could change if Mr. Gorbachev can persuade Russian agriculture to get its act together. Right now Russia is the world largest wheat grower -but somehow the wheat doesn't get to the consumer. Inefficiency and wastefullness are the two words most used to describe Russian farming. The American farmer is the most efficient farmer in the world, and if Gorbachev can get the Russian farmer to emulate the American farmer over the next 10 years, and it will take that long to turn that agricultural dinosaur around, then Russia will become a large exporter of wheat. Some of the best wheat fields in the world are in the East European countries e.g. Romania. So one of the possibilities is there.

The second possibility is more important. It is genetic plant engineering. Genetic methods of influencing plants have been priorities in many universities for years, and soon these new discoveries will be coming out of the laboratories and into the fields for testing under real conditions. A decade from now will see new strains of wheat and other grains. These new strains will be more resistant to disease, insects, drought and frost. We will also see the wheat yield go to new highs. It will be a second "Green Revolution" such as we had in the 60's and 70's. Right now it is estimated that about 25% of all world wheat production is being lost to insects, rodents, weeds, and disease -the third world countries have the greatest loss. You can see how progress in this direction will greatly enhance the prospects for more wheat production. But before this will happen we will see tight wheat supplies worldwide and much higher prices in the decade coming up.

To sum up. New high wheat prices are ahead. We are in a new upward price trend caused by the scarcity of wheat. The American farmer will finally be reaping a profitable crop ***every year*** and it's about time after all these years of low prices. By using the year round investment method and by using the Forecasting Graphs, you will be one of the big winners in the profitable years ahead.

GRAPHS AND CHARTS

COMBINED % MARCH Estimated Chicago MARCH WHEAT PRICE on MARCH 1st

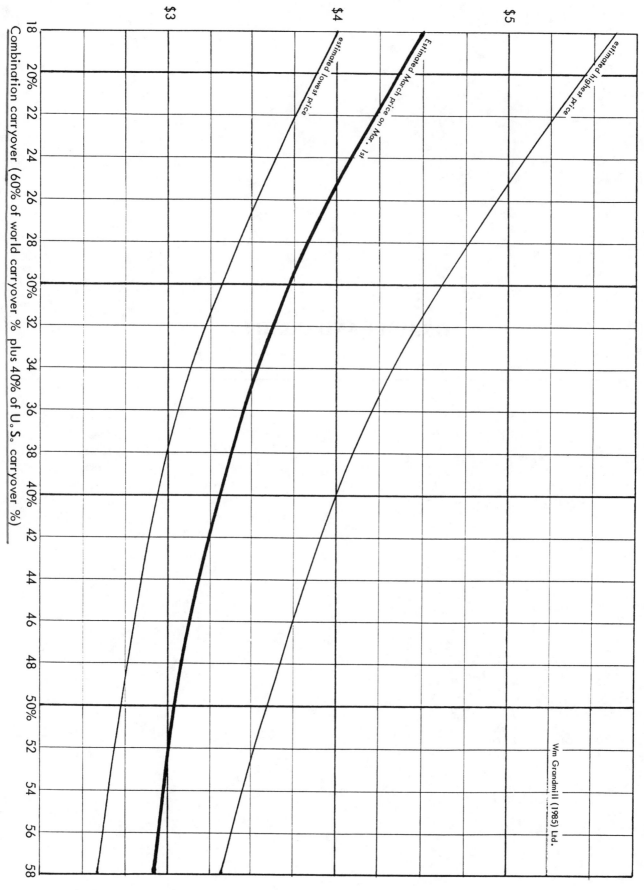

estimated highest price

Estimated March price on Mar. 1st

estimated lowest price

Combination carryover (60% of world carryover % plus 40% of U.S. carryover %)

Wm Grandmill (1985) Ltd.

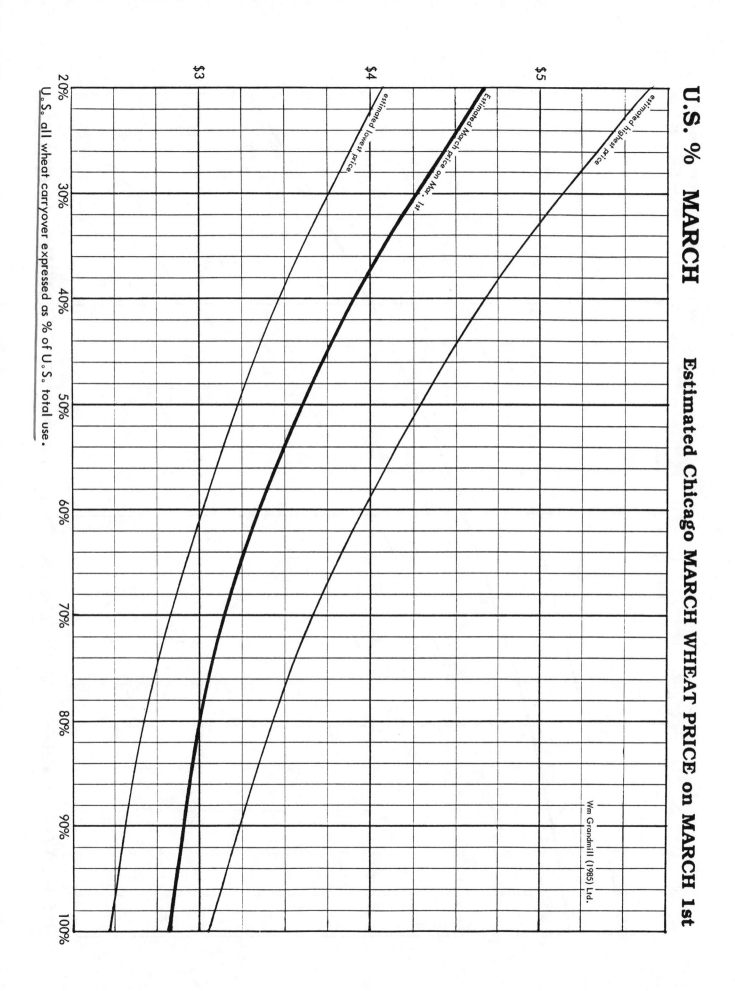

U.S. % MARCH   Estimated Chicago MARCH WHEAT PRICE on MARCH 1st

U.S. all wheat carryover expressed as % of U.S. total use.

estimated lowest price

Estimated March price on Mar. 1st

estimated highest price

Wm Grandmill (1985) Ltd.

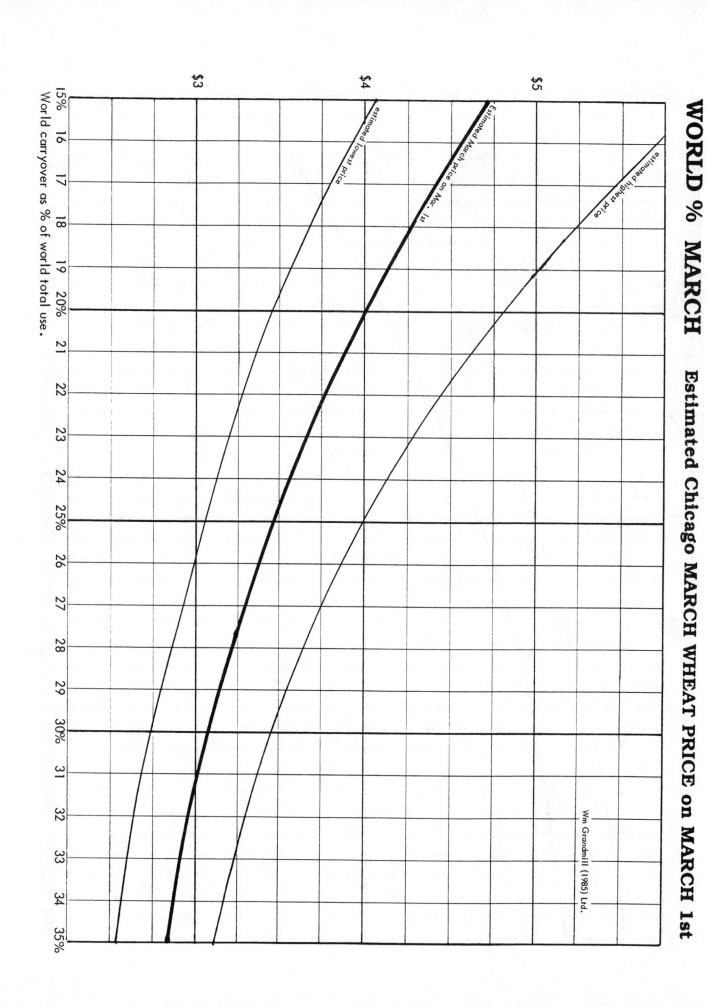

WORLD % MARCH Estimated Chicago MARCH WHEAT PRICE on MARCH 1st

World carryover as % of world total use.

estimated lowest price

Estimated March price on Mar. 1st

estimated highest price

Wm Grandmill (1985) Ltd.

$3

$4

$5

15%
16
17
18
19
20%
21
22
23
24
25%
26
27
28
29
30%
31
32
33
34
35%

65

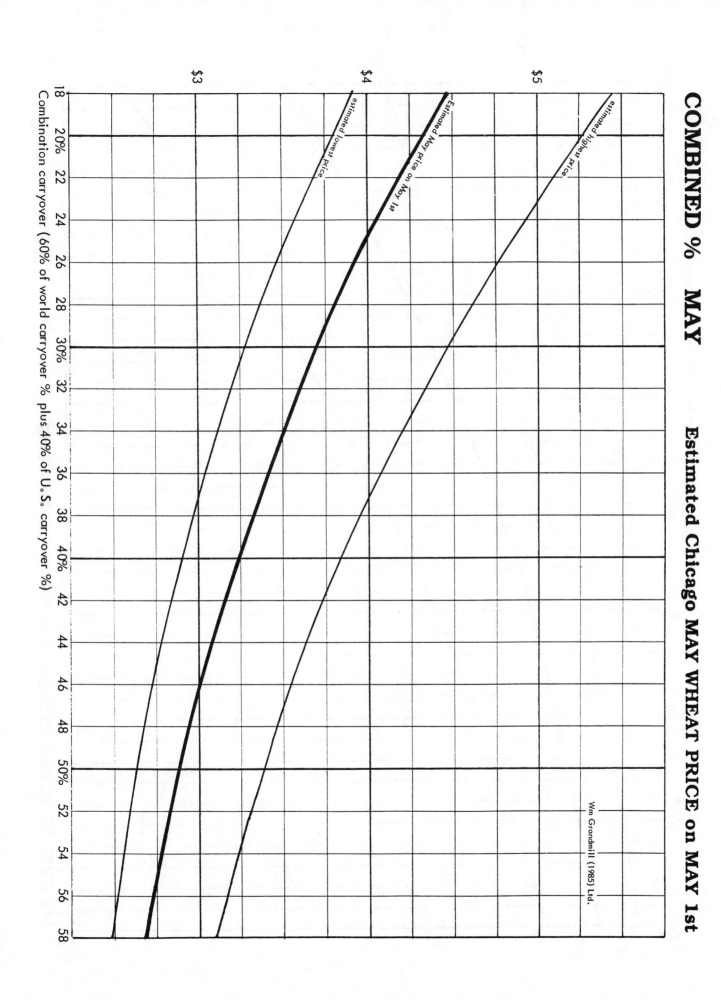

COMBINED % MAY

Estimated Chicago MAY WHEAT PRICE on MAY 1st

Combination carryover (60% of world carryover % plus 40% of U.S. carryover %)

estimated lowest price

Estimated May price on May 1st

estimated highest price

Wm Grandmill (1985) Ltd.

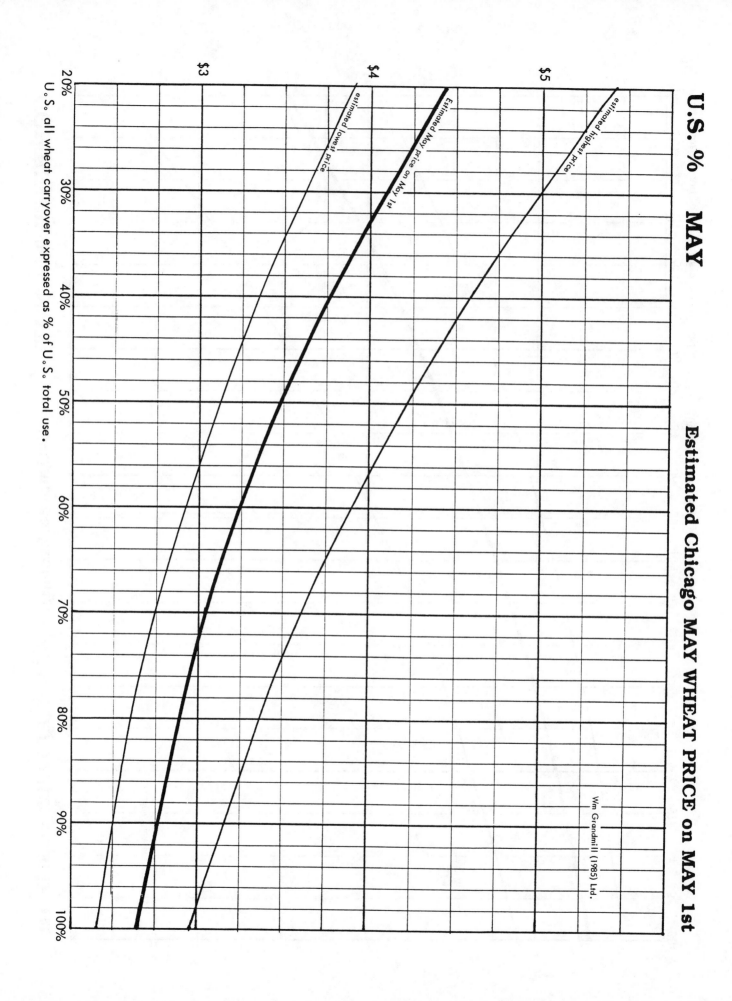

U.S. % MAY

Estimated Chicago MAY WHEAT PRICE on MAY 1st

U.S. all wheat carryover expressed as % of U.S. total use.

estimated lowest price

Estimated May price on May 1st

estimated highest price

Wm Grandmill (1985) Ltd.

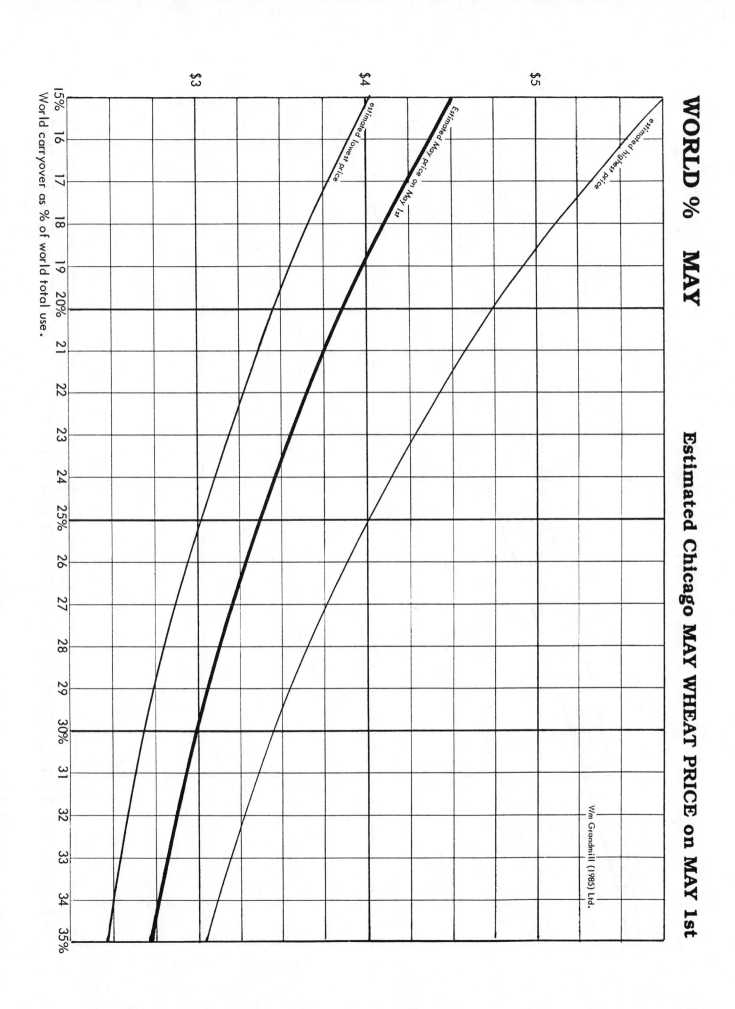

WORLD % MAY — Estimated Chicago MAY WHEAT PRICE on MAY 1st

World carryover as % of world total use.

estimated lowest price

Estimated May price on May 1st

estimated highest price

Wm Grandmill (1985) Ltd.

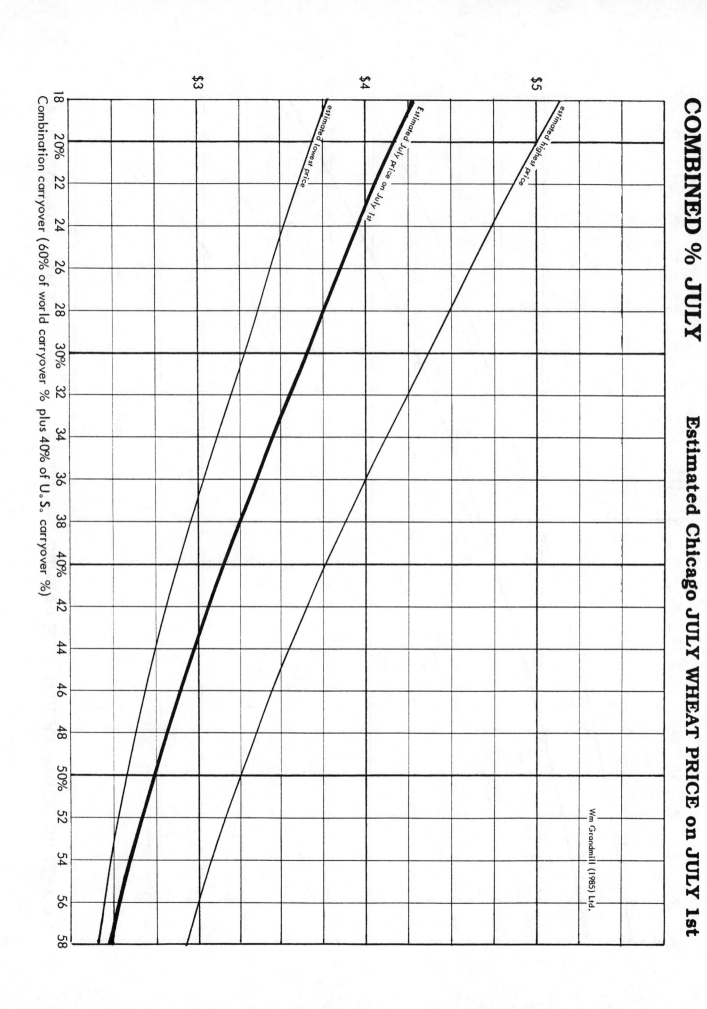

COMBINED % JULY

Estimated Chicago JULY WHEAT PRICE on JULY 1st

estimated highest price

Estimated July price on July 1st

estimated lowest price

Combination carryover (60% of world carryover % plus 40% of U.S. carryover %)

Wm Grandmill (1985) Ltd.

69

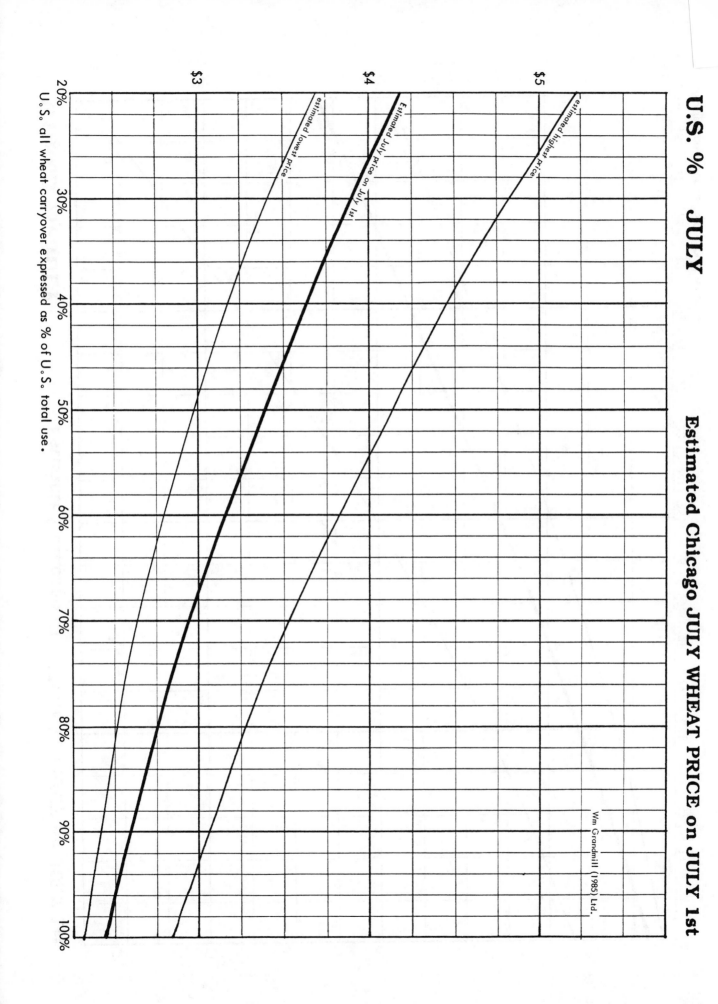

U.S. % JULY

Estimated Chicago JULY WHEAT PRICE on JULY 1st

U.S. all wheat carryover expressed as % of U.S. total use.

estimated highest price

Estimated July price on July 1st

estimated lowest price

Wm Grandmill (1985) Ltd.

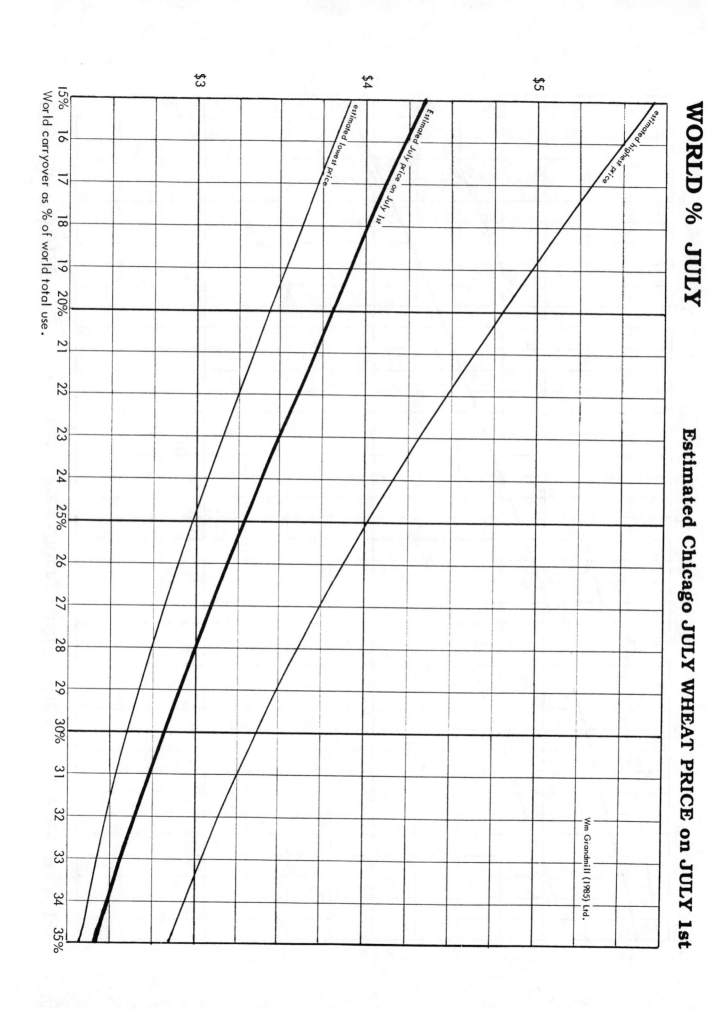

WORLD % JULY

Estimated Chicago JULY WHEAT PRICE on JULY 1st

estimated highest price

Estimated July price on July 1st

estimated lowest price

World carryover as % of world total use.

Wm Grandmill (1985) Ltd.

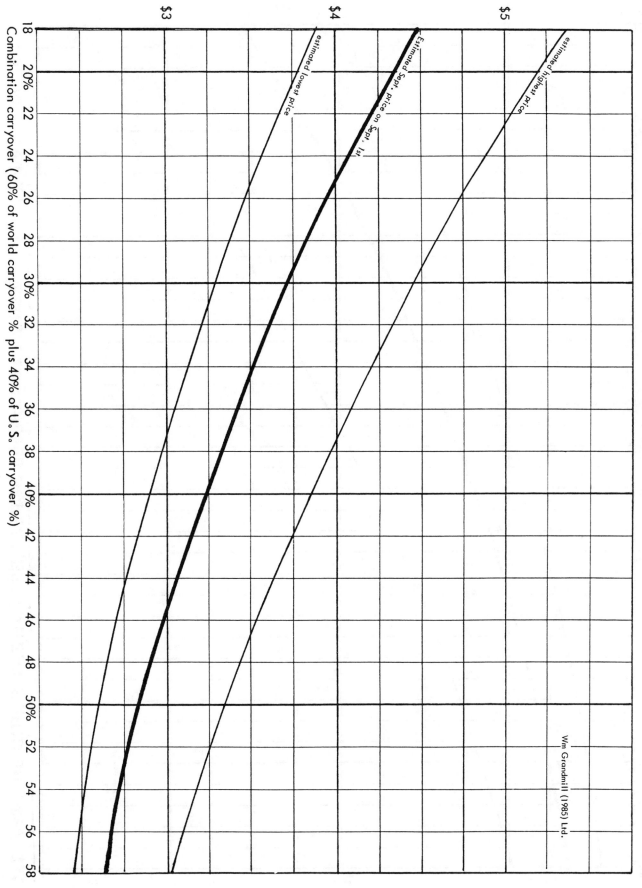

COMBINED % SEPT. Estimated Chicago SEPTEMBER WHEAT PRICE on SEPT. 1st

estimated highest price

Estimated Sept. price on Sept. 1st

estimated lowest price

Combination carryover (60% of world carryover % plus 40% of U.S. carryover %)

Wm Grandmill (1985) Ltd.

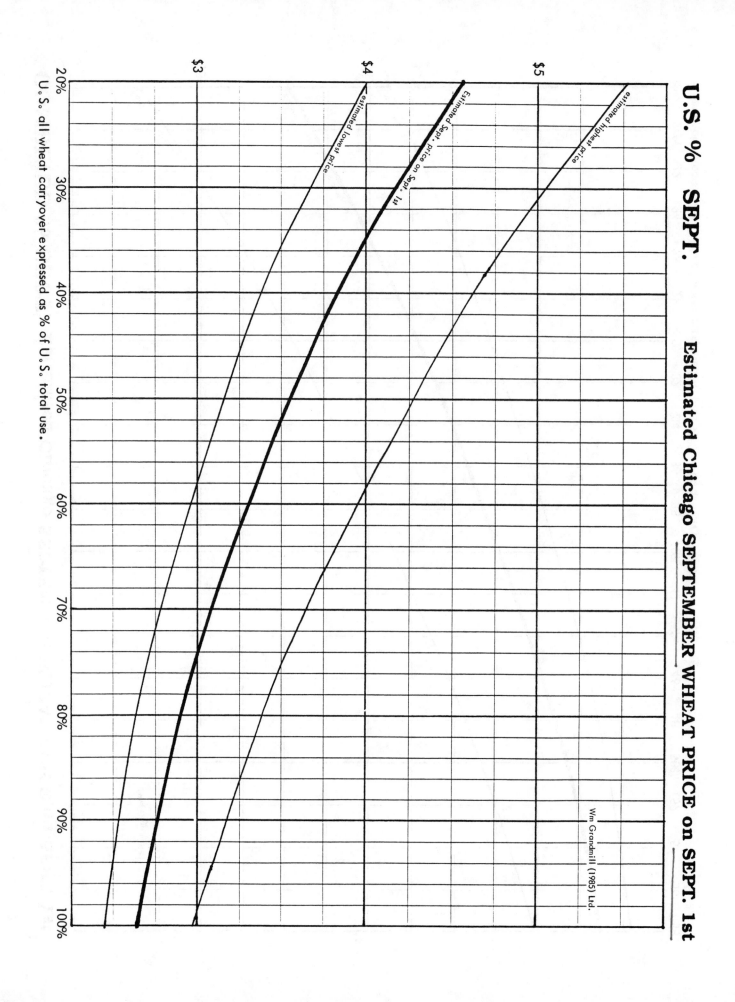

U.S. % SEPT.   Estimated Chicago SEPTEMBER WHEAT PRICE on SEPT. 1st

U.S. all wheat carryover expressed as % of U.S. total use.

estimated lowest price

Estimated Sept. price on Sept. 1st

estimated highest price

Wm Grandmill (1985) Ltd.

73

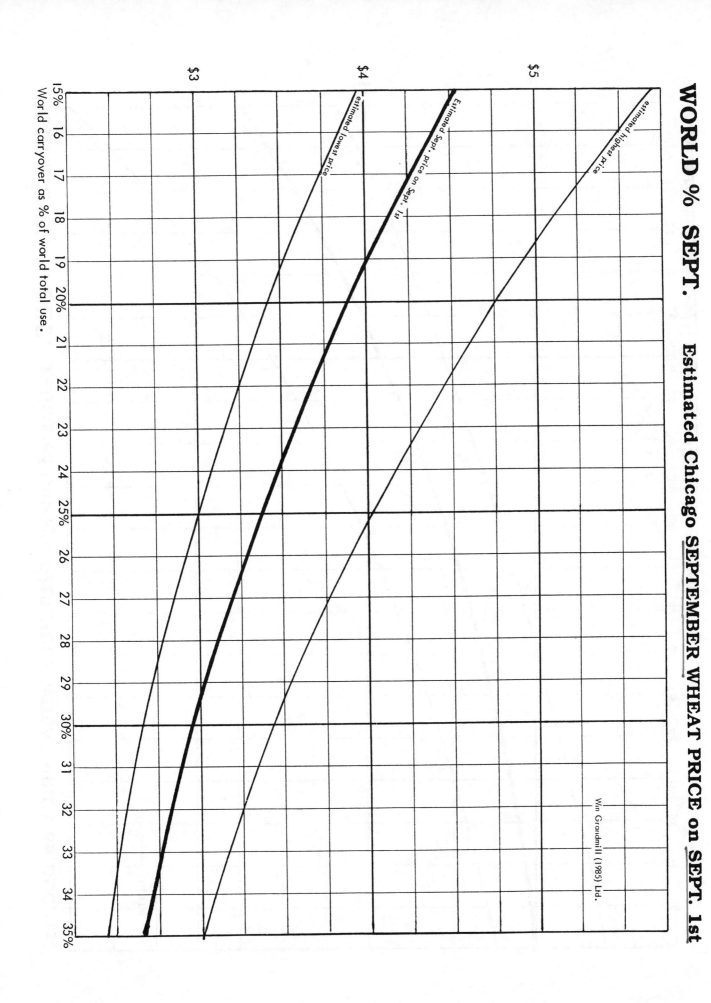

WORLD % SEPT. Estimated Chicago SEPTEMBER WHEAT PRICE on SEPT. 1st

World carryover as % of world total use.

estimated highest price

Estimated Sept. price on Sept. 1st

estimated lowest price

Win Grandmill (1985) Ltd.

74

COMBINED % DEC. Estimated Chicago DECEMBER WHEAT PRICE on DEC. 1st

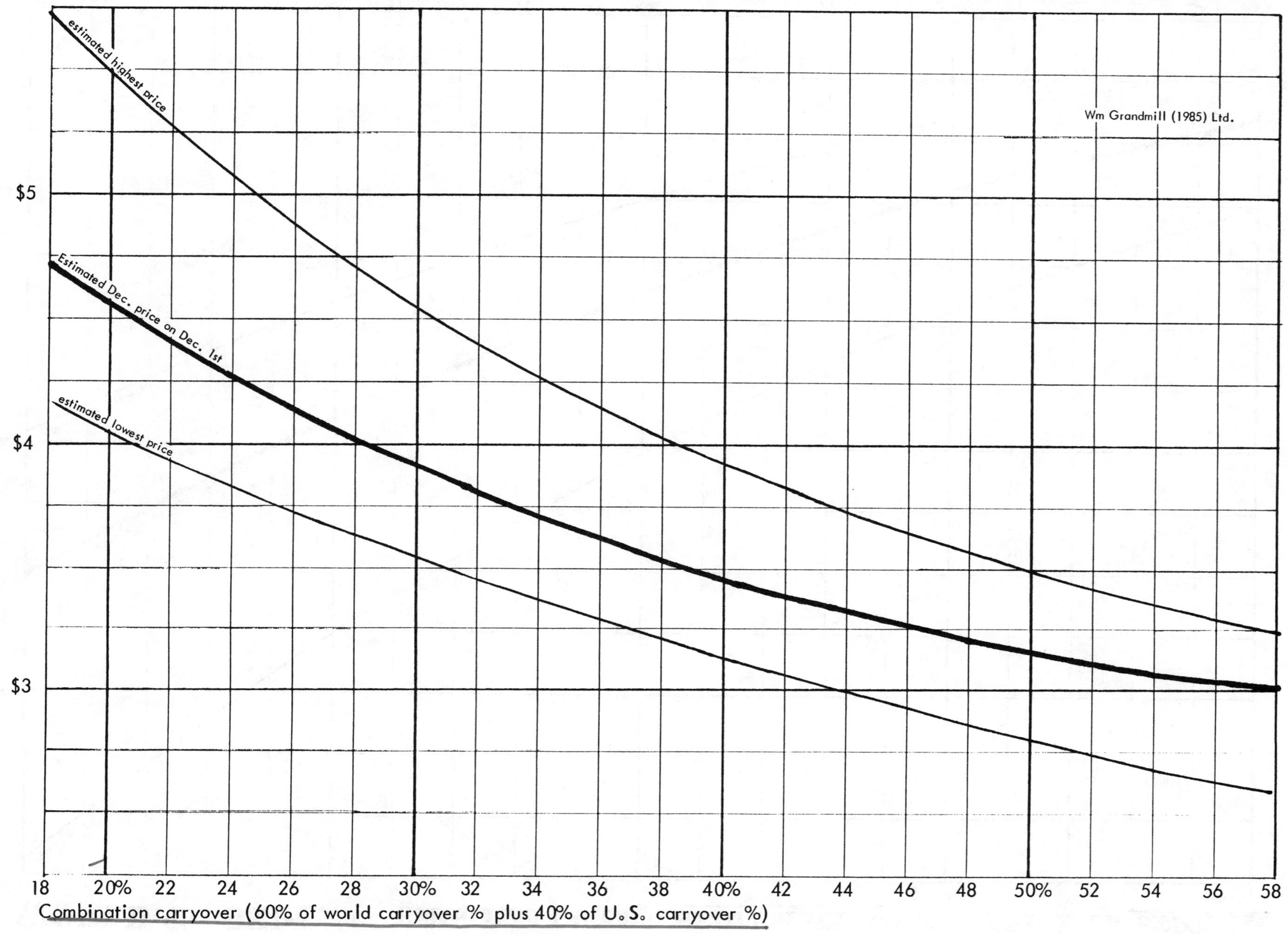

estimated higher price

Estimated Dec. price on Dec. 1st

estimated lowest price

Wm Grandmill (1985) Ltd.

Combination carryover (60% of world carryover % plus 40% of U.S. carryover %)

$5

$4

$3

18
20%
22
24
26
28
30%
32
34
36
38
40%
42
44
46
48
50%
52
54
56
58

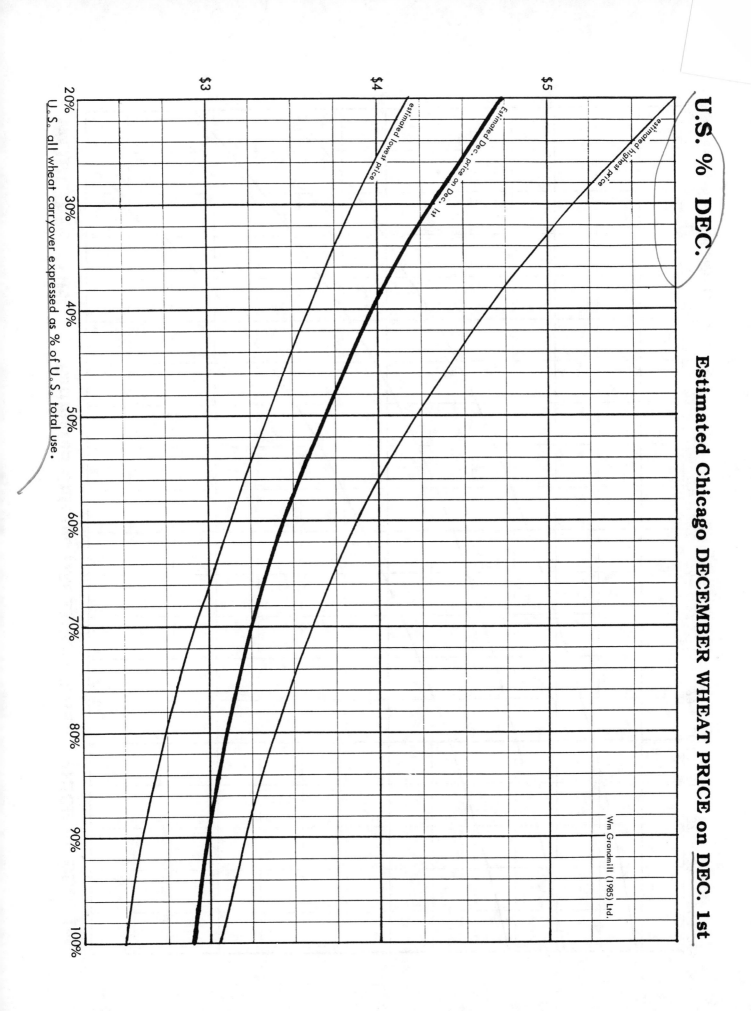

U.S. % DEC.

Estimated Chicago DECEMBER WHEAT PRICE on DEC. 1st

estimated highest price

Estimated Dec. price on Dec. 1st

estimated lowest price

U.S. all wheat carryover expressed as % of U.S. total use.

Wm Grandmill (1985) Ltd.

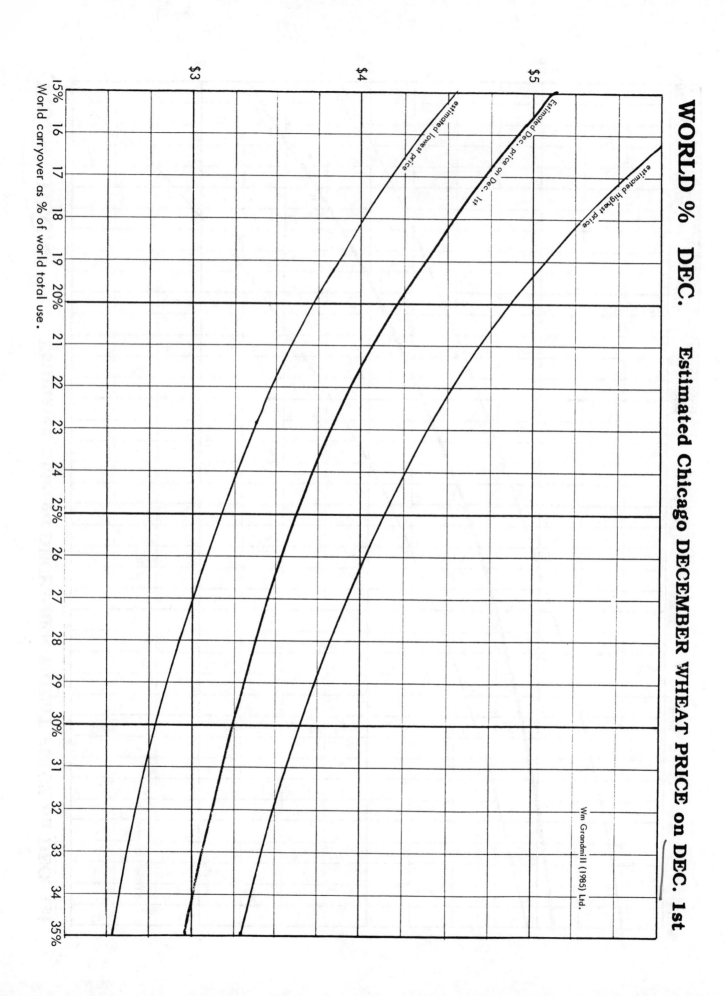

WORLD % DEC. Estimated Chicago DECEMBER WHEAT PRICE on DEC. 1st

estimated lowest price

Estimated Dec. price on Dec. 1st

estimated highest price

Wm Grandmill (1985) Ltd.

World carryover as % of world total use.

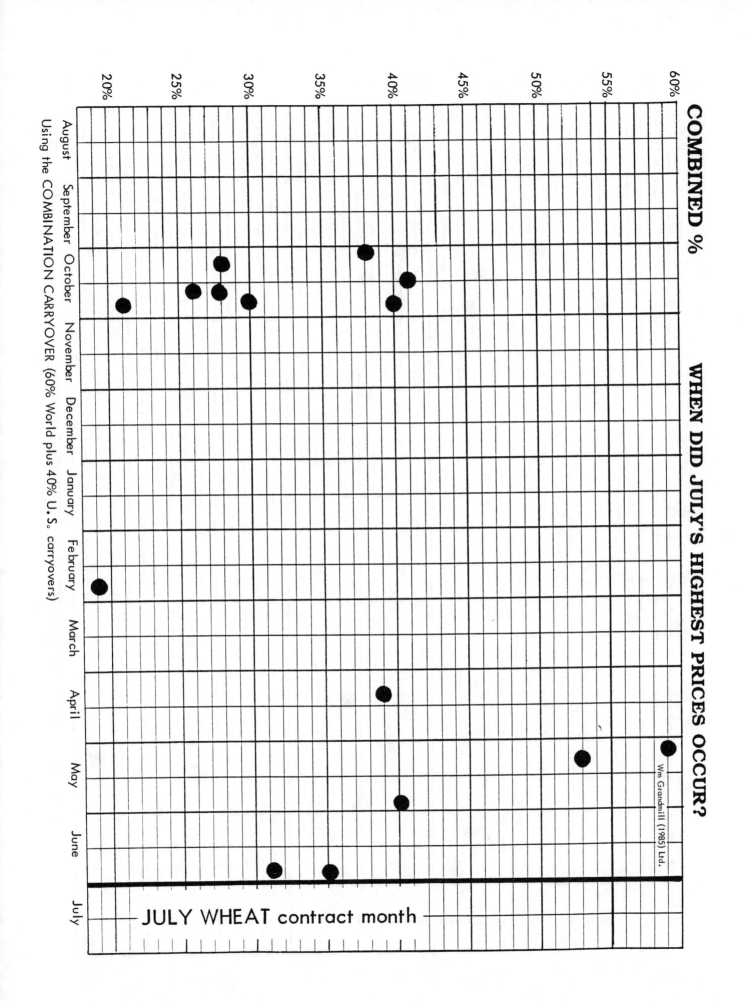

COMBINED %

WHEN DID JULY'S HIGHEST PRICES OCCUR?

Wm. Grandmill (1985) Ltd.

JULY WHEAT contract month

Using the COMBINATION CARRYOVER (60% World plus 40% U.S. carryovers)

78

U.S. %

WHEN DID JULY'S HIGHEST PRICES OCCUR?

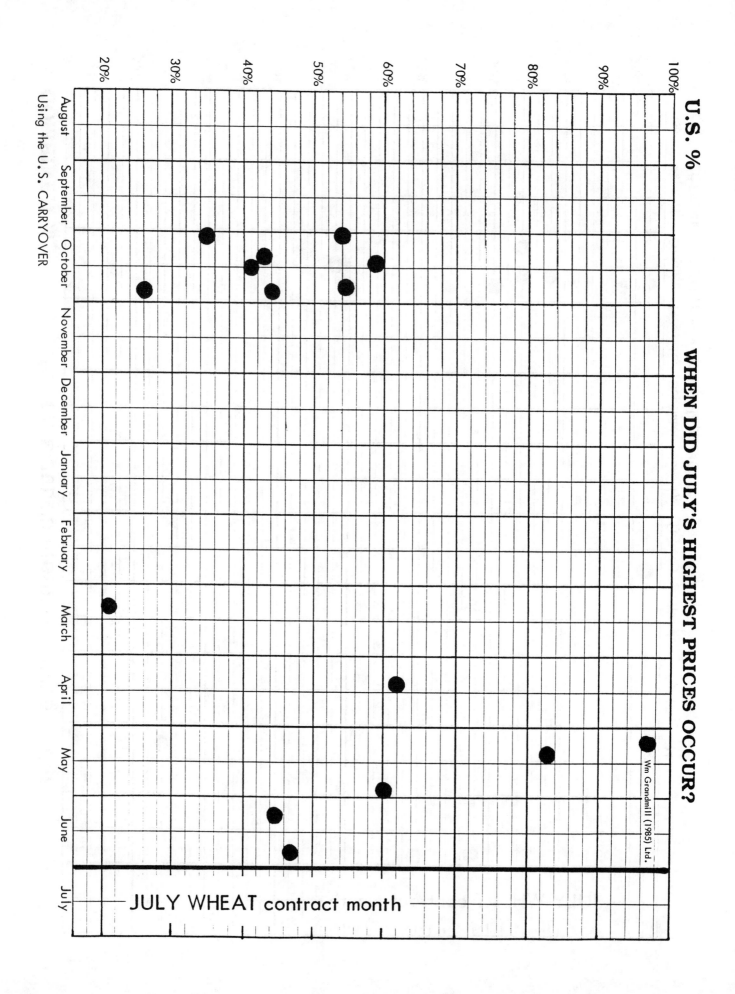

Wm Grandmill (1985) Ltd.

Using the U.S. CARRYOVER

JULY WHEAT contract month

79

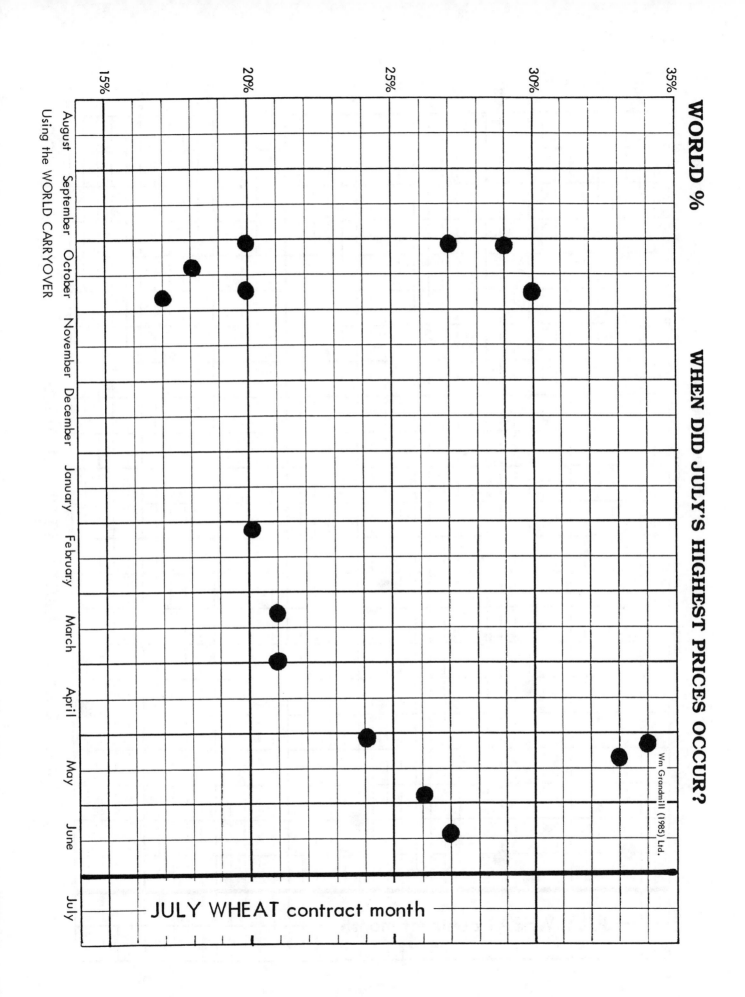

WORLD %

WHEN DID JULY'S HIGHEST PRICES OCCUR?

Using the WORLD CARRYOVER

JULY WHEAT contract month

Wm Grandmill (1985) Ltd.

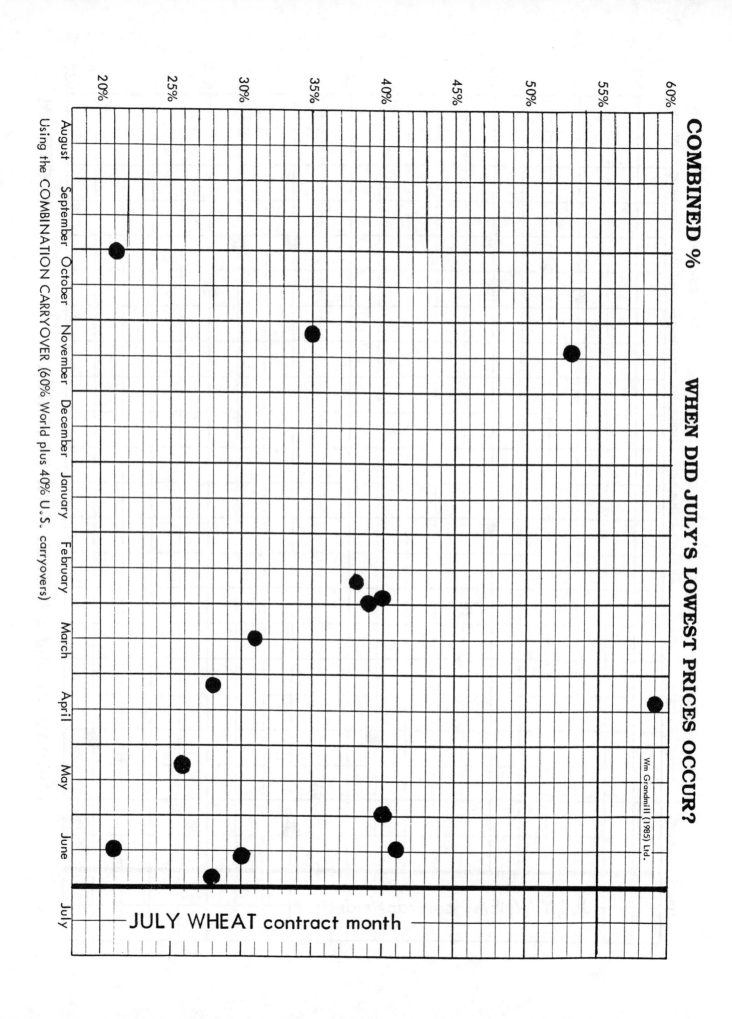

COMBINED %

WHEN DID JULY'S LOWEST PRICES OCCUR?

JULY WHEAT contract month

Using the COMBINATION CARRYOVER (60% World plus 40% U.S. carryovers)

Wm Grandmill (1985) Ltd.

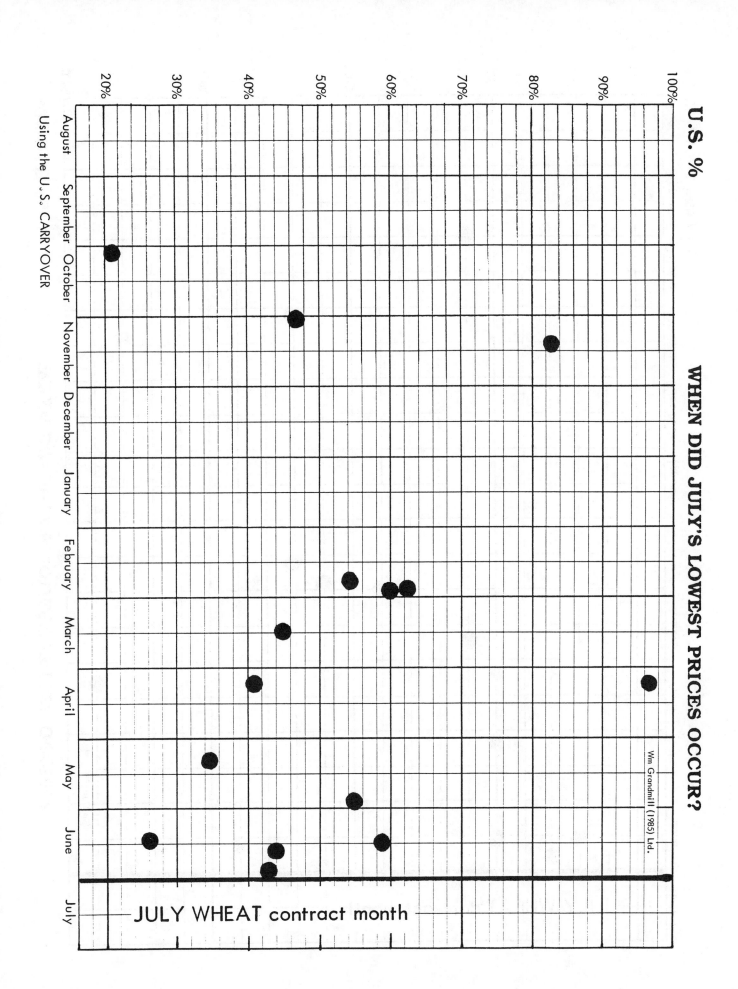

U.S. %

WHEN DID JULY'S LOWEST PRICES OCCUR?

Using the U.S. CARRYOVER

Wm Grandmill (1985) Ltd.

JULY WHEAT contract month

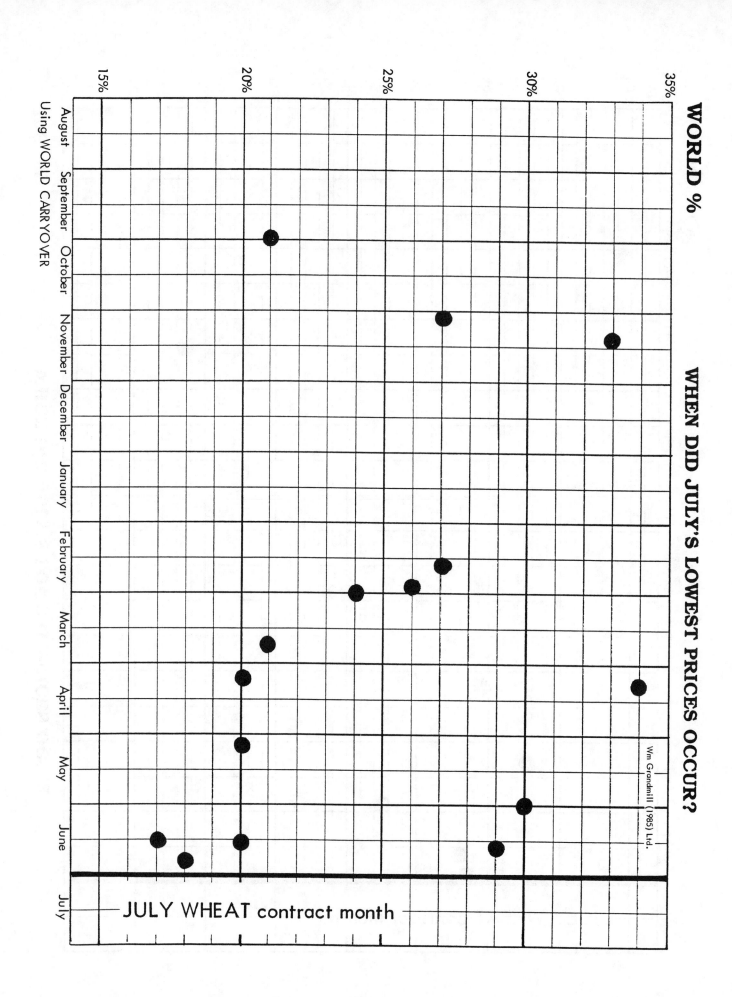

WORLD %

WHEN DID JULY'S LOWEST PRICES OCCUR?

Using WORLD CARRYOVER

JULY WHEAT contract month

Wm Grandmill (1985) Ltd.

83

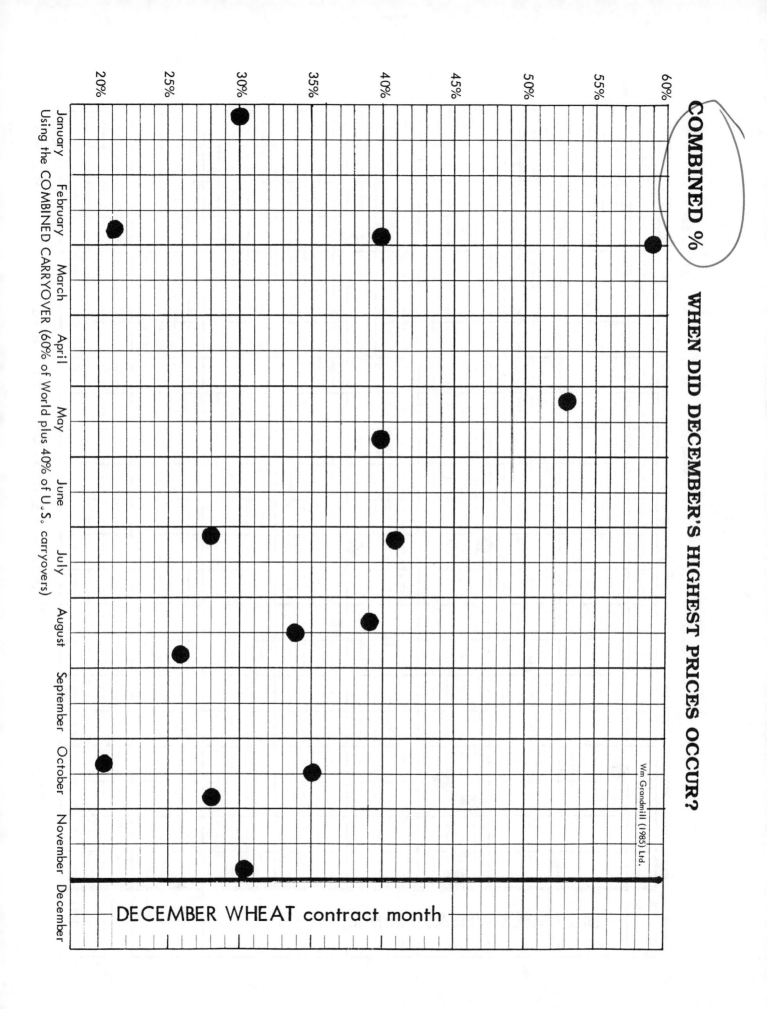

COMBINED %

WHEN DID DECEMBER'S HIGHEST PRICES OCCUR?

Using the COMBINED CARRYOVER (60% of World plus 40% of U.S. carryovers)

DECEMBER WHEAT contract month

Wm Grandmill (1985) Ltd.

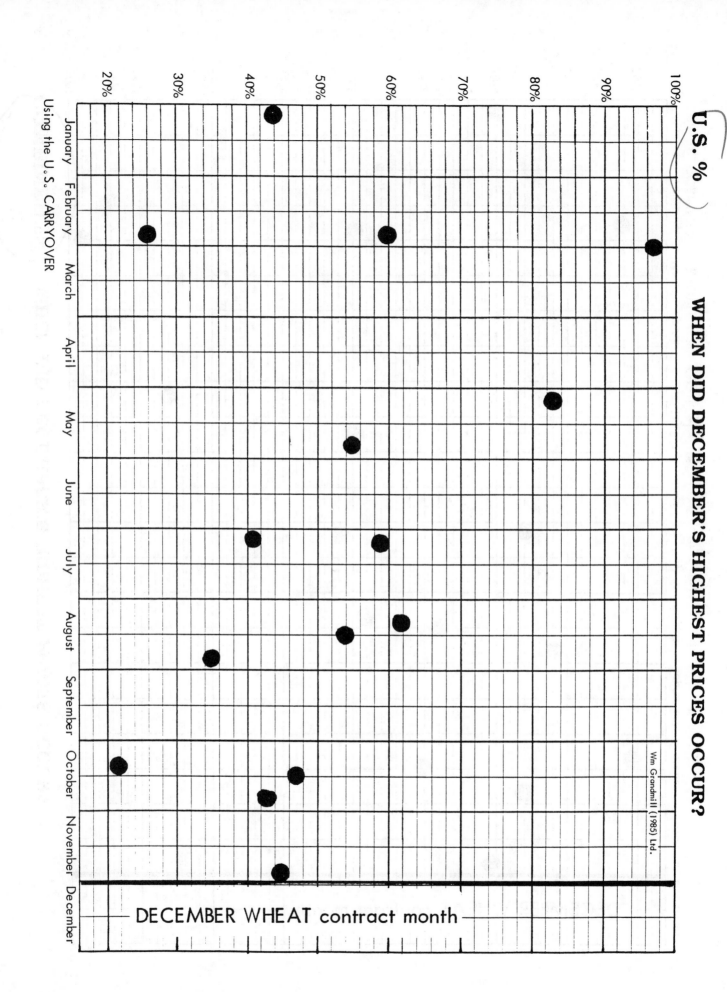

WHEN DID DECEMBER'S HIGHEST PRICES OCCUR?

U.S. %

Wm Grandmill (1985) Ltd.

DECEMBER WHEAT contract month

Using the U.S. CARRYOVER

85

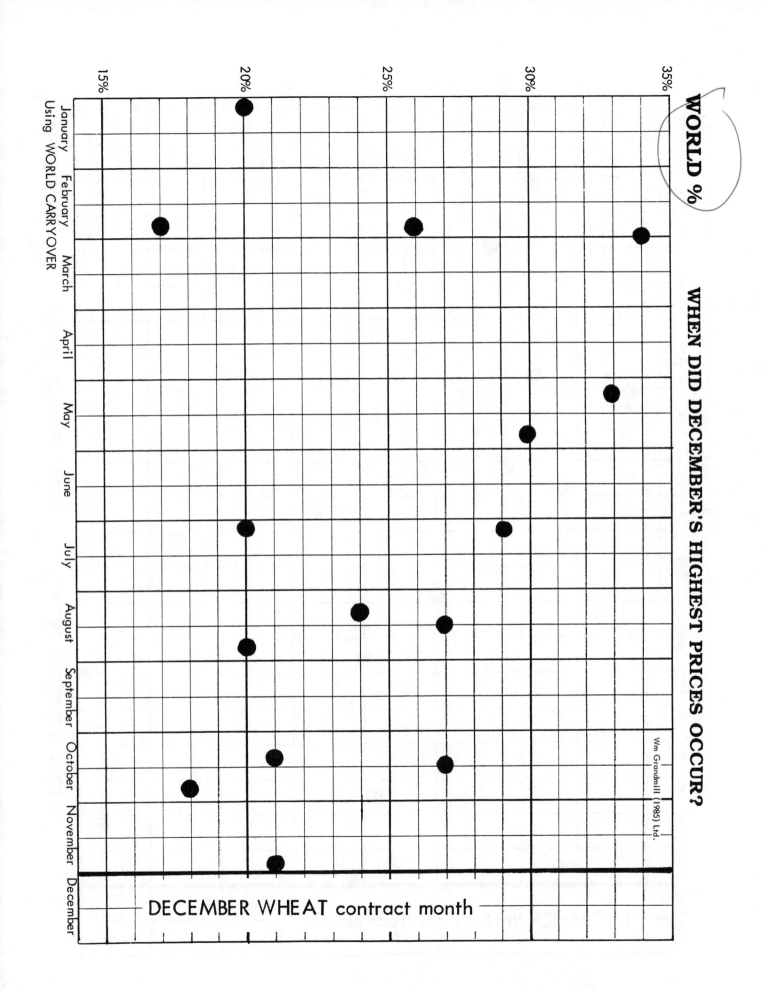

WORLD %

WHEN DID DECEMBER'S HIGHEST PRICES OCCUR?

Using WORLD CARRYOVER

DECEMBER WHEAT contract month

Wm Grandmill (1985) Ltd.

86

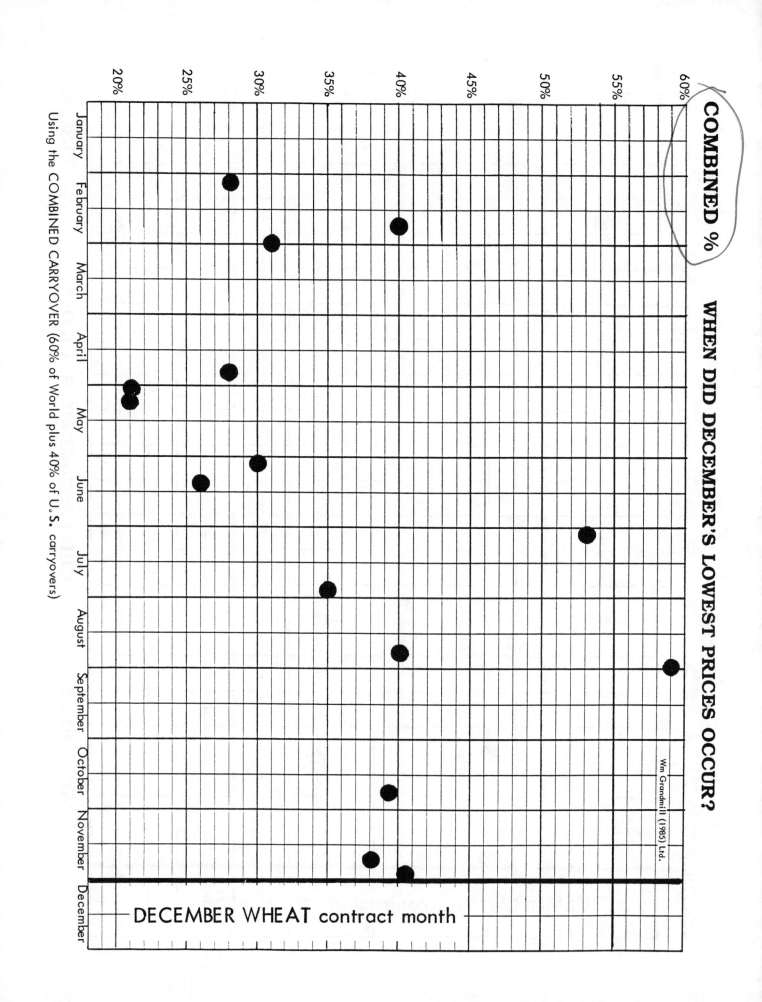

COMBINED %

WHEN DID DECEMBER'S LOWEST PRICES OCCUR?

Wm Grandmill (1985) Ltd.

Using the COMBINED CARRYOVER (60% of World plus 40% of U.S. carryovers)

DECEMBER WHEAT contract month

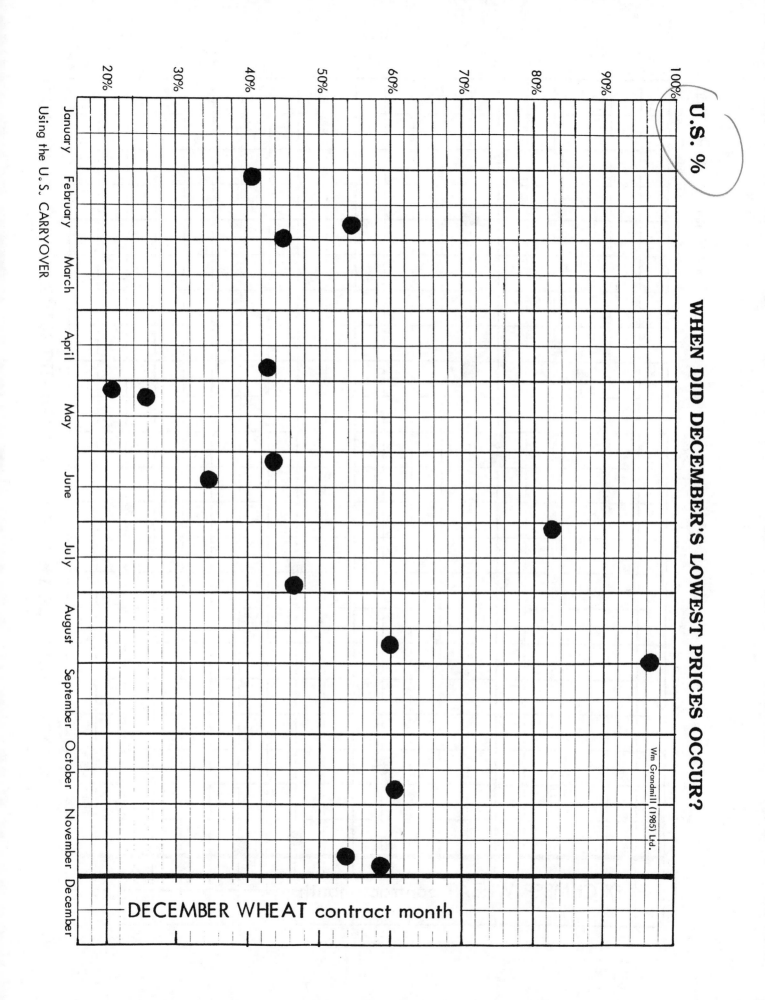

WHEN DID DECEMBER'S LOWEST PRICES OCCUR?

U.S. %

Using the U.S. CARRYOVER

DECEMBER WHEAT contract month

Wm Grandmill (1985) Ltd.

WHEN DID DECEMBER'S LOWEST PRICES OCCUR?

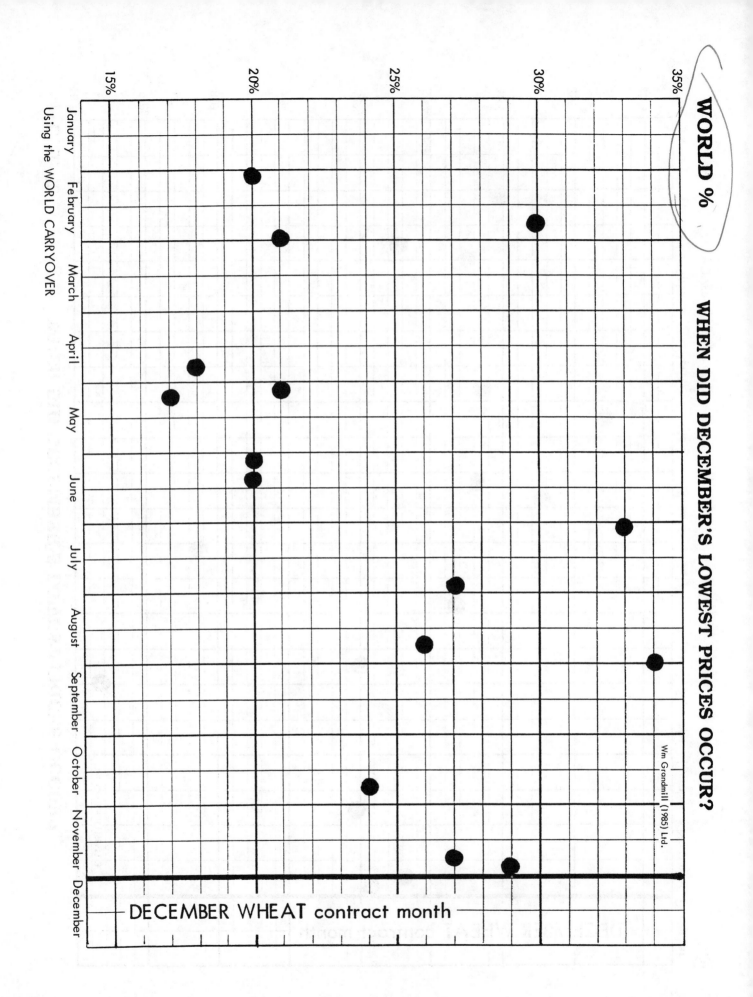

Wm Grandmill (1985) Ltd.

Using the WORLD CARRYOVER

DECEMBER WHEAT contract month

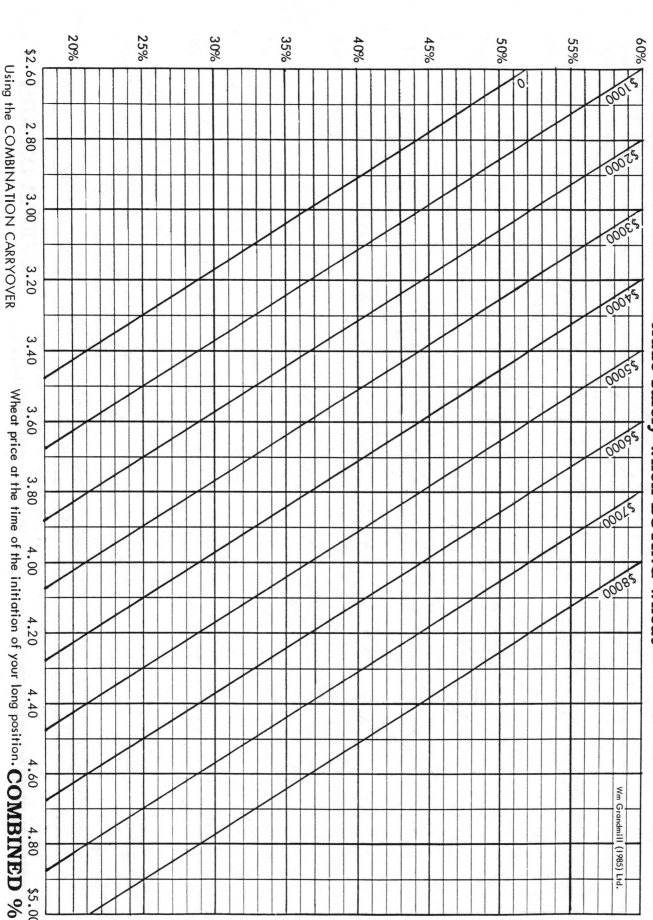

BUYING WHEAT

Estimated MAXIMUM AMOUNT of Backup Capital needed to trade safely when BUYING wheat

Wm Grandmill (1985) Ltd.

Using the COMBINATION CARRYOVER

Wheat price at the time of the initiation of your long position. **COMBINED %**

90

BUYING WHEAT

Estimated MAXIMUM AMOUNT of Backup Capital needed to trade safely when BUYING wheat

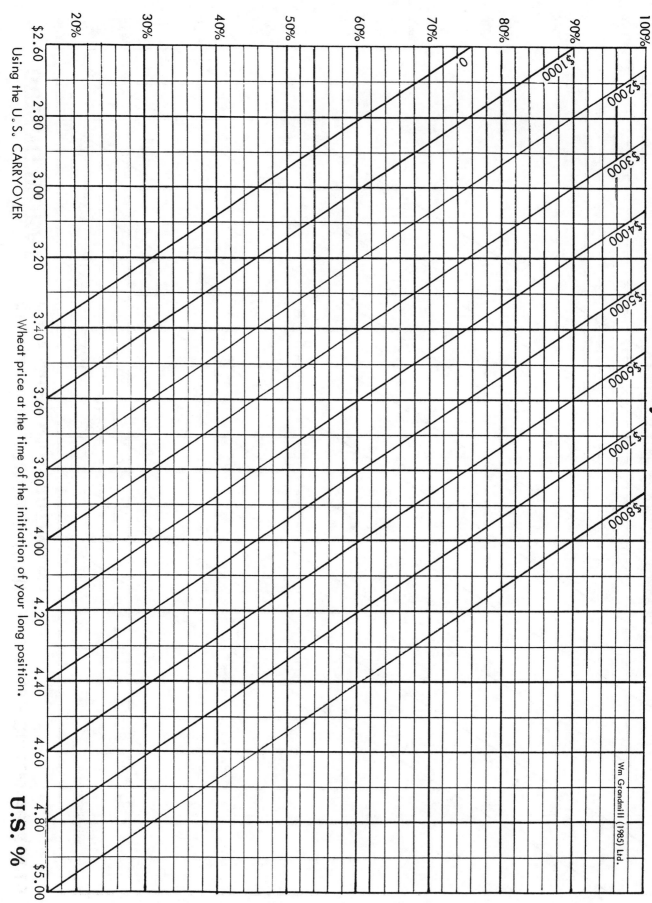

Using the U.S. CARRYOVER

Wheat price at the time of the initiation of your long position.

Wm Grandmill (1985) Ltd.

U.S. %

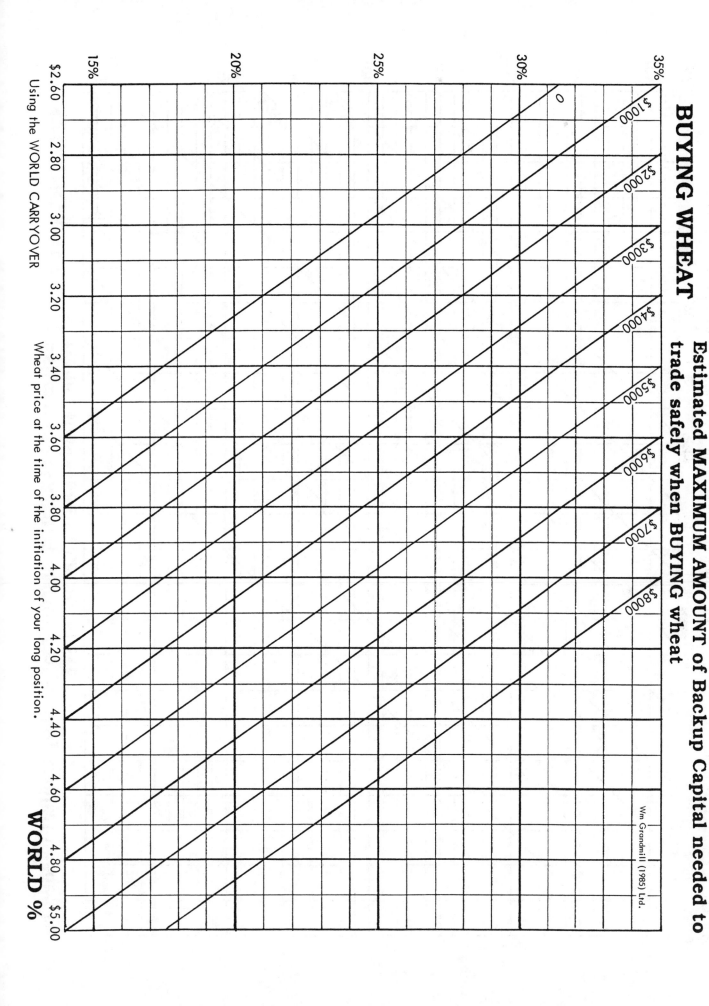

BUYING WHEAT

Estimated MAXIMUM AMOUNT of Backup Capital needed to trade safely when BUYING wheat

Wm Grandmill (1985) Ltd.

Using the WORLD CARRYOVER

Wheat price at the time of the initiation of your long position.

WORLD %

92

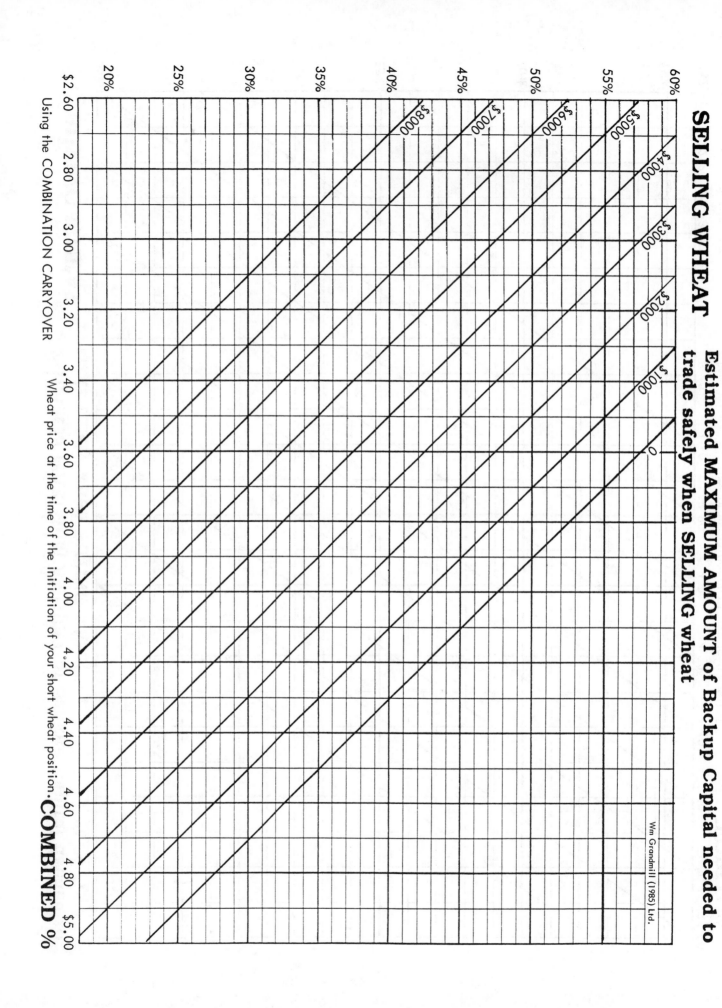

SELLING WHEAT

Estimated MAXIMUM AMOUNT of Backup Capital needed to trade safely when SELLING wheat

Wm Grandmill (1985) Ltd.

Using the COMBINATION CARRYOVER

Wheat price at the time of the initiation of your short wheat position. **COMBINED** %

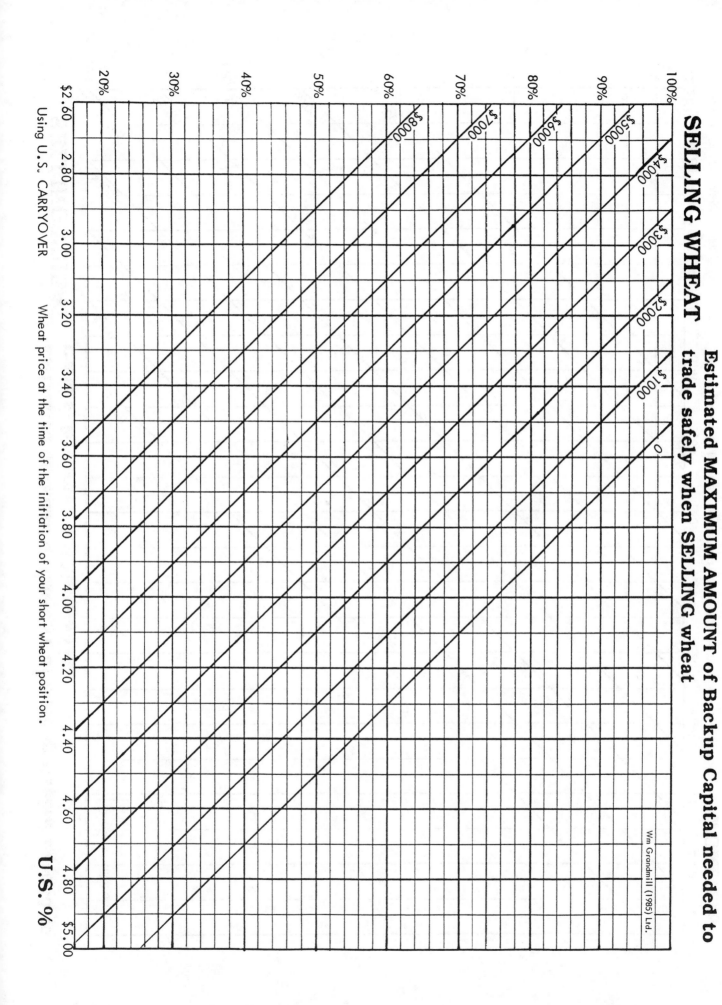

SELLING WHEAT

Estimated MAXIMUM AMOUNT of Backup Capital needed to trade safely when SELLING wheat

Using U.S. CARRYOVER   Wheat price at the time of the initiation of your short wheat position.

Wm Grandmill (1985) Ltd.

U.S. %

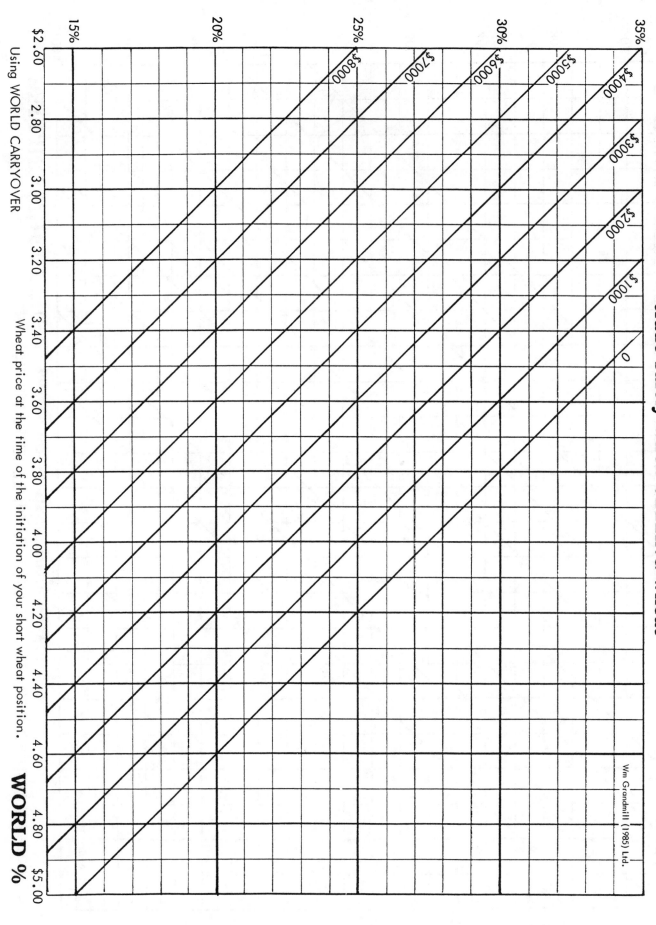

SELLING WHEAT Estimated MAXIMUM AMOUNT of Backup Capital needed to trade safely when SELLING wheat

Wm Grandmill (1985) Ltd.

Using WORLD CARRYOVER

Wheat price at the time of the initiation of your short wheat position.

WORLD %

$4000
$3000
$2000
$1000
0
$5000
$6000
$7000
$8000

35%
30%
25%
20%
15%

$2.60 2.80 3.00 3.20 3.40 3.60 3.80 4.00 4.20 4.40 4.60 4.80 $5.00

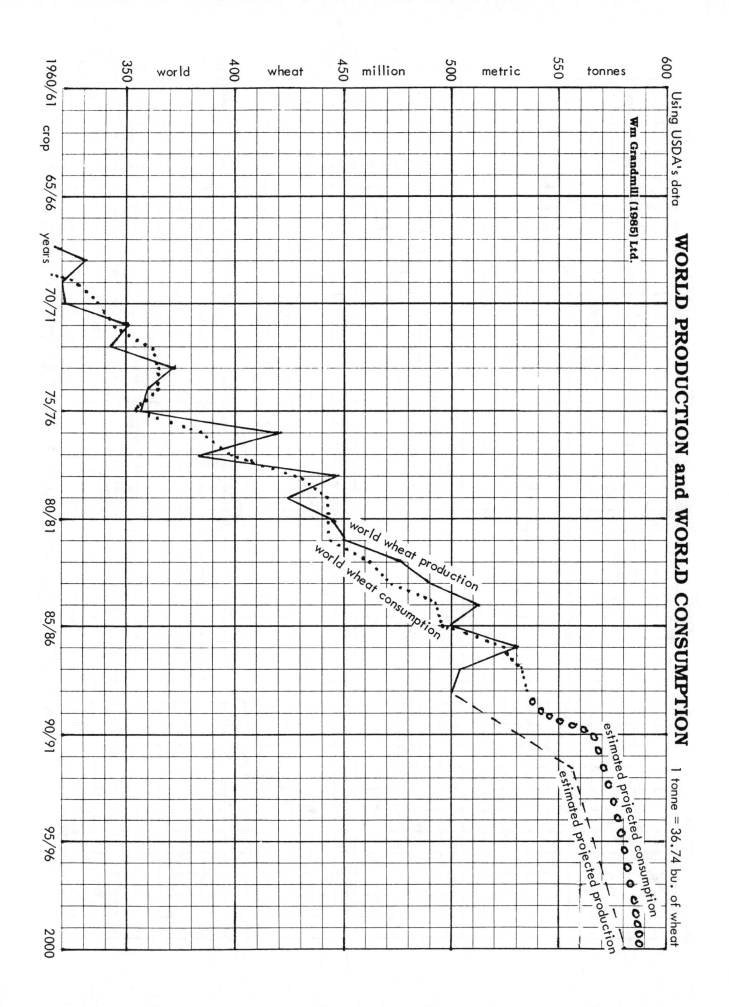

WORLD PRODUCTION and WORLD CONSUMPTION

Using USDA's data

Wm Grandmill (1985) Ltd.

1 tonne = 36.74 bu. of wheat

world wheat million metric tonnes

600
550
500
450
400
350

world wheat production

world wheat consumption

estimated projected consumption

estimated projected production

1960/61
crop
65/66
years
70/71
75/76
80/81
85/86
90/91
95/96
2000

96

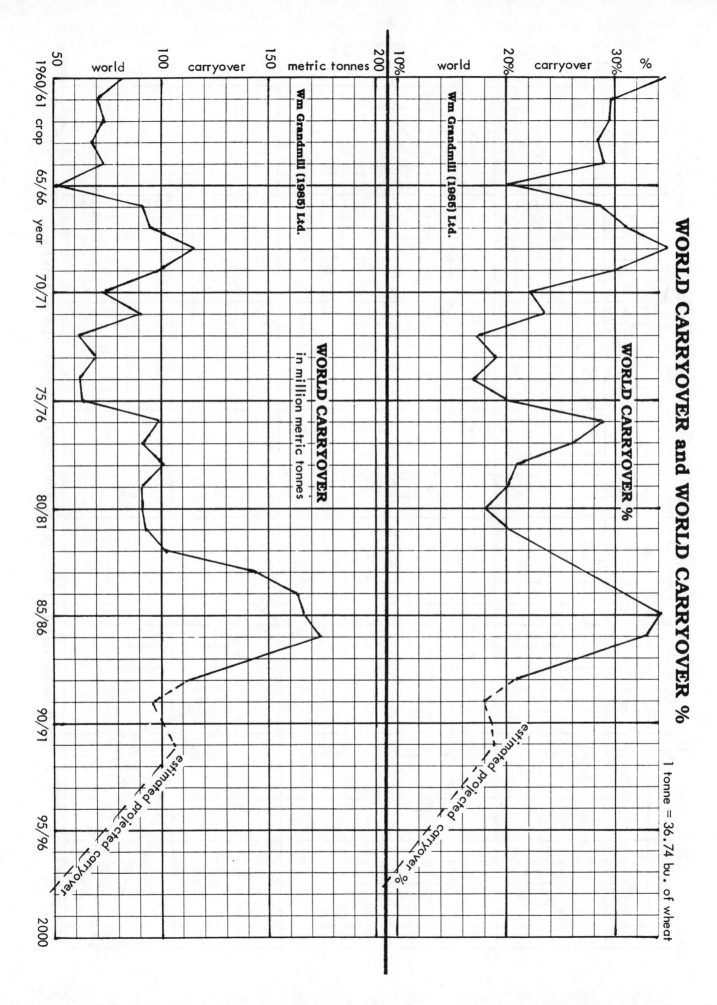

WORLD CARRYOVER and WORLD CARRYOVER %

1 tonne = 36.74 bu. of wheat

WORLD CARRYOVER %

Wm Grandmill (1985) Ltd.

estimated projected carryover %

WORLD CARRYOVER
in million metric tonnes

Wm Grandmill (1985) Ltd.

estimated projected carryover

97

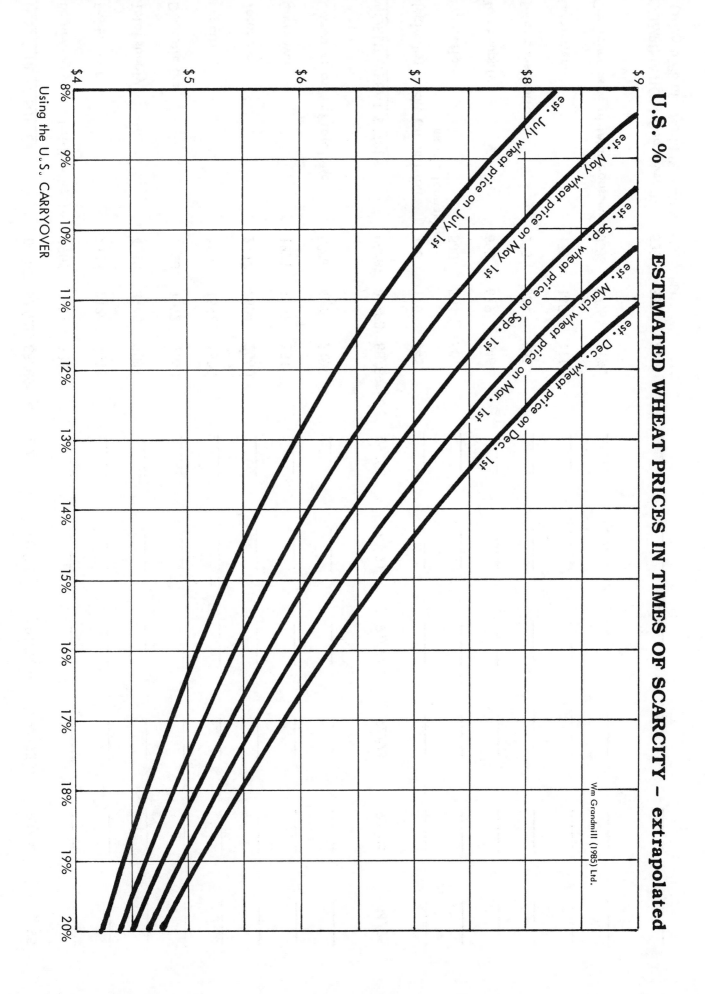

U.S. % ESTIMATED WHEAT PRICES IN TIMES OF SCARCITY – extrapolated

Using the U.S. CARRYOVER

est. July wheat price on July 1st

est. May wheat price on May 1st

est. Sep. wheat price on Sep. 1st

est. March wheat price on Mar. 1st

est. Dec. wheat price on Dec. 1st

Wm Grandmill (1985) Ltd.

98

U.S. WHEAT SUPPLY

	86/87	87/88	88/89*est.	89/90	90/91	91/92	92/93	93/94	94/95
Beginning stocks (million bu.)	1905	1821	1261	—	—	—	—	—	—
Production	2113	2124	1833	—	—	—	—	—	—
Total supply	4018	3945	3094	—	—	—	—	—	—
Domestic use	1193	1092	1060	—	—	—	—	—	—
Exports	1004	1592	1500	—	—	—	—	—	—
Total use	2197	2684	2560	—	—	—	—	—	—
Carryover	1821	1261	534	—	—	—	—	—	—
Carryover as % of total use	83%	47%	21%	—	—	—	—	—	—

WORLD WHEAT SUPPLY (in million metric tonnes)

	86/87	87/88	88/89*est.	89/90	90/91	91/92	92/93	93/94	94/95
Beginning stocks	168	175	145	—	—	—	—	—	—
Production	530	504	501	—	—	—	—	—	—
Total supply	698	679	646	—	—	—	—	—	—
Total consumption	523	534	535	—	—	—	—	—	—
Carryover	175	145	111	—	—	—	—	—	—
Carryover as % of total consump.	33%	27%	21%	—	—	—	—	—	—

	86/87	87/88	88/89*est.	89/90	90/91	91/92	92/93	93/94	94/95
COMBINATION Carryover % (using 60% of World % + 40% of U.S. %)	53%	35%	21%	—	—	—	—	—	—

PART III

INVESTING IN
SOYBEANS

SOYBEANS – WHAT TO EXPECT

You are about to invest in soybean futures. You will likely already know that soybeans are considered to be one of the most speculative of all commodities, with unexpected price fluctuations and trend reversals occurring frequently. A person who uses a stop price will suffer both financially and emotionally when he trades soybeans because there are plenty of 20¢ and 30¢ counter price moves during the summer which usually touch off most stop prices. However, it won't happen to you if you follow the suggestion of this book because this book recommends that you do not use a stop price at all. Instead, it suggests that you use backup money or an option to support your future's position and thus you will be in a position to any temporary trend reversal. It is this author's opinion that a stop price does more harm than good.

Another way in which this book differs from other soybean trading books is the use of Grandmill's new soybean Forecasting Graphs which were constructed specifically for this book. These graphs will indicate whether you should ***buy*** soybeans, ***sell*** soybeans, or ***stay out of the market*** because the size of the profit is not worthwhile. Not only will the Forecasting Graphs tell you whether to buy or to sell, but the graphs will give you the estimated soybean price at the end of the contract month. A subtitle of this book says,"Self Help Book – Be Your Own Advisor." That's what is happening here – you are being advised of the market direction and of the estimated price at the end of the contract. That's a real trading advantage.

An Automatic Year Round Soybean Investment Plan is another feature of this book. There are some people who prefer a simple approach to a problem. There are lots of soybean traders who enjoy the thrill of completing a successful position but who become frustrated when they have to pick the right time to buy or to sell the bean contract. Some brokers advise their clients to buy soybeans when prices are low, likely around harvest time. That's good advice for some of the time, but all lows don't occur at harvest, as you will see when you come to the Timing Charts. So such advice leaves you undecided and you could easily get the feeling that there is no one to help you, no one to whom you can turn for advice.

But this book is your personal advisor and it is full of good advice. The Automatic Year Round Investment Plan is but one example of the help you will get. In this plan, you will take two soybean positions per year. You will take a May position on Nov. 15th and a November position on May 15th. The Forecasting Graphs will tell you whether to buy or to sell. You will be informed whether to use an option or backup money. And if you are to use backup money, you will be told how much is needed. You will also be given, before you take the trade, the estimated price which the soybean position will reach when it comes time to liquidate the position. You will also know the estimated profit, before you take the trade. Everything is laid out for you no uncertainties, no tension.

But the proof is the size of the profit! How profitable is the Automatic Year Round Investment Plan? It was researched by using the soybean price data of the past 15 years. During those 15 years, you would have been told to stay out of the market for 3 of those years because the profit was too small or it was too risky. The remaining 12 years had an average annual return of over 200% on your investment. Sometimes the "investment" was backup money and sometimes it was the cost of an option.

The mystery of the popular July/November soybean spread is solved here,. If you had taken this spread every year (and some people did) by selling July and buying Nov., you would have lost money about 50% of the time. Why? What's the secret of success? Research found a key determinant which would make this a successful, profitable spread. This information was put into an easy-to-use table. You are told when to take the spread, what to do, and the likely date to take your profit and get out. Sometime you are told to ***not*** take the spread because it is too risky. It's all laid out for you and the profits are BIG.

Soybeans or Meal ? Did you know that sometimes it is more profitable to invest your money in soybean meal rather than in the soybeans themselves? There are times when the soybean meal market is hot, while the soybeans themselves are only luke-warm. When that happens the profits shift in favor of meal and if you can detect when that situation occurrs, then you can make extra money by investing in the meal rather than in beans. How can you detect that occurrence? By using a special graph made specifically for this book. The graph will tell you whether you should invest in soybeans or in meal. Not only does it do that, but it takes the crush margin into account – the crush margin is the fee charged by the soybean crushing company. This is important because if the crushing margin was not included, one's profit calculations would be away out. Not only does the graph take the crush margin into account, but it uses a ***variable*** margin. By "variable margin" is meant that the crusher charges different fees as determined by the price and need. Thus, if soybeans are plentiful, then prices will be low and so will the crushing margin – it could be 28¢ a bushel, for example. But if beans are scarce and prices high, then the crushing fee could be high, maybe about 80¢ a bushel. This variable margin is incorporated into the graph, and thus contributing to its accuracy.

There are other new features, too. But to sum it up, this book is your personal long term grain advisor. It covers all the bases. It's like having an expert grain advisor at your elbow as you plan your long term investment.

THE CARRYOVER AS A KEY PRICE DETERMINANT

Everyone knows that when soybeans are plentiful, then soybean prices are low, and when soybeans are scarce, prices are high. That's simple supply and demand affecting prices. Therefore if we could find out in June (just after the planting) how large the soybean crop will probably be when it is harvested in the coming fall, then we will be able to get a good estimate of the price range for the coming crop year. (A soybean crop year dates from Sept. 1st to Aug. 31st of the following year. Thus, an 89/90 crop year represents the time between Sept. 1/89 to Aug. 31/90.)

The most common way to describe whether soybeans are plentiful or scarce is by quoting the **carryover number.** The carryover is the amount of soybeans remaining after the **total use** (all the sales, crush, and exports) has been subtracted from the **total supply.**

To sum it up: **total supply** = the carryover from the previous crop year + the new crop which is harvested in the fall. **Total use** = the amount of soybeans used during the crop year such as exports, crush, seed. **Carryover** = total supply − total use.

So far, we have arrived at the **carryover number** (which is really the surplus amount of soybeans which is not needed or used during the crop year). Why is it important to know the size of the carryover? What is its significance ? Why does the carryover size affect prices? Up to now you may have thought along these lines " I can't see why the size of a carryover should affect prices. A carryover is a surplus of soybeans, and so what if the surplus is large or small, it still means that there are more beans than can be sold – so prices will not rise."

But the soybean trade (the whole grain trade, for that matter) looks at it differently. Here's what is different: **the commodity grain trade looks a year ahead.** To the trade, the carryover (the surplus) is a form of insurance against tough times in the **next** crop year if there is a crop failure.

For example, if the carryover of the current crop year was calculated to be 100 million bushels (historically, that's a small carryover) then soybean prices would rise rapidly right from before early harvest time because experienced traders know that if there is less than normal moisture **next year,** then next year's crop will be reduced by much more than the 100 m.bu. – thus creating a scarcity of soybeans.

On the other hand, if the carryover of the current crop year was calculated to be 700 million bu. (historically, that is a large carryover) then there is no fear of a bean shortage next crop year, even under drought conditions – so prices would stay low all year. (As an example of drought damage, the devastating drought of 1988 reduced the normal crop size by about 500 m.b.)

You can see now that the size of the soybean carryover will indicate whether prices will be low or high in the months following harvest. **But some further refinement** is needed. The words "small carryover" and "large carryover" are relative terms which mean different things to different people. What is needed is a more precise indicator of the carryover size. Therefore,to prevent confusion, the carryover is expressed in percent.

The carryover is expressed as a percentage of the Total Use. For example, if the Total Use was 2000 m. bu. and if the carryover was 400 m. bu., then the carryover is 20% of the Total Use (2000 ÷ 400 X 100 = 20%) . There is no confusion about 20% – it means the same to everyone. But that 20% carries a special message. It says that there are enough surplus beans on hand to last for 2.4 months in case of emergency(12 months x .20 = 2.4) Historically, that's a bigger than average carryover – so prices would likely be less than average . (The 15 year average is a carryover of 15%.)

This book uses a carryover expressed as %. All the graphs use a % carryover. To give you an idea of the size of the carryovers in the past 15 years, the smallest carryover was 7% in the crop year 76/77 and soybean prices rose to a high of $10.76 that year. The largest size carryover was 29% in 85/86 and the highest price that year was $5.67. From the above you can see that the difference between a 7% and a 29% carryover can cause a price difference of about $5 ($25,000 in contract value) .

Now follow this theoretical reasoning. If a 7% carryover caused a high price range, then an 8% carryover should cause a slightly lower price range than a 7% carryover. And a 9% carryover should produce a price range slightly lower than the 8% carryover. And a 10% carryover should produce a price range slightly lower than the 9% carryover...etc....etc. *In other words, there is a RIGHT PRICE for each carryover percentage, theoretically.* This is the basis of the Forecasting Graphs – that there is a "Right Price" for each carryover percent, for each contract month.

HOW TO USE THE FORECASTING GRAPHS

The Forecasting Graphs are the cornerstones of this book. These are the graphs which will tell you whether you should buy soybeans or whether you should sell soybeans or whether you should stay out of the market. Your opportunity to make a profit depends on the Forecasting Graphs. Therefore a great deal of care and research went into their construction. The utmost care was taken to arrive at the **Right Price** for each carryover percent.

HOW THE FORECASTING GRAPHS WERE MADE

Every soybean price for every crop year, for every contract month was analyzed from 1973 to 1989. Every carryover % was matched with its soybean prices for every contract month. To illustrate how it was done, let's use the Nov. soybean price on Nov. 1st with an 18% carryover as an example. All the Nov. 1st prices with the 18% carryovers had prices which were maybe from $5.60 to $6.05 . An average was taken so that there would be only one **right price** for 18% on the Nov. contract. This price was $5.79. An 18% carryover for the May contract would give a different estimate because only May prices were analyzed for the May Forecasting Graph.

You can see from the above that the estimated price which you get from a Forecasting Graph will not be 100% accurate because it was formed from **an average of related numbers.** But it will be close, and, most importantly, you get the direction of the market. Below is an example of what is meant by "getting the direction of the market".

Example: Suppose the date is May 12th and the latest USDA crop estimate is in your hands. You are thinking of taking a Nov. soybean position – but up to now, you don't know whether you should buy or sell Nov. beans. From the crop report you calculate the estimated carryover % for the upcoming new crop year. Let's say that you get an 18% carryover (just as in the example above). Here are the steps which follow. (1)You look in the morning newspaper and see that Nov. soybeans closed yesterday at $6.50. (2) You use the November Forecasting Graph at 18% and you get an estimated Nov. 1st price of $5.79. (3) To repeat, Nov. beans are now at $6.50 and are likely to fall to an estimated $5.79 on Nov. 1st. (4) That says,"Sell Nov. soybeans" in plain language because the Nov. price will decline, according to the Forecasting Graph. As mentioned above, the Nov. graph price of $5.79 is an **average price** so it will not be 100% accurate, but it will likely be close. So let's say that the Nov. 1st price finished up as $5.90 or maybe $5.65, instead of the $5.79 previously estimated. Even though the size of your profit may be different from what you expected, the important thing is that you sold soybeans; in this case if you had **bought** soybeans it would have been disastrous. The point being made here is that it is just as important to get the **direction of the market,** maybe more important, than it is to get the exact size of the estimated profit.

In the following pages you will see a Forecasting Graph for each of the contract months. If you are intending to take a future's position or an option position in July soybeans, for example, then you would consult the July Forecasting Graph. And the estimated price which you would get from the graph would be the estimated price of July soybeans on July 1st. That doesn't mean that you have to keep the position until July 1st. If prices reach you price objective before July 1st, take it – or place a stop price under it if you think there is more profit likely. This is the proper use of a stop price – to protect a profit already made.

This book considers the November and the May contracts to be the most important of all the soybean contracts. Why? For two reasons. *First,* November and May are the two months used in the Automatic Year Round Investment Plan. *Second,* these two month separate two completely different soybean trading periods from one another. Here is an explanation of that statement.

The date is May 15th. You are going to take a Nov. soybean position. What kind of "trading weather" are you heading into? The answer is,"Turbulent". Right ahead of you are the summer months with the wild speculations and weather scares which are prevalent during this season, sending soybean prices up and down erratically. Often the weather rumors are false and the price moves have no factual basis. Therefore, *the summer is the turbulent period* for prices with the most turbulent times being from mid June to mid September.

By contrast is the trading period from mid November to about mid April. *This is the "quiet period".* Why? Because the soybean crop has been made by mid November. It is too late for weather rumors to have an effect on the prices. Harvest will be near completion. A few months of peace and tranquility lie ahead. Any rise or fall in soybean prices will depend entirely on the size of the crop and the carryover. A new crop year began in September. The serenity will be punctuated occasionally in January or February by a weather rumor about soybean crop conditions in Brazil. This is the "quiet period". You will find that you will need less backup money in this period because there are almost no disturbing elements to interfere with the price trend .

The Automatic Year Round Investment Plan tackles these two different trading periods in a different way. One half of the plan is taken on Nov. 15th which is the beginning of the quiet period and the other half of the plan is taken on May 15th which is the beginning of the turbulent period. But you will get the details later, in the chapter on the Automatic Year Round Investment Plan.

The following paragraph gives you some practice with the use of the Forecasting Graphs. There are some questions. Try them for practice. The answers are at the end of the paragraph .

Do these: 1. The carryover is 10%. What is the estimated Nov. price on Nov. 1

2. The date is Nov. 15th. You wish to take a May position. The present price of beans is $7 and the carryover is 16%. (a) what is the estimated price of May beans on May lst? (b) Will you buy or will you

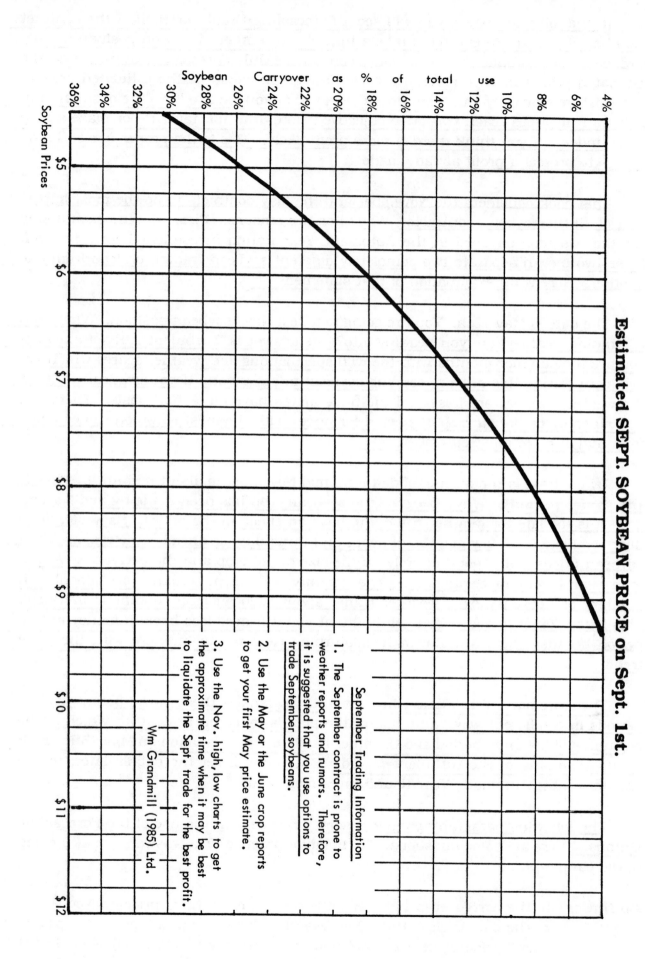

Estimated SEPT. SOYBEAN PRICE on Sept. 1st.

September Trading Information

1. The September contract is prone to weather reports and rumors. Therefore, it is suggested that you use options to trade September soybeans.

2. Use the May or the June crop reports to get your first May price estimate.

3. Use the Nov. high, low charts to get the approximate time when it may be best to liquidate the Sept. trade for the best profit.

Wm Grandmill (1985) Ltd.

Estimated NOV. SOYBEAN PRICE on Nov. 1st.

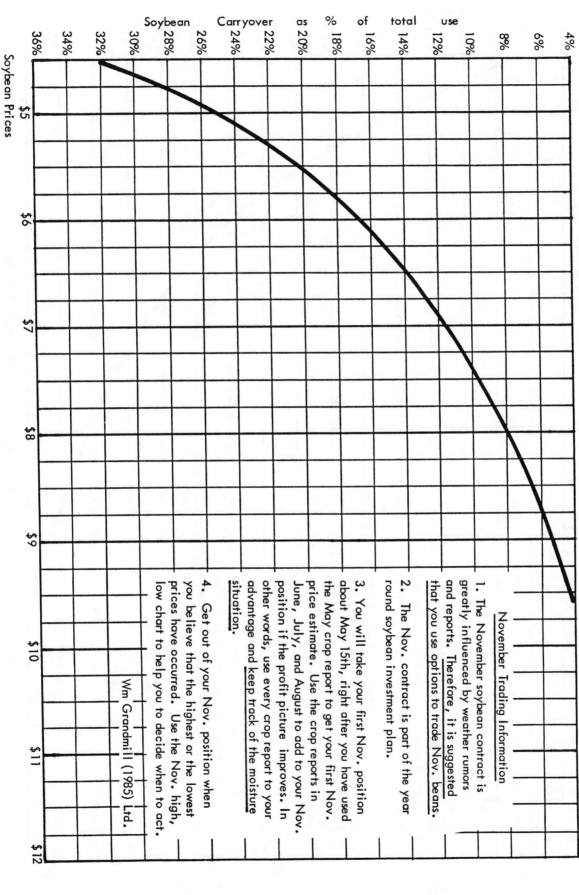

Soybean Carryover as % of total use

Soybean Prices

November Trading Information

1. The November soybean contract is greatly influenced by weather rumors and reports. Therefore, it is suggested that you use options to trade Nov. beans.

2. The Nov. contract is part of the year round soybean investment plan.

3. You will take your first Nov. position about May 15th, right after you have used the May crop report to get your first Nov. price estimate. Use the crop reports in June, July, and August to add to your Nov. position if the profit picture improves. In other words, use every crop report to your advantage and keep track of the moisture situation.

4. Get out of your Nov. position when you believe that the highest or the lowest prices have occurred. Use the Nov. high, low chart to help you to decide when to act.

Wm Grandmill (1985) Ltd.

108

Estimated JAN. SOYBEAN PRICE on Jan. 1st.

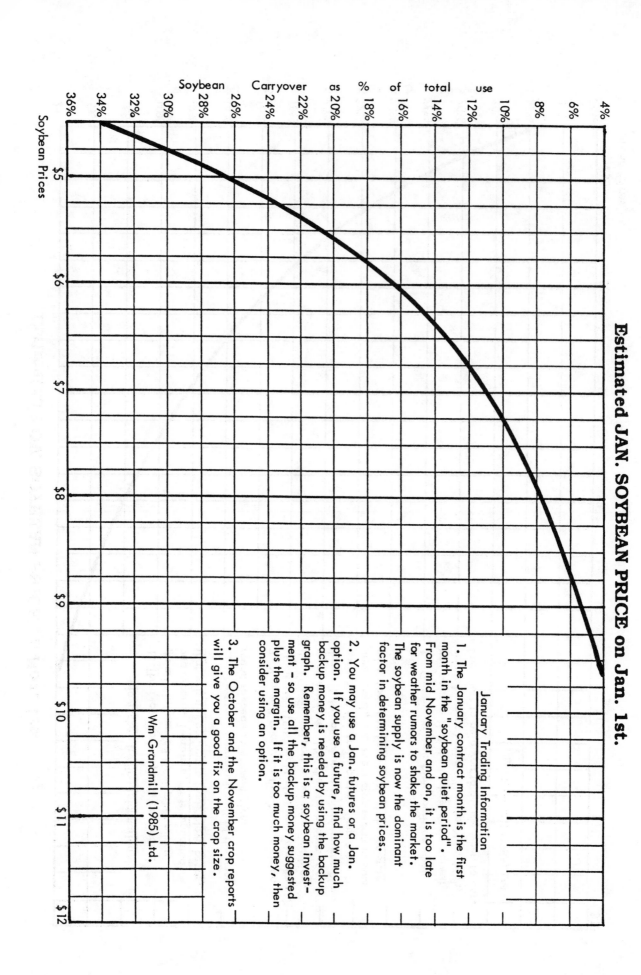

Soybean Carryover as % of total use

Soybean Prices

January Trading Information

1. The January contract month is the first month in the "soybean quiet period". From mid November and on, it is too late for weather rumors to shake the market. The soybean supply is now the dominant factor in determining soybean prices.

2. You may use a Jan. futures or a Jan. option. If you use a future, find how much backup money is needed by using the backup graph. Remember, this is a soybean investment – so use all the backup money suggested plus the margin. If it is too much money, then consider using an option.

3. The October and the November crop reports will give you a good fix on the crop size.

Wm Grandmill (1985) Ltd.

Estimated MARCH SOYBEAN PRICE on March 1st.

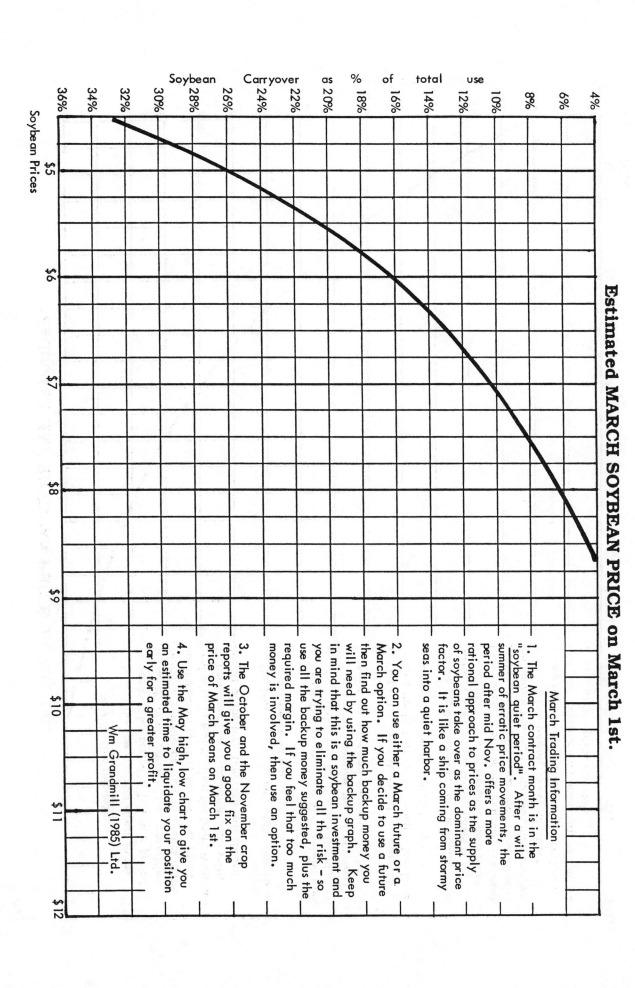

Soybean Carryover as % of total use

Soybean Prices

4% 6% 8% 10% 12% 14% 16% 18% 20% 22% 24% 26% 28% 30% 32% 34% 36%

$5 $6 $7 $8 $9 $10 $11 $12

March Trading Information

1. The March contract month is in the "soybean quiet period". After a wild summer of erratic price movements, the period after mid Nov. offers a more rational approach to prices as the supply of soybeans take over as the dominant price factor. It is like a ship coming from stormy seas into a quiet harbor.

2. You can use either a March future or a March option. If you decide to use a future then find out how much backup money you will need by using the backup graph. Keep in mind that this is a soybean investment and you are trying to eliminate all the risk – so use all the backup money suggested, plus the required margin. If you feel that too much money is involved, then use an option.

3. The October and the November crop reports will give you a good fix on the price of March beans on March 1st.

4. Use the May high, low chart to give you an estimated time to liquidate your position early for a greater profit.

Wm Grandmill (1985) Ltd.

Estimated MAY SOYBEAN PRICE on May 1st.

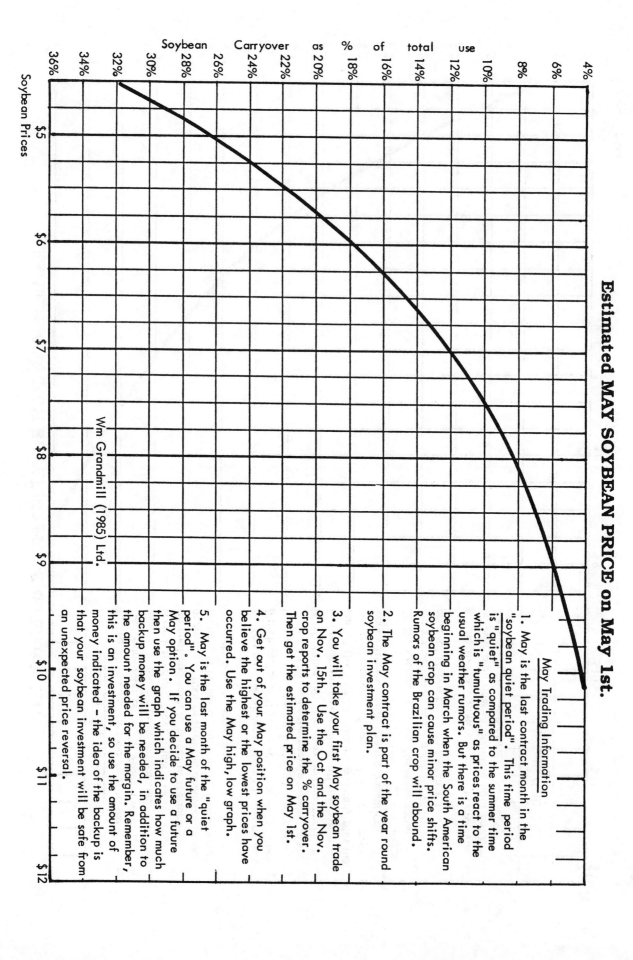

Wm Grandmill (1985) Ltd.

May Trading Information

1. May is the last contract month in the "soybean quiet period". This time period is "quiet" as compared to the summer time which is "tumultuous" as prices react to the usual weather rumors. But there is a time beginning in March when the South American soybean crop can cause minor price shifts. Rumors of the Brazilian crop will abound.

2. The May contract is part of the year round soybean investment plan.

3. You will take your first May soybean trade on Nov. 15th. Use the Oct and the Nov. crop reports to determine the % carryover. Then get the estimated price on May 1st.

4. Get out of your May position when you believe the highest or the lowest prices have occurred. Use the May high, low graph.

5. May is the last month of the "quiet period". You can use a May future or a May option. If you decide to use a future then use the graph which indicates how much backup money will be needed, in addition to the amount needed for the margin. Remember, this is an investment, so use the amount of money indicated – the idea of the backup is that your soybean investment will be safe from an unexpected price reversal.

Estimated JULY SOYBEAN PRICE on July 1st.

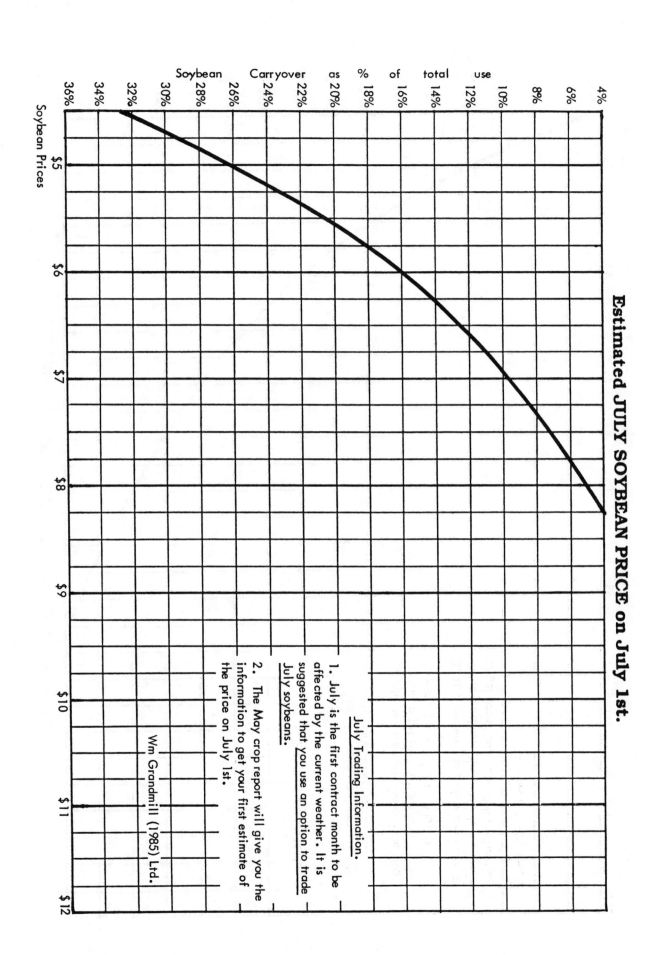

Soybean Carryover as % of total use

Soybean Prices

July Trading Information.

1. July is the first contract month to be affected by the current weather. It is suggested that you use an option to trade July soybeans.

2. The May crop report will give you the information to get your first estimate of the price on July 1st.

Wm Grandmill (1985) Ltd.

Estimated AUG. SOYBEAN PRICE on Aug. 1st.

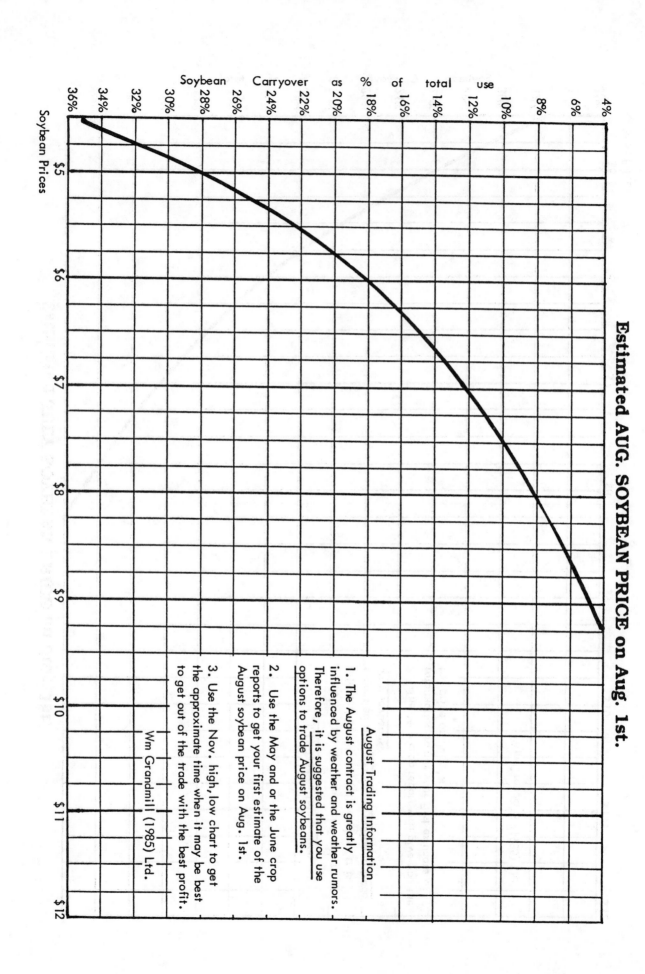

Soybean Carryover as % of total use

Soybean Prices

$5
$6
$7
$8
$9
$10
$11
$12

4%
6%
8%
10%
12%
14%
16%
18%
20%
22%
24%
26%
28%
30%
32%
34%
36%

August Trading Information

1. The August contract is greatly influenced by weather and weather rumors. Therefore, it is suggested that you use options to trade August soybeans.

2. Use the May and or the June crop reports to get your first estimate of the August soybean price on Aug. 1st.

3. Use the Nov. high,low chart to get the approximate time when it may be best to get out of the trade with the best profit.

Wm Grandmill (1985) Ltd.

sell May beans? 3.The date is May 15th. You are going to take a November position. The present Nov. soybean price is $6. The carryover is 22%. (a) What is the estimated Nov. price on Nov. 1st? (b) Will you buy or sell Nov. beans? Answers: 1.about $7.40 2.(a) $6.25 (b) sell 3.(a) about $5.30 (b) sell

The following problems have a little more work to them. Below are consecutive crop years A,B,and C. The supply and demand figures are provided for each of them, in millions of bushels.

	A	B	C
Beginning stocks	300	400	300
Production	2000	1800	1900
Total supply	2300	2200	2200
Crush, seed, etc.	1200	1100	1250
Exports	700	800	550
Total use	1900	1900	1800
Carryover	400	300	400
Carryover %	21%	16%	22%

Do these:

1. Using Crop Year A. (a) What is the carryover amount? (b) What is the carryover %? (c) What is the estimated price of July soybeans on July 1st?

2. Using crop year B. (note that the carryover for one crop year becomes the 'Beginning stocks" of the following crop year) (a) What is the total supply? (b) What is the total use? (c) What is the carryover? (d) What is the carryover %? (e) The date is Nov. 15th. The present price of May beans is $5.50. Will you buy or sell May?

3. Using crop year C. (a) What are the "Beginning stocks" ? (b) What is the total supply? (c) What is the total use? (d) What is the carryover? (e) What is the carryover %? (f) The date is May 15th. The present price of Nov. soybeans is $6.19. Will you buy or sell Nov. soybeans? (g) How much profit is indicated?

Answers: 1. (a) 400 (b) 21% (c) about $5.45

2. (a) 2200 (b) 1900 (c) 300 (d) 16% (e) buy

3. (a) 300 (b) 2200 (c) 1800 (d) 400 (e) 22% (f) sell (g) about 89¢ approx.

How did you do? If you had all correct or only 1 wrong, you deserve a A+!

USING SOYBEAN OPTIONS

There is option information in Part 1 of this book. If you have never traded options before, it would be wise to reread it. But don't let your lack of option knowledge prevent you from using options. They are easy to do. This book uses only the simple types, such as: buying a call or buying a put. Nothing could be easier. You'll get lots of help. Remember, this book is your advisor. **Buy a call** when you believe that soybean prices will rise. **Buy a put** when you believe that soybean prices will decline. That's all there is to it.

There are a few option terms with which you should be familiar. (1) **Premium** – a premium is the price of the option – the price which you pay to your broker when you take the option position. It is quoted in cents e.g. 37¢ – so in this case, you would pay your broker $1850 for the option. You do not need to put up any margin when you take an option. (2) **At- the- money,** an option is based on its underlying future's price. Thus, if a July soybean future closed at $6.00 then you would buy a $6.00 at- the- money July option. So, at- the- money means that you will match the closing price of the future with a strike price of the option. (3) **Strike price** – soybean option prices are quoted in increments of 25¢ e.g. $7.00, $7.25, $7.50, etc. These are called "strike prices". An example below will hopefully make these definitions clear to you.

Here is a typical set of soybean call option quotes, just like the quotes which you see in your newspaper or on the quote machine in your broker's office.

Soybean Options — 5000 bu., cents per bu.

strike price	Mar.	calls May	July
650	27	32	53
675	15	26	46
700	10	13	37
725	6	10	32

Look at the quote page above. (1) Note that the "Strike Price" column is in increments of 25¢. (2) Note that there is a premium (price) column for each of the contract months of March, May, and July. (3) And under each month you will see the prices (premiums) for each call option.

Here are some problems for you to solve. They will help you to understand how the option quote page works.

1. If March soybeans futures are $6.75, how much money will you pay to your broker for a March at- the- money call?

2 If July soybeans are $7.25, what is the premium for a July at- the- money call ?

3. If March soybeans are $6.70, which strike price would you use to buy a March call? What is the premium?

4. If July soybeans are $7.09, which strike price would you use to buy a July call ? What is the premium ?

Answers: (1) 15¢ ($750) (2) 32¢ (3) 675, 15¢ (4) 700, 37¢

USING THE FORECASTING GRAPHS TO BUY AN OPTION

Sometimes the best way to explain is to use an example. ***Example:*** The date is May 15th and you have just used the data from the latest USDA crop report to estimate the carryover for the upcoming new crop year which will begin on Sept. 1st. You estimate that the new carryover will be 20%. You think that you will take a Nov. option if the profit is sufficient. The present Nov. soybean price is $6.50. You look in the morning paper on the option page and you see that the premium for a $6.50 call is 38¢ and a $6.50 put is 40¢. Now that you have all the necessary information, you can take the following steps: (1) Use the 20% carryover on the Nov. Forecasting Graph and you get $5.50 as the estimated Nov. price on Nov. 1st. (2) You saw in the paper that the present Nov. price is $6.50 and the Forecasting Graph indicates that the price will likely fall to an estimated $5.50 – so you will buy a put, expecting a $1.00 decline. (3) You check out the option trade on the Soybean Option Graph (you will learn to use it soon) to see if the option trade meets the safety and profit standards. The Option Graph indicates that you should earn about 140% net on your investment (the investment is the 40¢ premium). (4) It's a good deal so you phone your broker and say," Buy a $6.50 Nov. soybean put".

Here again are the steps to take when using a soybean option.
1. Find the present future's price of the month in which you are interested.
2. Find the price objective by using the Forecasting Graph.
3. From the above information, decide whether to buy a call or a put.
4. Find the option premium from the newspaper or from your broker.
5. Use the Soybean Option Graph to see if the option is worth taking.

HOW TO USE THE SOYBEAN OPTION GRAPH

Below is the Soybean Option Graph. Note that the premium is on the left side of the graph. The bottom line represents the price difference between the soybean future's price at the time of taking the option, and the estimated price objective obtained from the Forecasting Graph.

Example: (follow this on the Option Graph) The date is June 15th and you intend to buy a September option.
1. You have to assemble certain information beforehand.
2. Let's say that the present Sept. future's price is $6.70.
3. Let's say that the Sept. Forecasting Graph's estimated price is $5.70.
4. That's a price difference of $1 between the two prices above .
5. We will have to use the premium for a 675 strike price.
6) Let's say that the premium for the Sept. option put is 45¢.

Solution: Trace along the 45¢ premium line to meet the vertical $1 line. Read the % net profit from the slanting lines. In this example, the net profit will be about 110% (that's a net profit of 110% on your investment of 45¢). That's a good return on

SOYBEAN OPTION GRAPH

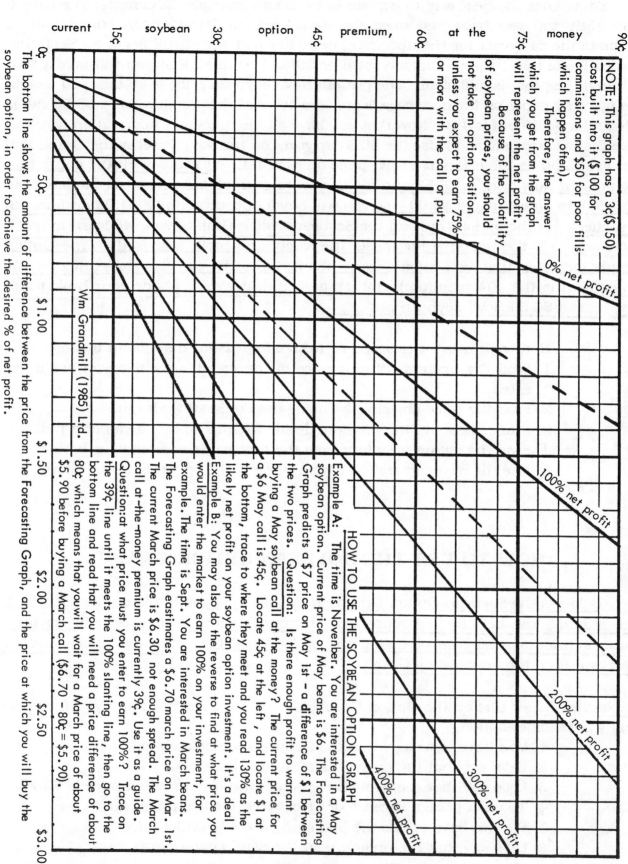

NOTE: This graph has a 3¢ ($150) cost built into it ($100 for commissions and $50 for poor fills which happen often).

Therefore, the answer which you get from the graph will represent the net profit.

Because of the volatility of soybean prices, you should not take an option position unless you expect to earn 75% or more with the call or put.

current soybean option premium, at the money

90¢ · 75¢ · 60¢ · 45¢ · 30¢ · 15¢ · 0¢

0¢ · 50¢ · $1.00 · $1.50 · $2.00 · $2.50 · $3.00

0% net profit · 100% net profit · 200% net profit · 300% net profit · 400% net profit

Wm Grandmill (1985) Ltd.

HOW TO USE THE SOYBEAN OPTION GRAPH

Example A: The time is November. You are interested in a May soybean option. Current price of May beans is $6. The Forecasting Graph predicts a $7 price on May 1st - a **difference** of **$1** between the two prices. Question: Is there enough profit to warrant buying a May soybean call at the money? The current price for a $6 May call is 45¢. Locate 45¢ at the left, and locate $1 at the bottom, trace to where they meet and you read 130% as the likely net profit on your soybean option investment. It's a deal!

Example B: You may also do the reverse to find at what price you would enter the market to earn 100% on your investment, for example. The time is Sept. You are interested in March beans. The Forecasting Graph eastimates a $6.70 march price on Mar. 1st. The current March price is $6.30, not enough spread. The March call at-the-money premium is currently 39¢. Use it as a guide. Question:at what price must you enter to earn 100%? Trace on the 39¢ line until it meets the 100% slanting line, then go to the bottom line and read that you will need a price difference of about 80¢ which means that youwill wait for a March price of about $5.90 before buying a March call ($6.70 - 80¢ = $5.90).

The bottom line shows the amount of difference between the price from the Forecasting Graph, and the price at which you will buy the soybean option, in order to achieve the desired % of net profit.

117

your investment, especially when you consider that you will be in the market for only about 3 months. The graph gives you a **net profit** percentage – that's because the graph has a built in cost of a full commission of 2¢ and a poor fill on your order of 1¢, which is a realistic cost. But if you are using a discount broker, then your profit will be larger by the difference between the two commission rates.

You can also use the graph in reverse order. In other words, you might wish to know by how much should soybean prices change so that you can earn 100% on your option investment.

Example: The date is Nov. 15th and you wish to take a May option. But you want to be sure that you will earn 100% or more on the option investment. (l)The present May soybean price is $6.00. (2) You want to know this: by how much must the May price rise so that you can earn 100% on a call or by how much must the May price fall so that you can earn 100% on a put. (3) The May 600 strike price has a premium of 30¢.

Solution: (follow this on the graph) Trace along the 30¢ premium line to the 100% slanting line. Go straight down to the bottom line and you can read 64¢. This means that at the present time, May will have to rise to $6.64 if you are buying a call or May will have to decline to $5.36 if you are going to buy a put. Because the premiums and soybean prices change, it will be necessary to redo the process frequently.

WHEN TO USE A SOYBEAN OPTION

The Forecasting Graphs were designed to function with both futures and options. In fact, the Forecasting Graphs work hand in hand with the Option Graph to help make your option trade to be successful and have enough profit to make it worthwhile to do. It is very important to have some sense of the market direction and the likely profit size so that you can check it out on the Option Graph to ensure that it is up to the standards for both safety and profit. This brings us to the point where one asks the question,"When should one use an option instead of a future's position?" A few guidelines will help you to decide.

Option Guide-lines:
1. *Always use options to trade soybeans between May and the beginning of September.*
The Reason: A few pages back you were told that soybean tradingcould be divid-edinto two distance periods. One was called "The Turbulent Period" and it covered the summer months with its erratic price movements prompted by weather rumors. The other was called "The Quiet Period" and it encompassed the months after the crop was in, from Nov. to the end of March. So you are being advised to use options during the turbulent period because research has found that you need almost twice as much backup money for a soybean future in the summer as you would need in the "quiet

period" – and this can amount to a lot of money – so by using an option you are accomplishing two advantages (1) it cuts down on the amount of money required (2) the Forecasting Graph will likely have given you a good fix on the final soybean price, so by using an option, you are not worried by the wild antics of the prices in the summer because you are interested only in the price at the end, at the date of expiration.

2. *Don't take a soybean option position unless the Option Graph indicates that you can earn at a 75% net profit.*

The Reason: Soybeans are a speculative commodity. Consequently, the profit size may not turn out to be what you expected. So play it safe by buying a call or a put only when it appears that the profit is large enough to warrant the risk. So a 75% minimum profit seems like a reasonable guideline to ensure a safe option trade.

3. *Use an option if the amount of backup money is too large for you.*

The Reason: Some people will always use a future's position because it has no direct cost to it if the trade is successful. An option has a direct cost, the premium, no matter whether the option trade is successful or not. So some people will not mind putting up a large amount of money as backup. But if you find that the amount of backup suggested by the Backup Graph is likely to take too big a bite out of your capital, then use an option-in fact you may be able to take 2 options for less than the backup money suggested.

4. *Do not use an option to take a soybean spread.*

The reason: You need two option positions for a spread, which means that you will spend about 60¢ to 80¢ on premiums. Most spreads don't earn anywhere near 60¢ – so it is nearly always a waste of money. Use futures for a spread because the margin is small, not usually over $300.

5. *Do not use an option as backup for a future's position.*

The reason: You have probably already seen a suggestion which goes something like this,"Use an option to protect a future's position against undue loss. For example, suppose you were long a July future. Instead of putting up backup money, **buy a put.** This way, if prices go against your long future's position, the put will be making money when the future is losing money. Also, if prices go in your favor, then the long position will be making money when the put is losing money, and the most you can lose is the cost of the put, the premium." It certainly sound good, but alas, it doesn't work out so good in real life. In fact, in this example, **you are just as far ahead to buy a call, only.** You make just as much money as in the deal above, and in addition, you will have only one commission to pay instead of two commissions in the example above. So, in a sense, you are further ahead to just use an ordinary call, in this case. **Keep it simple,** is a good motto. **Explanation:** Did you know that a future position makes a profit twice as fast as an option position? Yes, it's true that a future makes money twice as fast as an at- the- money option. (A future can also lose money twice as fast if prices go against it.) But later on, when in- the- money, the option starts to gain on the future. **Example:** Lets say that July soybeans are now at $6. So we will have a race. We will buy a July future and buy a $6 July call, and set them side by side as in a race. At the end of a day's trading, let's say that July prices advanced by 10¢. What happened to the values of the future and of the call option? Well, the future gained the whole 10¢, but the option premium only increased by 5¢. For this example, let's use numbers instead of names. Let's call the **call option a 1.** Then the **future would be a 2** because it earned twice as fast as the call. Then a **put option would be a -1** because it lost 5¢ when the July price rose by 10¢. At the beginning of this paragraph, we were discussing "buying a future and buying a put instead of using backup money". Let's put those words into numbers. Here's what we get: 2 +(-1) = 1, and the 1 represents a call option (see above). In other words, a call option will earn as much as a future plus a put (and save the cost of a commission, too).

To Sum Up. Options are a very relaxing form of investment because you are concerned only with the value at the expiration date, and you are unaffected by those wild fluctuations in the summer. The Forecasting Graph will give you an estimate of the final price, approximately, for the expiration date. If one of those wild fluctuations should suddenly reach your price objective then you should take it. It is always a good idea to get out of your position early if possible because it frees your capital to be used again. When is the expiration date? *The last trading day* for options is the second last Friday in the preceding month, usually. The **expiration day** is usually the following day, a Saturday. **For example,** for the Nov. 89 contract, the last trading day was Friday, Oct. 20th and the expiration date was Oct. 21/89.

AUTOMATIC YEAR ROUND SOYBEAN INVESTMENT PLAN

This is called a "Year Round Investment Plan" because it runs for one year – from harvest to harvest. It consists of 2 halves – with one half being taken on Nov. 15th and liquidated on May 1st, and the other half being taken on May 15th and liquidated on Nov. 1st. The 15th of the month was chosen as the date to take the positions because the 15th is right after important USDA crop reports are issued.

The Automatic Year Round Investment Plan is called "automatic" because the soybean future's positions and the option positions are taken at set dates, on Nov. 15th and May 15th automatically. These two dates immediately follow important USDA crop reports. Also, these two dates represent the beginning of the "Quiet Period" and the "Turbulent Period" in soybean trading. Research showed that you will have more safety and profit by using Nov. 15 and May 15th than any other dates used in the research.

The dates for the liquidation of the soybean position are normally as follows: the position taken on Nov. 15th would normally be liquidated on the following May 1st or the last day of trading which might be April 30th and the position taken on May 15th would normally be liquidated on the following Nov. 1st or the last day of trading which might be Oct. 31st. Note that the words "*normally* liquidated on May 1st" and "*normally* liquidated on Nov. 1st" were used. The word "normally" means that you will get out of the position if nothing unusual happens. But if there was a sudden price fluctuation which put prices at your price objective which you had received from the Forecasting Graph, then you should seize the opportunity and take your profit by liquidating the position then and there. It is usually a wise move to get out early with your profit if you can because it frees your capital to be used on a new position.

The word "Automatic" used in the title is psychologically pleasant. It takes the pressure off a trader who doesn't know when or how to enter the market. If you are an experienced trader, you will know the mental agony that one can go through when one searches for the right time to initiate a position. Timing is so crucial that it becomes a big problem. Well, the pressure is off if you wish to use the Automatic Year Round Investment Plan. Everything is laid out for you in this plan, and the profits are BIG. It's a relaxing way to invest. All you have to do is to put up the money and take the profits. This book, your personal advisor, will do the rest.

WHAT TO DO WHEN TAKING A SOYBEAN POSITION ON NOV. 15th

1. You will buy or sell May soybeans on Nov. 15th. It's up to you whether you use a future or an option. But this is the beginning of the "quiet period" and it is the

best time to use a future because the amount of backup money needed is smaller, on the average, in the "quiet period".

2. You will hold the position until May 1st **unless** your price objective is reached earlier, and this happens often.

3. Here is the procedure to follow on Nov. 15th. Look in the morning newspaper and note yesterday's closing price for May soybeans – or ask your broker. Also note the latest carryover % number which you got from the crop report of a couple of days ago.

4. Use the May Forecasting Graph to get the estimated soybean price on May 1st.

5. Compare the two prices, the closing price from the newspaper and the estimated price from the Forecasting Graph, and decide whether you will be buying or selling May beans.

6. Again compare the two prices and ask yourself,"Is the potential profit large enough to make the transaction worthwhile?" If the profit is too small, consider a position in wheat or corn. Use the rule below to help you to decide.

7. **Rule:** If you are going to use a **future's position,** use 40¢ as the minimum acceptable profit.

   If the estimated profit is less than 40¢, consider a wheat or corn position, and stay out of the soybean market. (Past research has shown that you would be out of the soybean market about 1 year in 4 or 25% of the time. And further research has shown that if you had taken a position when the rule said to stay out, you would have lost money 85% of the time.) So it is a rule worth following. Remember, this rule applies only to taking a future's position on Nov. 15th.

8. **Rule:** If you are going to use an **option position,** use the Option Graph and use a 75% net profit as the minimum acceptable profit. If it is less than 75%, don't take it but check out the option possibilities for wheat and corn.

9. If you decided to use a future's position, then the next step is to find out how much backup money is needed to invest safely without using a stop price. To find out, you will use the Backup Graph which you will see soon.

10. You have all the information that you need if you are intending to use a future's position
    (a) You know whether to buy or to sell May soybeans or to stay out.
    (b) You know your price objective from the May Forecasting Graph.
    (c) You know the estimated size of the profit.
    (d) You know how much backup money is needed.
    (e) You know that there is a good chance that you will reach the price objective early because of a price fluctuation, and to get out.

11. You have all the information that you need if you are intending to use an <u>option</u> position.

      (a) You know whether to buy a call or a put or to stay out of the market.
      (b) You know the price objective on the May Forecasting Graph.
      (c) You know the premium and you use it in the Option Graph.
      (d) You know there is a good chance that you will reach the price objective early because of a price fluctuation, and to get out.

12. <u>Now you need to learn how to use the Timing Charts and the Backup Graph.</u>

HOW TO USE THE TIMING CHARTS

On the following pages are the "Timing Charts" for Nov. soybeans and for May soybeans. One chart shows you when the highest soybean prices have occurred, in relation to the carryover %. The other chart tells you when the lowest soybean prices have occurred, in relation to the size of the carryover %. *Note* that it is the size of the carryover % which determines when the highs and the lows occur, most of the time. Take a look at the charts now.

The black dots represent when the highest or the lowest prices happened, as related to the size of the carryover % for the crop year. At first glance the black dots seem to form a random pattern but a closer look reveals a more deliberate relationship with the carryover %.

Look at the chart titled "When did Nov. soybean's highest prices occur?". Note that the highest prices tend to occur in the fall when soybean supplies are tight, as signified by a carryover of 5% to 10%. Whereas, when soybean supplies are plentiful as signified by carryovers of 20% or more, then the highest prices tend to occur in late Winter or early spring. The medium range percentages are the problem (11% to 19%) because they seem to spread over from June to October. Anyway, that's the way it happened over the past 15 years. Granted that one has to look hard to see a pattern, but the charts are of some help. For example, suppose on May 15th you had calculated that the carryover for the upcoming crop would be 8%. That means a tight supply of beans for sale. Then you can be very sure that the highest price will happen before all the soybean crop is harvested. Why? Well, for one, the chart shows it. But there is a reasonable explanation as well. If you found out in May that the crop will be small, then you can be sure that the whole world will know that the U.S. soybean crop will be small, by early June. Then the rush starts as crushers and foreign importers struggle to get their share of beans, pushing prices up rapidly, sometimes before the harvest starts. That's why soybean prices peak early in times of a tight supply.

WHEN DID NOV. SOYBEAN'S LOWEST PRICES OCCUR?

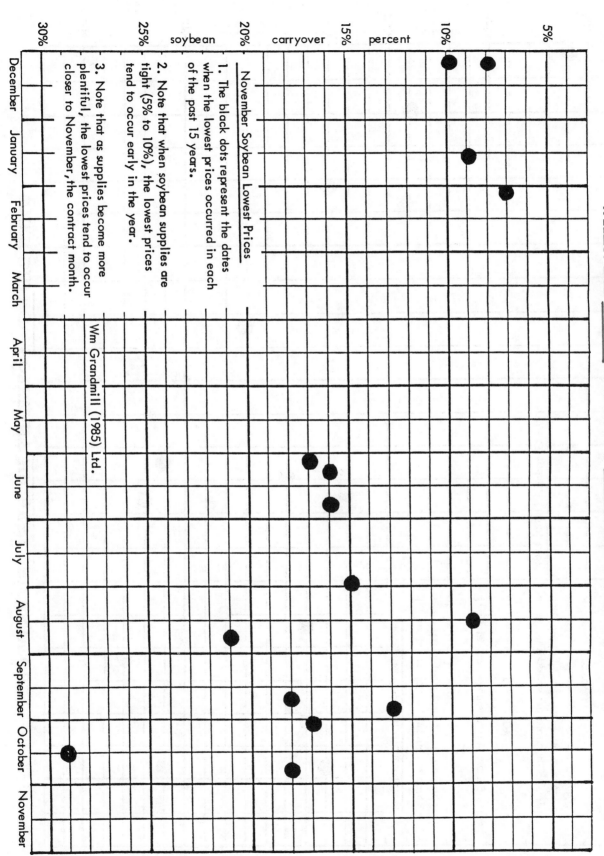

November Soybean Lowest Prices

1. The black dots represent the dates when the lowest prices occurred in each of the past 15 years.

2. Note that when soybean supplies are tight (5% to 10%), the lowest prices tend to occur early in the year.

3. Note that as supplies become more plentiful, the lowest prices tend to occur closer to November, the contract month.

Wm Grandmill (1985) Ltd.

WHEN DID NOV. SOYBEAN'S HIGHEST PRICES OCCUR?

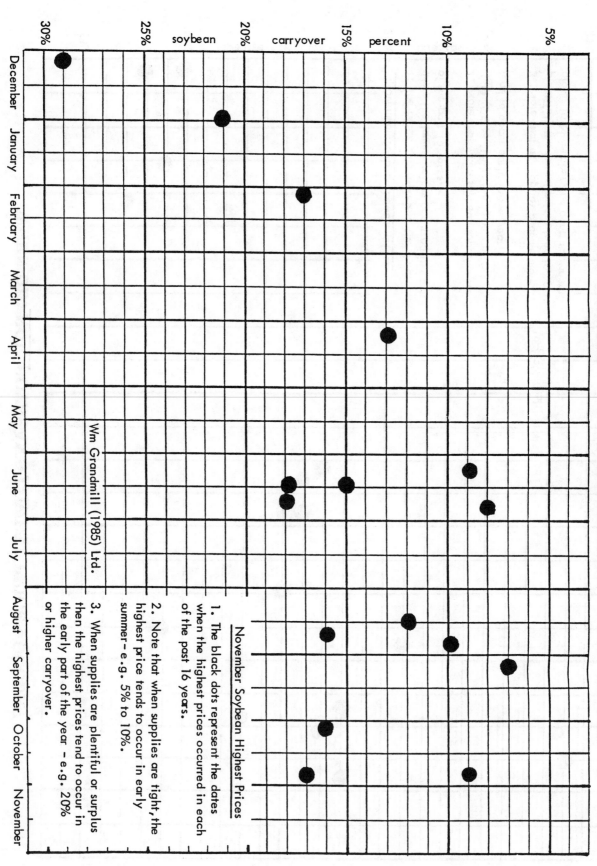

Wm Grandmill (1985) Ltd.

November Soybean Highest Prices

1. The black dots represent the dates when the highest prices occurred in each of the past 16 years.

2. Note that when supplies are tight, the highest price tends to occur in early summer – e.g. 5% to 10%.

3. When supplies are plentiful or surplus then the highest prices tend to occur in the early part of the year – e.g. 20% or higher carryover.

WHEN DID MAY SOYBEAN'S LOWEST PRICES OCCUR?

soybean carryover percent

5% 10% 15% 20% 25% 30%

June July August September October November December January February March April May

May Soybeans Lowest Prices

1. The black dots represent the dates when the lowest price occurred in each of the past 15 years.

2. Note that when supplies are tight (5% to 10%) the lowest prices tend to occur in July, Aug. and early Sept., and then to rise thereafter to March and April.

3. Note that when supplies are plentiful, the lowest prices tend to cluster in March and April.

Wm Grandmill (1985) Ltd.

WHEN DID MAY SOYBEAN'S HIGHEST PRICES OCCUR?

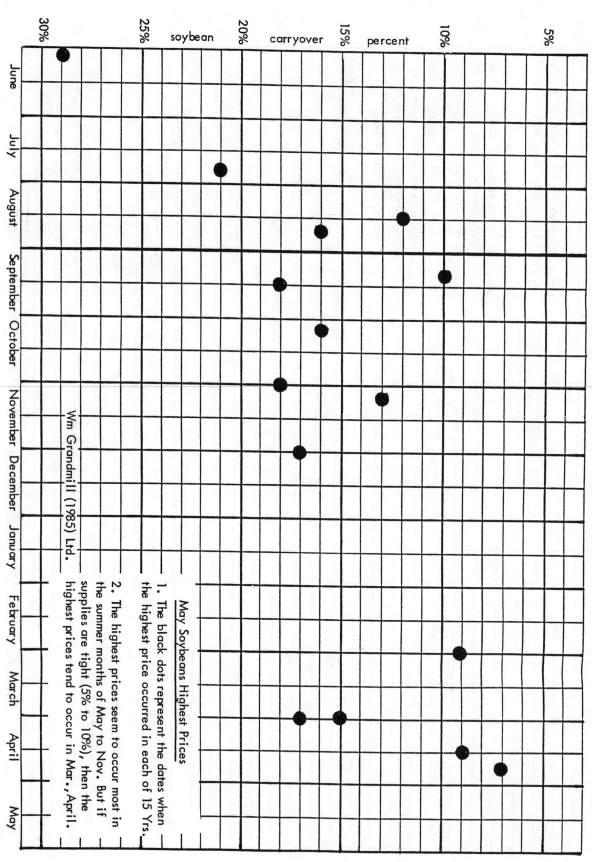

May Soybeans Highest Prices

1. The black dots represent the dates when the highest price occurred in each of 15 Yrs.

2. The highest prices seem to occur most in the summer months of May to Nov. But if supplies are tight (5% to 10%), then the highest prices tend to occur in Mar., April.

Wm Grandmill (1985) Ltd.

HOW TO FIND THE AMOUNT OF BACKUP MONEY NEEDED

Take a look at the Backup Graph below. Along the left side are the carryover percentages and along the bottom line are the soybean prices. The two curved lines represent the lowest ever and the highest ever soybean prices which have occurred in the past 15 years. These two curved lines will your guide as to how much backup money is needed to invest safely without using a stop price .

To give you some information about the two curved lines, here's how the **lowest price** line was made. Only the lowest of the low prices were used. **For example,** here's how the lowest price for the 18% carryover was found. There were two crop years which had an 18% carryover, and each crop year had 7 contract months and each contract month had about 230 days of price quotes, and each day has a lowest price and a highest price. To form the lowest price line on the graph for the 18% carryover, all the low prices were scrutinized and the lowest price of all was selected . It was $4.79. The $4.79 was placed opposite the 18%. And so all the carryover % were done the same way. Therefore, the "Lowest Price Line" was formed by using the lowest of all the low prices which have occurred over the past 15 years. Similarly, the "Highest Price Line" was formed by using only the highest of all the highest prices over the past 15 years.

You can see from the above that if you were taking a long soybean position in a crop year which had an 18% carryover (as in the example above) and if you protected your long position with enough money to protect yourself all the way down to $4.79, then you are safe, using a base below which prices are never likely to fall

But you still may not feel 100% safe. "Hold it!", you say," Look, if the soybean price fell to $4.79 once already in the past 15 years, what's to stop it from doing it again? Or maybe falling to $4.78? Nothing is for sure in the soybean business!" True. You're right.

But don't forget that you also have margin money in your account. A soybean margin is usually between $1000 and $1500 – so let's use $1200 which is about average. Therefore the margin money provides you with another 24¢ protection. In other words you are actually covered all the way down to $4.55 ($4.79 – 24¢) for an 18% carryover in this example. This is much farther that the lowest of all low prices has ever gone. Thinking of the future, inflation will automatically raise the lowest limits up by a few cents. That $4.79 lowest of all low prices occurred about 10 years ago – so that low price will never be touched again for an 18% carryover.

You may think that the amount of backup money which you get on the Backup Graph is too much money to be used to protect your soybean position. Don't think that way! **This is an investment,** not a speculation. You are **investing** in soybeans! Don't skimp on the amount of backup money needed! Use the full amount which the backup graph indicates, or use an option .

HOW MUCH BACKUP MONEY IS NEEDED TO INVEST IN SOYBEANS?

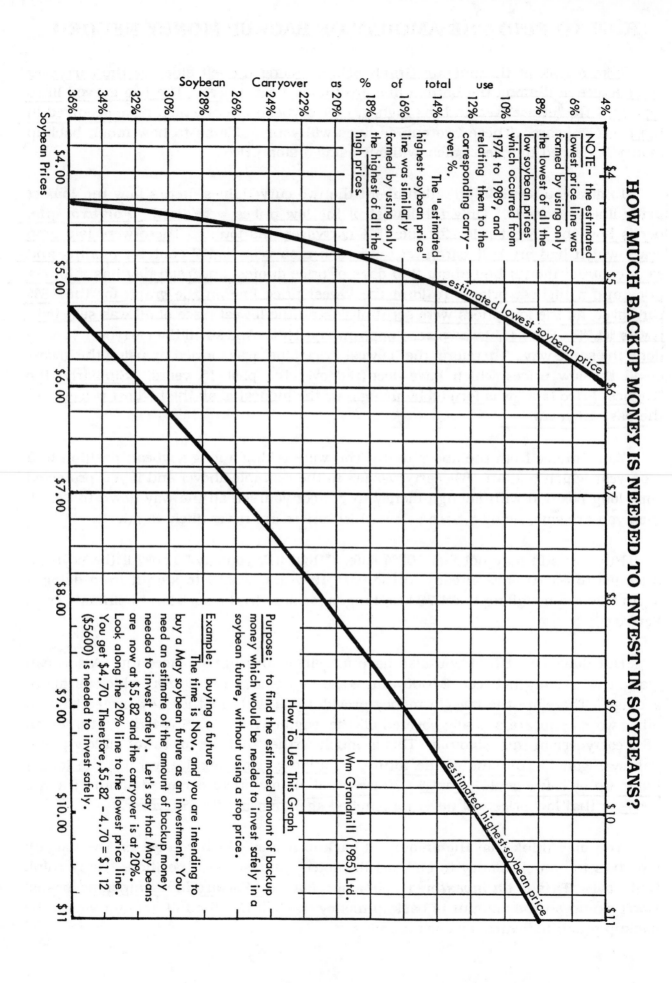

NOTE - the estimated lowest price line was formed by using only the lowest of all the low soybean prices which occurred from 1974 to 1989, and relating them to the corresponding carry-over %.

The "estimated highest soybean price" line was similarly formed by using only the highest of all the high prices.

Soybean Carryover as % of total use

estimated lowest soybean price

estimated highest soybean price

Soybean Prices

How To Use This Graph

Purpose: to find the estimated amount of backup money which would be needed to invest safely in a soybean future, without using a stop price.

Example: buying a future

The time is Nov. and you are intending to buy a May soybean future as an investment. You need an estimate of the amount of backup money needed to invest safely. Let's say that May beans are now at $5.82 and the carryover is at 20%. Look along the 20% line to the lowest price line. You get $4.70. Therefore, $5.82 - 4.70 = $1.12 ($5600) is needed to invest safely.

Wm Grandmill (1985) Ltd.

To further drive home the point that you must use the full amount of backup for real safety in soybean investing, *a preposterous example* will be used. Follow the line of thought in it because it has a lesson in it.

Example: The date is Nov. 15th. You are going to buy May soybeans. The carryover is 18% (just as in the example above). The present price of May beans is $6.00 per bushel.

Note this. You are very conservative in your trading of soybeans. You don't want to expose yourself to any risk at all. You say,"I'm going to protect my long soybean position all the way down from $6.00 to 0¢. That way there is no chance at all that soybean prices will fall below 0¢. I will have achieved the ultimate safety!"

Yes, it will be the ultimate safety alright, but let's see how much money is involved here. There are 5000 bushels of soybeans in one contract – so, 5000 x $6 = $30,000. So, $30,000 will be used here as backup for the long May position. Now, soybean prices move by more than $1 on the average, twice a year. But, let's be conservative here and say that prices in this example rise by exactly $1. Therefore the rate of profit is: $1 + $6 x 100 = 16.7% in 6 months – or an annual rate of 33.4%, which is not too bad and better than many blue chip stocks.

But what has happened in the example above is this: You have really bought 5000 bushels of soybeans outright – you own them all. You are like a farmer who has 5000 bushels of soybeans stored on his farm and he is waiting for higher prices. Except that you are in a better position than a farmer because you do not have the trouble of handling and storing them, nor do you have to take them to an elevator to sell them – you just phone your broker.

Here is the point of the story. The Backup Graph has a message, and it says,"Look, you don't need to use that $6 as backup. In fact, you don't need the first $4.79 of that $6. In fact, you just need the bit on the end, the $1.21 ($6 – $4.79 = $1.21) and you will have just as much safety when the carryover is 18%, from the $1.21 plus the margin money, as you would have had by using $6 as the backup"

But look at the difference in the profit rate ! Using the same $1 price rise as in the example above, and using the backup of $1.21, here is the profit rate: $1.00 + $1.21 x 100 = 83% profit in 6 months, or 166% on an annual basis.

But you may have an objection, saying "O.K., I can see that I need to put all the backup money into my commodity account for safety's sake – but something bothers me. It's the fact that only a portion of the backup is likely to be needed because the amount obtained from the graph is the *maximum amount* required, and in most cases I will need less than half of it. I hate to have my money sitting idle by earning no interest." Good point and something can be done about it.

Use T-Bills or some other liquid financial instrument as a method of "parking" some of your backup money until it is actually needed. Your broker will phone you to put in more money, if needed, and you can easily change a T-Bill into cash to replenish your backup. Let's say, **as an example,** that the Backup Graph indicated that you will need a maximum of $6000 as backup . You could deposit $3000 into your commodity account and put the other $3000 into T- Bills, or even into a bank account if you can get a good rate of interest. But you must be sure that you have set aside the whole amount of backup somewhere, in some form. This book recommends that you have at least $3000 in your commodity account, as a start. Research has shown that $3000 will cover over 3/4 of all soybean investments because the Forecasting Graph gets you pointed in the right direction before you take the soybean position.

To sum up. Set aside the **whole amount** of backup money as indicated by the Backup Graph. Don't skimp on the proper amount. Do not take half measures. Go all the way. If you find that the size of the backup is more than you can manage, then use an option. This way you are investing safely. A half measure exposes you to danger. Play it safe.

FINISHING THE AUTOMATIC YEAR ROUND INVESTMENT PLAN BUYING OR SELLING NOV. SOYBEANS ON MAY 15th

So far we have learned about the first half of the Year Round Plan – that is, taking a May soybean position on Nov. 15th. It is now time to finish off the Year Round Plan by learning how to handle the second half – that is, taking a November soybean position on May 15th.

Use options only on this half of the investment plan. Here's why. You'll remember away back it was mentioned that soybean trading could be separated into two distinct periods – a "quiet period" and a "turbulent period". The quiet period represents November to May. The turbulent period represents the months of May to November. You are heading into the turbulent period when you take a November soybean position on May 15th because you will be holding your position during the summer months when prices are tossed about by weather rumors.

Summer is the season for erratic price upheavals and it is the time when many thousands of futures' stop prices are touched off, leaving a trail of financial and emotional problems behind. But that won't happen to us because we will avoid the "stop price trap" by using an option or adequate backup instead.

Here is why an option is recommended for the turbulent summer months. More backup money is needed during the summer than during the quiet period of the first half of the Year Round Plan because of the uncertainties in the market, such as the possibility of a drought. Therefore because so much backup is needed one should use an option. An option's premium on May 15th for the November contract usually costs between $1500 and $2000. It is likely that you could take 2 options for less than the amount of backup that you would need for a future's position.

But there is one kind of situation when you might be better off to use a soybean future during the summer months. It is this: if the Nov. Forecasting Graph indicated that you should buy a Nov. future. Here's why. Often Nov. prices decline towards the harvest time. But if the Nov. Forecasting Graph indicates that prices will **rise** during the summer then it is likely indicating a tight soybean supply is being forecast for the coming crop year – which means that prices are already bullish and any sign of dryness or drought will cause prices to rise even further. So, in this case, weather rumors and drought would work in your favor. This is about the only kind of situation where futures are better than options in the summer. Of course, buying a Nov. call option will also produce a good profit.

Here are the steps to follow when taking a November position on May 15th.

1. Use the latest crop report about May 12th to estimate the carryover % for the new crop year which begins on Sept. 1st.

2. Consult the Nov. Forecasting Graph to find whether you should buy a call or buy a put. Remember the safety rule that there must be at least 75% potential profit possible – otherwise, stay out of the soybean market and consider wheat or corn.

3. Consult the soybean option graph. Remember the safety rule that you should be able to earn a 75% profit or better – otherwise stay out of the soybean market.

4. It may be possible for you to reach your % profit target early. The Nov. Timing Charts will help you to see when the highest and lowest prices might occur. It is an advantage to take your profit early if you can do so.

HOW WOULD THE AUTOMATIC YEAR ROUND SOYBEAN INVESTMENT PLAN HAVE FARED IN THE PAST 15 YEARS ?

Looking at the first half of the plan – taking a May futures position on Nov.15th.

1. By using the soybean price data of the past 15 years, here's what happened.
2. The May Forecasting Graph indicated that one should **stay out of the soy bean market** for 3 of those 15 years – because it was too risky.
3. One would have **bought** a May future in 6 of those 15 years.
4. One would have **sold** a May future in 6 of those 15 years.
5. Of the 12 years in which a May future was taken, there was one loss of 22¢ ($1100).
6. The **maximum** backup needed in all of those 12 years was 65¢ ($3250).
7. The **average** profit for each of those 12 years in which a May position was taken was 114¢ ($5700).

8. This represents a profit rate of 175%, using the maximum backup of $3250 as the investment money ($5700 ÷ $3250 x 100 = 175%),in 6 months.

Looking at the second half of the plan – taking a Nov. option on May 15th.

1. Options were used on every one of the 15 years, and the premium used was 40¢.

2. One would have **stayed out** of the market in 4 of those 15 years because there was insufficient profit potential. That leaves 11 years of the 15 years in which an option was taken.

3. A Nov. **call** was bought in 6 of those 11 years.

4. A Nov. **put** was bought in 5 of those 11 years.

5. There was one losing year of those 11 years (the 40¢ premium was lost).

6. The average net profit for each of those 11 years in which an option position wastaken, was 72¢ ($3600 net) which represents a 180% net return in 6 months, based on an investment of 40¢, the option premium.

7. **To sum up.** This finishes the information on the Automatic Year Round Investment Plan. This is a relaxed, safe method of trading the wild soybean market. The profits were good. The bad trades were filtered out by using the standards for safety and profit. And the standards are the 40¢ rule when the Forecasting Graph was used, and the 75% rule when the Soybean Option Graph was used.

AVERAGE LOW AND HIGH SOYBEAN PRICES

There are two graphs on the following pages which depict the *average* low and high prices which you might experience during a soybean trade. The graphs are based on the soybean price data of the past 15 years, and the prices are correlated to the carryover %.

Look at the graph which shows the average lowest and highest prices for November soybeans. Look at the 22% carryover line. Here is the message that the graph indicates when the carryover is 22% – it says that you can expect a November price low of about $5.00 and a high of about $6.70, based on the price behavior of the past 15 years. This gives you a ballpark number for a possible price range and you can get that price range before you take your soybean position, which is helpful. A 22% carryover represents a fairly large supply of soybeans on hand.

Look at the 8% carryover line. (8% represents a scarce supply of soybeans on hand) The lowest price here is about $6.65 and the average highest price is about $9.10. You can expect a wild trading year with a price range that wide.

How can you use this information? Here is an example – using the 8% carryover of the paragraph above. Let's say that you calculated an 8% carryover just after the May or the June crop reports, and you were intending to buy a November future. *First,* you check the November Forecasting Graph and note that the price on November 1st is estimated to be $8.00. *Second,* you check this new graph and you see that an 8% carryover could mean that the price could go as high as $9.10. *Third,* you check the November timing charts and note that the highest prices will likely occur in the summer, likely in July, August, September.

From the information above, you now have a sort of approximate agenda of how and when November prices could occur. You can now keep a watchful eye out for these events by being forewarned. Of course these prices are based on normal weather. A drought would push prices much higher. These graphs, then, are just one more item which will help you to gain an insight into your soybean position.

Don't confuse these new graphs with the Backup Graph. Turn back to the Backup Graph and compare the two graphs. The Backup Graph uses only the *lowest* of all the low prices in the past 15 years, and the other line uses only the *highest* of all the high prices. This new graph which you have here uses the *average* low and high prices.

These two graphs, the November and the May, will keep your "soybean price perspective" in focus. Here is what is meant. Some traders, new soybean traders in particular, get carried away by their enthusiasm. For example, when the carryover is 14%, some enthusiasts who are revelling in euphoria, might actually believe that May soybeans might actually go over $10 that year. Not a chance ! The May graph with a 14% carryover indicates a high of about $8.60 as the likely top price – and the Timing Chart will give a hint of when that top price might occur. These two graphs, then, keep your price perspective within reasonable limits.

AVERAGE RANGE OF NOV. SOYBEAN'S HIGHEST AND LOWEST PRICES

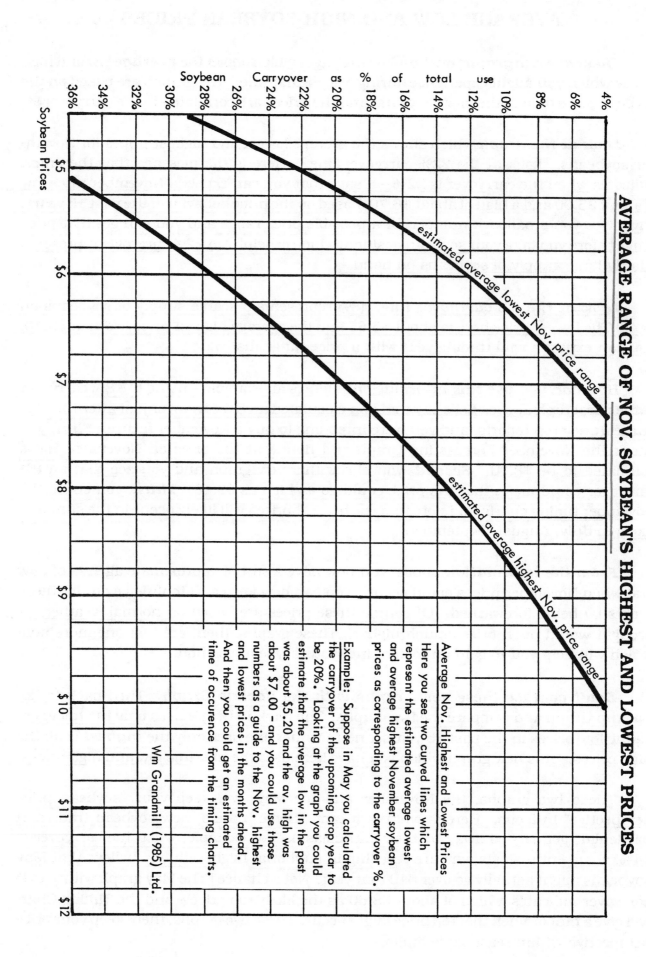

Average Nov. Highest and Lowest Prices

Here you see two curved lines which represent the estimated average lowest and average highest November soybean prices as corresponding to the carryover %.

Example: Suppose in May you calculated the carryover of the upcoming crop year to be 20%. Looking at the graph you could estimate that the average low in the past was about $5.20 and the av. high was about $7.00 – and you could use those numbers as a guide to the Nov. highest and lowest prices in the months ahead. And then you could get an estimated time of occurence from the timing charts.

Wm Grandmill (1985) Ltd.

AVERAGE RANGE OF MAY SOYBEAN'S HIGHEST AND LOWEST PRICES

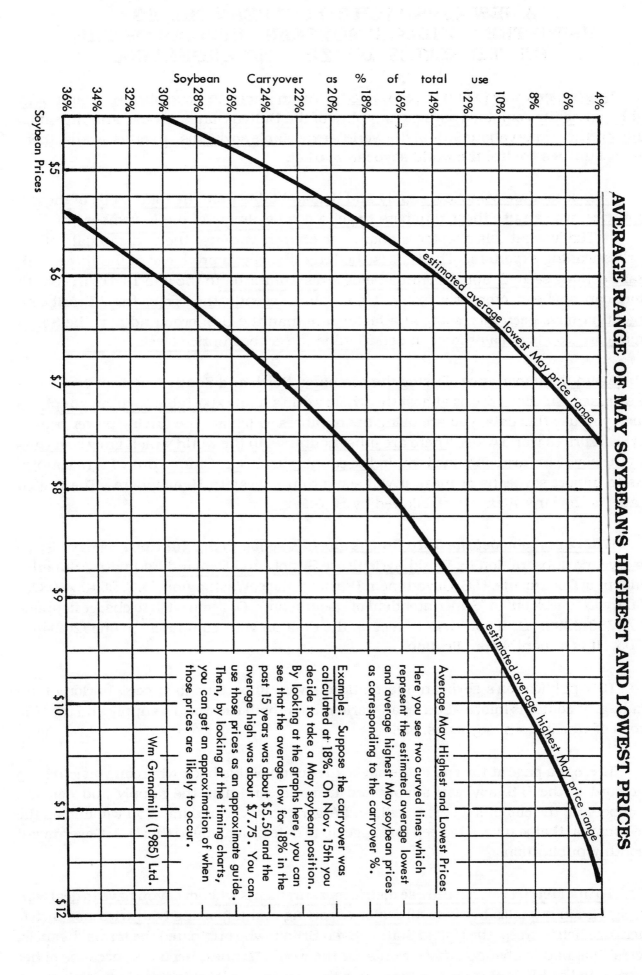

Soybean Carryover as % of total use

estimated average lowest May price range

estimated average highest May price range

Soybean Prices

Average May Highest and Lowest Prices

Here you see two curved lines which represent the estimated average lowest and average highest May soybean prices as corresponding to the carryover %.

Example: Suppose the carryover was calculated at 18%. On Nov. 15th you decide to take a May soybean position. By looking at the graphs here, you can see that the average low for 18% in the past 15 years was about $5.50 and the average high was about $7.75. You can use those prices as an approximate guide. Then, by looking at the timing charts, you can get an approximation of when those prices are likely to occur.

Wm Grandmill (1985) Ltd.

A NEW APPROACH TO SOYBEAN PRICES
USING THE COMBINED SOYBEAN SUPPLIES OF THE
UNITED STATES, BRAZIL, AND ARGENTINA

This is a new way to find the estimated soybean prices on November 1st, about May 1st by using the combined soybean supplies of the United States, Brazil, and Argentina who together export about 90% of the world's exportable soybeans. In other words, these three countries control the world soybean market.

Therefore, if we compile a supply and demand table from the total crops of these 3 countries, we can use these numbers to get a good estimate of the November prices.

That's what this chapter is about – to show how to use the soybean data of the world's leading exporters. The U.S. is the largest soybean producer of the three, with Brazil coming second, and Argentina being a distant third. In the late 1970's the South American soybean crop was insignificant. But recently the crops from Brazil and Argentina have been increasing at a faster rate than the U.S. crop and now the South American crop is a major force in determining the soybean price levels.

Again the importance of using the combined North and South American crop must be stressed. In effect, this is almost the whole world's total exportable soybean supply. So when you use this data, you are using the numbers which are the driving power behind soybean prices world wide. There are other countries in the world which grow soybeans but the soybeans are consumed within the country itself, e.g. China. But when a country has to import soybeans or meal, it will some to the Western Hemisphere. The United States is the largest exporter, followed by Brazil .

Where can you get the data for the world's soybean production? By paying $18 for a year's subscription to: World Agriculture Supply and Demand Estimates, Superintendent of Documents, U.S. Government Printing Office, Washington, D.C. 20402 – 9372. Make your check out to "Superintendent of Documents". Or if you wish to charge it, phone (202)783-3238. Or if you wish to receive the data on your computer, phone (202)447-5505. It is a monthly publication .

This publication's soybean information is very important to successful long term trading. It contains information on all world grains- both the world's supply and the U.S. crops of wheat, corn, soybeans, etc.

There is a page at the end of the soybean section of this book whereon you can keep a record of the U.S. soybean supply and demand, and also the supply and demand numbers for the combined U.S..Brazil, and Argentina soybean data. You will find all the information that you need to keep this page up to date by looking in this U.S. Government monthly publication.

Think Metric! You have to use metric measurements whenever you have to deal with foreign grain supplies because all major exporting and importing countries use metric measurements except the United States. Even Britain who originated the terms "bushels, acres" has had to abandon those words for the words "tonnes, hectares" because of her entry into the EEC. But we need only use the metric words which apply to grains.

Grains are measured in **metric tons** or **tonnes** instead of in bushels. A metric ton = 2204.6 lbs. A bushel of soybeans (and wheat) weighs 60 lbs. Therefore a metric ton has 2204.6. ÷ 60 = 36.74 bushels of soybeans (or wheat). **The conversion number, then, is 36.74.** Thus, 5 tonnes of soybeans = 5 x 36.74 = 183.7 bu. Likewise a contract of 5000 bushels of soybeans = 5000 ÷ 36.74 = 136.1 metric tons. The abbreviation is m.t. The supply and demand figures are expressed in millions of metric tons or m.m.t.

WHEN DOES THE SOUTH AMERICAN SOYBEAN CROP BEGIN TO AFFECT CHICAGO SOYBEAN PRICES?

The soybean crops of Brazil and Argentina are harvested mainly during March, April and early May. But you will hear rumors, true and false, of Brazil's soybean crop difficulties in January and in February which will affect soybean prices marginally. The only rumor worth looking into is a drought rumor because a drought in Brazil would have a big impact on the Chicago soybean prices. The other important piece of information is the size of the planted hectares.

You will learn of Brazil's planted hectares about January. Compare the amount with the planted hectares of last year, and you will know whether the crop is likely to be larger or smaller than last year's soybean crop. For example, a much larger crop would cause Chicago soybean prices to begin to weaken in early March, whereas a normal crop size would likely cause prices to be affected in late April or May.

Where do you get the information on Brazil's soybean crop? From the USDA. The first tentative crop estimate will likely come in the February report. Then the USDA March report will have a more definite figure on the estimated Brazilian crop size. You should a good estimate of the crops of Brazil and Argentina by the May 12th USDA crop report because **you will then be able to use the following graph** and the Forecasting Graphs to decide whether you will be taking an option position, or a future's position or whether you should stay out of the market. **The new graph which is on the following page, will enable you to get a good fix on the soybean prices in the months ahead, by using only the combined crop size estimates of the United States, Brazil, and Argentina.** You will not even need the carryover – just the crop size. The June crop report will be even better because the crop information will be more definite – especially the information on the estimated U.S. soybean crop which has just been planted. But you should take your soybean position by June 15 at the latest if you are planning on taking one. Use an option preferably because you are heading into the wild summer price rumors.

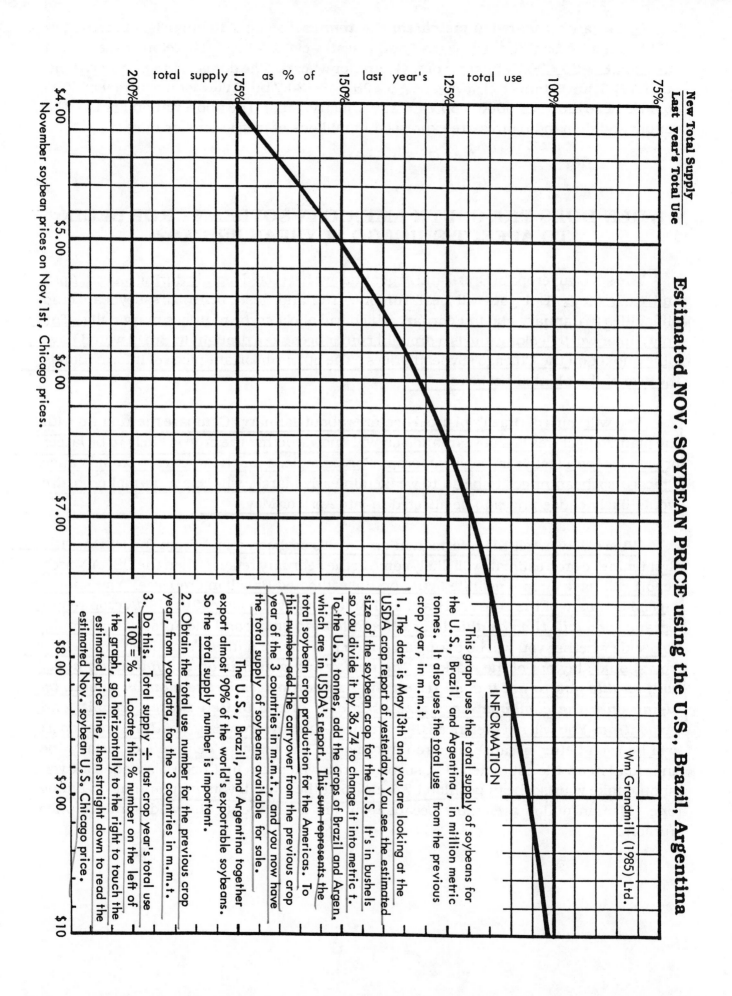

Estimated NOV. SOYBEAN PRICE using the U.S., Brazil, Argentina

Wm Grandmill (1985) Ltd.

New Total Supply
Last year's Total Use

total supply as % of last year's total use

November soybean prices on Nov. 1st, Chicago prices.

75%   100%   125%   150%   175%   200%

$4.00 $5.00 $6.00 $7.00 $8.00 $9.00 $10

INFORMATION

This graph uses the total supply of soybeans for the U.S., Brazil, and Argentina, in million metric tonnes. It also uses the total use from the previous crop year, in m.m.t.

1. The date is May 13th and you are looking at the USDA crop report of yesterday. You see the estimated size of the soybean crop for the U.S. It's in bushels so you divide it by 36.74 to change it into metric t. To the U.S. tonnes, add the crops of Brazil and Argen. which are in USDA's report. This sum represents the total soybean crop production for the Americas. To this number add the carryover from the previous crop year of the 3 countries in m.m.t., and you now have the total supply of soybeans available for sale.

The U.S., Brazil, and Argentina together export almost 90% of the world's exportable soybeans. So the total supply number is important.

2. Obtain the total use number for the previous crop year, from your data, for the 3 countries in m.m.t.

3. Do this. Total supply ÷ last crop year's total use × 100 = %. Locate this % number on the left of the graph, go horizontally to the right to touch the estimated price line, then straight down to read the estimated Nov. soybean U.S. Chicago price.

139

THE TOTAL SUPPLY / LAST YEAR'S TOTAL USE USING THE COMBINED CROPS OF THE U.S., BRAZIL, ARGENTINA

This new graph is based on making a comparison between the **total soybean crop supply** which will be available for the upcoming new crop year, and with the **total soybean use of the previous crop year.** And by supply, we mean the total crop sizes and the beginning stocks of the United States, Brazil and Argentina together.

Here's the theory. From the May and June crop reports we will be able to add together the crop estimates of the 3 countries, plus the beginning stocks, to come up with a number which represents the **total soybean supply** of the Western Hemisphere which controls the world soybean prices. Then, compare this number with the number which represents **last year's total use** of the 3 countries combined. Here's the point: (a) if the total supply for the upcoming crop year is **smaller** than the previous crop year's total use, then it is a sign that there may not be enough soybeans to supply the world market – and then prices will go sky high (b) if the total supply for the upcoming crop year is **larger** than the previous crop year's total use, then it is a sign that soybean supplies will not be tight – and so prices will be moderate or low.

One of the best ways to compare two numbers is to make a percentage number from them. That's what is done here. Here is the equation: **total supply ÷ previous crop year's total use x 100 = %** . There are 3 possible ways for the answer, and here is an example of each way. (a) **Let's say that you got 90%** as the answer to the equation above. That means that we have only 90% of the required number of soybeans on hand to supply the world. So some form of rationing must be done – and in the grain business, rationing is done by raising prices high enough to price some buyers out of the market. Therefore, a percentage below 100% means that prices will likely rise to over $10 per bu. at Chicago. (b) **Let's say that we get 100%** as the answer to the equation above. That means that there is exactly enough soybeans to go around, with none left over for emergency nor any for a new customer who wants to do some buying. This is a bullish situation and soybean prices should rise to over $9 per bu. (c) **Let's say that we got 150%** as the answer. That means that we have 50% more beans than we are likely to need in the new crop year. That's a bearish situation and prices will be low.

Look at the graph. Note that the % numbers are on the left side of the graph. Note also that this graph is for November soybeans – because you will be taking a decision in May or June which means that you will be likely to use the November contract. Remember that the graph is based on normal soil moisture during the summer. A drought would push prices higher than the graph indicates. To use the graph, locate the % number at the left, go horizontally to touch the heavy price line, then go straight down to read the soybean's estimated November Price on Nov. 1st.

It's time for some practice. Learn by doing. Below are 3 consecutive soybean crop years which uses the combined data of the U.S., Brazil, and Argentina soybean supply and demand figures. The information is in **million metric tons.** Below the supply and demand table are some questions .

	A	B	C
Beginning stocks (m.m.t.)	16.2	16.7	S
Production	81.7	83.0	76.1
Total Supply	97.9	Q	T
Domestic use	53.2	51.6	
Exports	28.0	27.0	
Total Use	81.2	78.6	
Carryover	16.7	21.1	
Carryover %	21%	27%	
Total supply/last yr. total use	118%	R	W

Questions. 1. Using crop year B (a) what number should occupy space Q? (b) what% should occupy space R? (c) Use the graph to find the estimated November soybean price on November 1st.

2. Using crop year C (a) what number should occupy space S? (b) what number should occupy space T? (c) what % should occupy space W? (d) use the graph to find the estimated November price on Nov. 1st for crop year C.

Answers. 1. (a) 99.7 (b) 123% (c) about $6.60 2.(a) 21.1 (b) 97.2 (c) 124% (d) about $6.55. You deserve an A+ if you had all those right.

GETTING A HEAD START ON THE MARKET

As you know, all soybean traders want to be first to "get the news". This way, they be able to get in on a big price move from the beginning because they know that once the general public catches on, then it is too late because prices may have advanced by almost half the move by then. This is particularly true when it comes to getting the size of the upcoming soybean crop because foreknowledge here means big profits if you get in at the start of the price move which comes when the new crop will be larger or smaller than the present crop size.

Therefore, the purpose of this chapter is to help you to be among the first to find the estimated new crop size, earlier than most soybean traders. Usually April is the earliest time to get the first estimate of the upcoming soybean crop. This is because the USDA usually gets its first estimate of the number of acres which will be planted in soybeans, in April.

The USDA takes a survey of soybean farmers to find out their **planting intentions.** From this information, USDA will calculate the expected number of soybean acres which will be planted. Usually this information is given in the April crop report which comes out about April 12th. You can see from the above that this first acreage estimate will be a tentative one, because the crop itself will not be planted for another 4 to 6 weeks.

Each succeeding crop report will contain a more accurate acreage estimate. The May crop report will be more accurate than the April estimate, and the June estimate will be more accurate still. However, the real number of acres which are planted will not be known until after the harvest is completed. This is too late for us (and for all soybean traders) so we will have to make do with the estimates in April and May. Our Automatic Soybean Investment Plan starts on May 15th so we should be ready by then.

Therefore, two graphs have been made for this book which will enable you to get an early estimate of the new upcoming soybean crop size and also an estimate of the Nov. soybean price on Nov. 1st. This way, you will be able to plan early and to get a soybean position in place before the masses invade the market.

Look at the two graphs now. One graph gives you the estimated U.S. soybeans based on the number of planted acres and on the amount of moisture in the soil (a detailed explanation soon). The other graph uses the information from the first graph to give you the estimated price of Nov. soybeans on Nov. 1st. Note that we are using only the U.S. soybean data here in these two graphs, and the production is in millions of bushels. Whereas, in the previous chapter we used the combined production of the United States, Brazil, and Argentina and the production was expressed in millions of metric tons.

The Soybean Production Graph. Here is the theory behind this graph. If one knows how many acres of soybeans were planted, and if one knows the soil moisture condition, then one can get a reasonably accurate estimate of the size of the upcoming soybean crop.

There are a couple of terms to understand. One is **planted acres.** These are the acres planted by the farmer. The other term is **harvested acres.** These are the acres which are actually harvested in the fall. Not all planted acres are harvested. Therefore the number of harvested acres is always less than the number of planted acres. Based on the data of the past 15 years, about 2% to 3% of the planted acres are never harvest for some reason.We are interested only in the number of harvested acres, not the number of planted acres, because it is the harvested acres which produce the soybean crop. This presents us with a problem because the number of harvested acres is not know until after the soybean crop has been harvested. But this is too late for us. We need that information in April or May. We need to know the estimated number of **harvested acres** in April or May so that we can calculate the estimated size of the upcoming soybean crop.

Here's how that problem was tackled for this book. An analysis was made on data of the past 15 years to establish the relationship between the number of planted acres and the number of harvested acres. Here's what was found. The amount of abandoned acreage depended upon the soybean price at the time. Thus, when soybean prices were high there were very few acres abandoned. In fact, when prices were high the harvested acres were about 99% of the planted acres. But when prices were low the harvested acreage was about 95% to 96% of the planted acres. This reflected the farmer's mood that showed that he was reluctant to give up a chance to make all he could from his crop when prices were high -whereas he was more easily persuaded to abandon acreage when prices were low.

As a result of the above analysis, it was decided to use the average acreage loss. Therefore, this book uses 97.5% of the planted acres, as the amount of harvested acres. Also, to save you from doing a calculation, this 97.5% was incorporated into the graph which gives the estimated production. In other words, you can use the **planted acreage number** – given by the USDA in the April and May reports directly on the Production Graph because the conversion into **harvested acres** has been built into the structure of the graph. This makes the graph easier for you to use.

Let's take a closer look at the Production graph. Note that the left side of the graph has the **planted** acres. Look at the interior of the graph and you will see 4 slanting lines, each with a title on it. The title represents the amount of soil moisture at the time when you are finding the estimated production. You see the words "Ideal Weather", "Average Weather", "Dry Weather", and " Severe Drought" . What follows is a more detailed description of each type of weather, and the criteria which you can use to decide which of those 4 lines to use when you are getting the production estimate.

Ideal Weather. It is the best condition that you could hope for. It means that there has been just the right amount of rain and sunshine in the spring (don't forget, you will be using this graph in April and May) – just the right amount of rain and snow in the winter – and the previous fall and summer were either average or ideal (the previous year is important for calculating the moisture – a lack of moisture in the

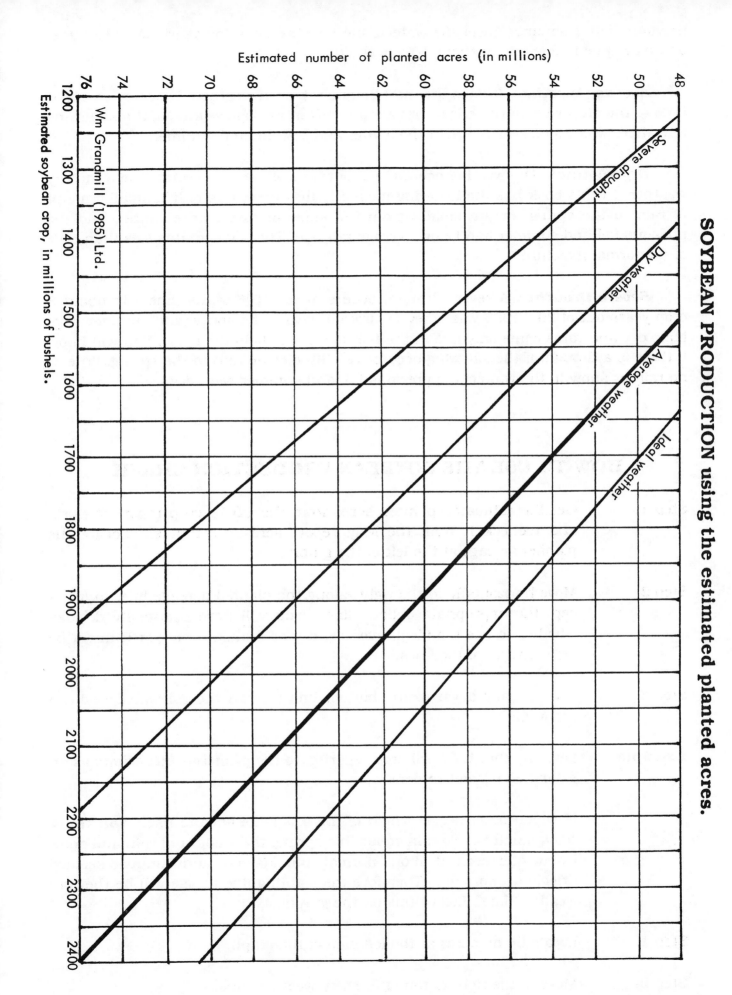

SOYBEAN PRODUCTION using the estimated planted acres.

Estimated number of planted acres (in millions)

Estimated soybean crop, in millions of bushels.

Wm Grandmill (1985) Ltd.

Severe drought

Dry weather

Average weather

Ideal weather

previous fall or summer affect the water table into the following year). An Ideal year doesn't happen often – only about 10% of the time.

Average Weather. This is the most common type of weather. It occurs in about 55% of the crop years. The crops thrive quite well in average weather. It also means that there was average moisture in the winter and last fall and summer.

Dry Weather. Dry weather occurs in about 20% of the crop years. The term "dry weather" in this book has the following meaning: that there was only a small amount of rain in the spring, only a small amount of snow or rain in the winter, and the previous fall and summer had below average rainfall. The soil contains less than 50% of its normal moisture.

Severe Drought. A severe drought occurs about 15% of the time – in about 3 crop years out of 20. 1988 was a severe drought year – the spring and summer were bone dry and rains came only late in the fall, too late to help the crop. You will know if there is a drought if the following occurs: very little or no rain in the spring, little or no rain or snow in the winter, the previous fall and summer were dry.

HOW TO USE THE SOYBEAN PRODUCTION GRAPH

Step 1.   Get the estimated planted acres from the USDA crop report of April, and recheck it from the May report acreage estimate. Locate the planted acreage at the left of the graph .

Step 2.   Move horizontally to the right, along the planted acreage line, to intercept the appropriate oblique line. You will have previously decided whether to use the ideal, average, dry or drought line – or it might be between two of the lines.

Step 3.   Go vertically down to the bottom line to read the estimated soybean production.

Example.   Let's say that the April crop report gave the *planting intentions* as an estimated 64 million acres.

Now you must decide which of the 4 oblique lines to use. **You think back** like this: "No rain so far this spring, the amount of rain and snow last winter seemed about normal, but last fall and summer seemed drier than normal". Therefore the slanting line to use will be the "dry weather" line. Follow this on the graph.

Step 1.   Locate 64 m. acres at the left side of the graph.

Step 2.   Move to the right to touch the "dry weather" line.

Step 3.   Go vertically down to the bottom line to read 1840 million bu. as the estimated soybean crop.

You don't always have to use one of the 4 oblique lines. Sometimes you will use a place between two of the oblique lines. Suppose, for example, that you believed that the present soil conditions were just a bit drier than average . Then, in this case, you would use a spot between the "average " and the "dry" lines – just how far between them is based on your judgement of the weather. In fact, most of the times that you use this graph, you will be using a place between two of the 4 weather lines.

What To Do Next.

So far you have found the estimated crop size for the new crop year by using the planting intentions from the April or May crop reports.

The next step is to find the estimated price of November soybeans on Nov. 1st. You will use the production number from the Production Graph to help find the November soybean price.

Look at the November price graph. Note that it uses the Total Supply/ the previous crop year's Total Use, expressed as %. This is just like the previous chapter's method, except that here we are using only the U. S. soybean data on this graph – whereas in the previous chapter we used the combined soybean production of the United States, Brazil, and Argentina, expressed in millions of metric tons.

You will remember that the **Total Supply** is made from the crop **production** plus the **beginning stocks** (which is actually the carryover from the previous crop year). To repeat: **Total Supply = the Beginning Stocks + the new crop Production.** Thus, by using the planted acreage estimate in the April crop report, and by using these two graphs, you will be able to get your first tentative November soybean price estimate by April 15th. This way, you will be among the very first to have an idea of whether prices will be higher or lower in the upcoming new crop year. You will be among the first to be able to take a market position early if a big price change is ahead. That's an advantage.

PRICE OF NOVEMBER SOYBEANS ON NOV. 1st – using $\dfrac{\text{new Total Supply}}{\text{last year's Total Use}}$

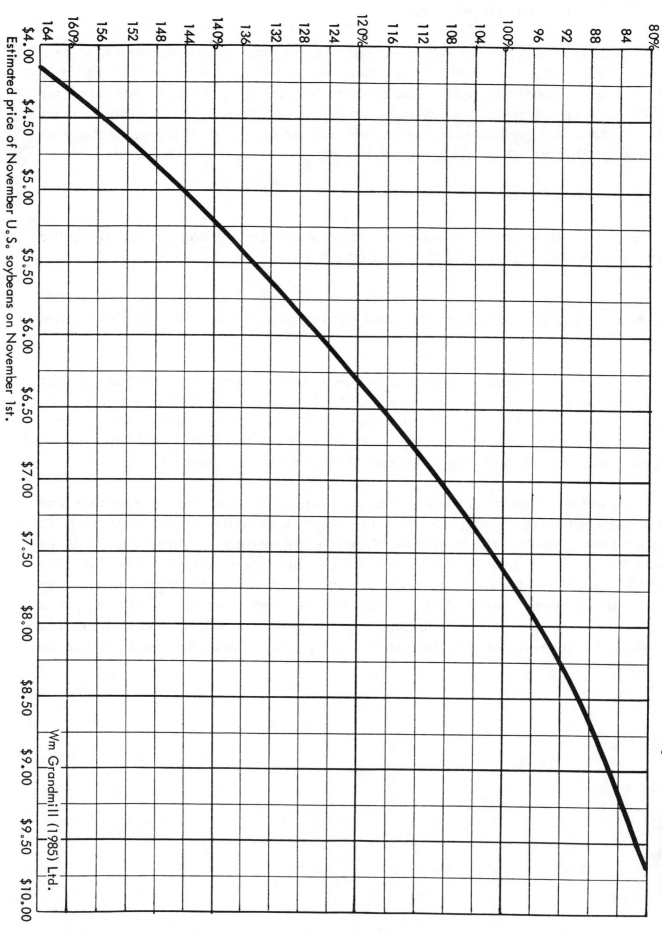

Estimated price of November U.S. soybeans on November 1st.

Wm Grandmill (1985) Ltd.

IT'S PRACTICE TIME !

It is time to get some experience using the two graphs in this chapter. Below are 3 consecutive crop years. Some of the data is missing (marked with a letter). Your job is to calculate the missing data. (all acres and bushels are expressed in millions)

Soybean crop years	X	Y	Z
Planting intentions (mil.ac.)	64	60	66
Beginning stocks (mi 1. bu.)	300	400	C
Production	2000	1890	D
Total Supply	2300	2290	E
Domestic use (crush,etc.)	1200	1100	
Exports	700	700	
Total Use	1900	1800	
Carryover	400	490	
Carryover as % of total use	21%	A	
New Total Supply _____ % Previous Year's Total Use	130%	B	F

Do these questions.

1. In crop year Y (a) what % is represented by A? (b) what % is B?

2. In crop year Z (a) what number is represented by C? (b) assume that there has been dry weather in the past several months – what is the crop production which is represented by D? (c) what number is E? (d) what % number is F?

3. What is the estimated November price on Nov 1st for crop year Z?

Answers.

1. (a)27% (b) 121% 2. (a)490 mil. bu. (b) 1900 mil. bu. (c)2390 m.b. (d) 133% 3. about $5.60

EXAMPLE – This example takes you through the whole process.

Data – 1. The date is April 12th and the USDA crop report has just been released and it says that the planting intentions are estimated to be 60 million acres.

2. The weather for the past several months has been a bit drier than average.

3. The beginning stocks for the new crop year are 200 million bu.

4. The Total Use for the previous crop year was 1800 m.b.

5. The present price for November beans is $6.00.

Question – What is the estimated November soybean price on Nov 1st?

Method – (follow this on the graphs)

1. Using the estimated 60 mil. acres. of planted soybeans on the Production Graph and noting that the weather was a "bit drier than average", we will go 1/4 of the way from the Average line to the Dry line. Doing so, we get an estimated ***production of 1850 mil. bu .***

2. By adding the 200 m.b. of beginning stocks to the production, we get: 200 + 1850 = ***2050 m. bu. as the Total Supply.***

3. The previous year's Total Use was 1800 m.b. Using the equation: Present Total Supply ÷ previous year's Total Use x 100%, we get 2050 ÷ 1800 x 100 = ***114%.***

4. Using the November price graph. Locate 114% at the left side of the graph, move horizontally to the right to touch the dark curved line. Then go vertically down to the bottom line to read about $6.65 as the estimated price on Nov 1st.

5. The present price of November beans is $6.00 – so we expect a price rise of 65¢. Therefore we should buy a November option call or a future.

6. It has been suggested that you should use an option during the volatile summer months. ***But this is a good time to buy a November future.*** Here's why. You can be almost 100% sure that there will be at least one weather rumor or scare during the summer which will send prices up. Therefore, if you are long a future position, then a price rise from a weather scare will add to your expected profit.

HOW DOES A CHANGE IN THE CARRYOVER %
AFFECT
SOYBEAN PRICES?

At first this chapter was to be omitted from this book because there was not enough data in the past 15 years of soybean prices to complete this table. There was enough information to complete only about half the table. The remainder of the table was completed by interpolation and by what this author believed was the "right price" for each circumstance.

It was finally decided to include this table because it provides two uses: (1) it provides a good insight into what happens to soybean prices as the size of the carryover changes. (2) it can be used as a forecasting tool, at the same time providing a price check on the other graphs.

As far as is known, this is the first time that there has been an attempt to correlate the rate of change in the carryover % to the rate of price changes. As a result you have a new type of forecasting method which forecasts the November price from an entirely different point of view. You now have   different methods of forecasting prices: (1) the original Forecasting Graph (2) the graph which uses the combined crops of the United States, Brazil, Argentina (3) this new table which uses a change in the carryover % to find the amount of change in the November price. Each is different and it is like having independent soybean advisors who gives you his price forecast, each from a different point of view. It is a good thing to have it this way because maybe the "Right Price" lies near the average of the   price forecasts. Use this table after the June report. Again, this table is based on normal soil moisture for the soybean crop. A drought would raise the prices above the prices quoted in this table.

Look at the table. At the left side are the changes in the carryover %. For example the date is June 12th, the day the crop report comes out. Let's say that you are in crop year A and the present carryover % is 18%. From the new data in the crop report you calculate that the carryover for the next crop year B will be 13% – which is 5% less than the present carryover. Locate -5 on the left side of the table. Let's say that the November soybean price on June 12th was $7. Locate $7 on the bottom row, and go straight up to intercept the -5 row. You read $7.55 as the estimated November price on November 1st.

That example was easy and neat. But often you will have to interpolate. For example, if the November price on June 12th was $6.87, then you would have to interpolate to arrive at the price. It was mentioned above that you will use November's price on June 12th. Let's amend that to read, "Use the November price of the time at which you take your position, and try to take it by June 15th if you are planning to take a position at all". There will be thousands of traders studying that report and they will act within a few days – so don't delay if the graphs indicate that it is a good investment.

What the research revealed. A lot of research went into the compilation of the table. A few significant points were noted which will be of interest to you.

HOW DOES A CHANGE IN CARRYOVER % AFFECT THE NOV. PRICE?

151

Example: The date is June 12th and the latest crop report. From the USDA data, you figure that the carryover for the upcoming crop year will be 14%. The current carryover is now 20%. The Nov. bean price on June 12th is $6.50. What will be the estimated price of Nov. beans on Nov. 1st? How to do it: the new crop carryover is 6% less than the current %. Look along the −6 row, to meet the $6.50 column and you get $7.10.

Wm Grandmill (1985) Ltd.

November Soybean Price On June 12th

%	$5.00	$5.50	$6.00	$6.50	$7.00	$7.50	$8.00	$8.50	$9.00	$9.50
−8	5.50	5.85	6.25	6.60	7.00	7.30	7.60	7.95	8.40	9.20
−7	5.35	5.65	6.00	6.35	6.70	7.00	7.30	7.60	8.00	8.70
−6	5.20	5.50	5.80	6.15	6.45	6.75	7.10	7.40	7.75	8.30
−5	5.10	5.40	5.65	6.00	6.30	6.60	6.95	7.20	7.55	7.85
−4	5.05	5.30	5.55	5.85	6.15	6.45	6.80	7.05	7.40	7.75
−3	4.95	5.20	5.45	5.75	6.05	6.35	6.65	6.90	7.25	7.60
−2	4.90	5.10	5.35	5.65	5.95	6.25	6.55	6.80	7.10	7.45
−1	4.85	5.05	5.30	5.55	5.85	6.15	6.45	6.70	7.00	7.35
0%	4.80	5.00	5.25	5.50	5.80	6.10	6.40	6.65	6.95	7.25
+1	4.80	5.00	5.25	5.50	5.75	6.05	6.35	6.60	6.90	7.20
+2	4.80	5.00	5.20	5.45	5.70	6.00	6.30	6.55	6.85	7.10
+3	4.75	4.95	5.20	5.40	5.65	5.95	6.20	6.45	6.70	7.00
+4	4.75	4.95	5.15	5.35	5.60	5.90	6.10	6.35	6.60	6.85
+5	4.70	4.90	5.10	5.30	5.50	5.80	6.00	6.25	6.45	6.70
+6	4.70	4.85	5.05	5.20	5.40	5.65	5.85	6.05	6.25	6.45
+7	4.65	4.80	5.00	5.10	5.30	5.50	5.65	5.85	6.05	6.20
+8%	4.60	4.75	4.90	5.00	5.15	5.30	5.45	5.65	5.85	6.00

DONE ON JUNE 12TH

1. Different dates were experimented upon to find which produced the best profit and reliability. The time immediately after the June crop report proved to be the best.

2. It was noted that the size of the November price when you take the position greatly affected the rate of change in the price. **Do this.** Look at the -2 row (which means that the new carryover is 2% smaller). Look in the $5 column and you will see that there is only a 10¢ change for the 0 row. Now look over to the other side of the table and you will see that there is a price change of $3.55 in the $9.75 column. The size of the November price makes a big difference to the rate of price change.

3. It was also noted that the larger the carryover % difference, the greater was the rate of price change. Look at the price difference between the -7 and the ~8 rows, in any column. Look now at the price difference between the -1 and the -2 rows. The larger carryover difference produce a grater rate of change.

YOU NOW HAVE 4 DIFFERENT NOVEMBER GRAPHS OR TABLES TO CONSULT

This book considers the month of November to be the key soybean investment month. Why? Three Reasons.

First, Even though September 1st is the official beginning of the crop year, the harvest has scarcely begun and weather rumors still plague the market. But by the time November has come, the harvest is nearly over and the weather rumors are obsolete and prices have settled down. The November USDA crop report is a good one to use for a position.

Second, November is the beginning of the "quiet period" when prices are stable and react mainly to the size of the soybean supply. Less backup money is needed during the quiet period because there are less price fluctuations. This is a nice time to take a position.

Third, November 15th is the beginning of the Automatic Year Round Investment Plan.

Because of November's importance, special attention has been paid to the process of trying to get as accurate a soybean price estimate for November 1st as possible. Consequently this book has 4 November Forecasting Graphs – each one viewing the November price from a different perspective. *One graph* uses the carryover % of the U.S. soybean crop to get an estimate of the November 1st price. *A second graph* uses the combined United States, Brazil, and Argentina soybean crops in a different way: the total supply / last year's total use. *The third* is a table which estimates the November price by using a change in the carryover %. *The fourth* uses the U.S. data only and the total supply/last year's total use. *There is an advantage here.* It is like getting a price estimate from 4 different soybean experts, each of whom uses a different method of analysis!

Therefore, you will get 4 price estimates for November 1st – **and they will all be different.** There are 2 forecasting graphs for the estimated price on May 1st – **and they will all be different.** But not different by a lot – they will be ballpark numbers.

What to do? A good solution is to calculate an average price. Using the 4 different November price forecasts as an example, add them together and divide by 4 to arrive at the average November estimated price. That is a good solution unless you have a reason to favor one graph over the others. For example, some people will believe that the forecasting graph which uses the combined North and South American soybean crops is the best one because it represents the world exportable soybean supply and we are in a world market. But there are others who would argue the other way, saying,"I prefer to use the Forecasting Graph which uses the U.S. supply and carryover only. We are using Chicago prices and I am familiar with the past history of the U.S. soybean price behavior. I feel more comfortable using our own information and our own words like "bushel" and "acre". Anyway, we are the biggest producers so we set the prices." These are good arguments on both sides of the question. If a compromise is the best solution, then use an average. **An average is a compromise.**

WHICH IS BETTER TO TRADE – SOYBEANS or MEAL ?

There are times when it is more profitable to invest your money in soybean meal rather than in the soybeans themselves.

Normally there is a balance of values between soybeans and the products – namely, meal and soybean oil. But once in a while this price alignment gets out of kilter, usually because there is a sudden demand for one of the products in the market. When that happens, it presents a profit advantage .

This chapter is dealing with the price relationship between soybeans and meal. When the price relationship between them gets out of line, it is not uncommon to be able to increase your profit by another 15% to 25%.

But how do you know when it is more advantageous to invest in meal ? By looking at the graph. Look at the graph now. On the left side you see the meal price and on the bottom line are the soybean prices. The heavy diagonal line represents the borderline between the profitability of meal and soybeans – the line is neutral, not favoring either the beans or the meal .

As you know, meal and oil are obtained by crushing the soybeans. The people who do the crushing charge a fee. When business is slow, the fee is small. When prices are really lively and the demand is great, the fee will be larger – that's business. Here's the point. This graph has the variable crushing fee incorporated into it. If the fee (also called the crush margin) was not taken into account, then the meal calculations would be incorrect.

WHICH IS BETTER TO TRADE – SOYBEANS or SOYBEAN MEAL?

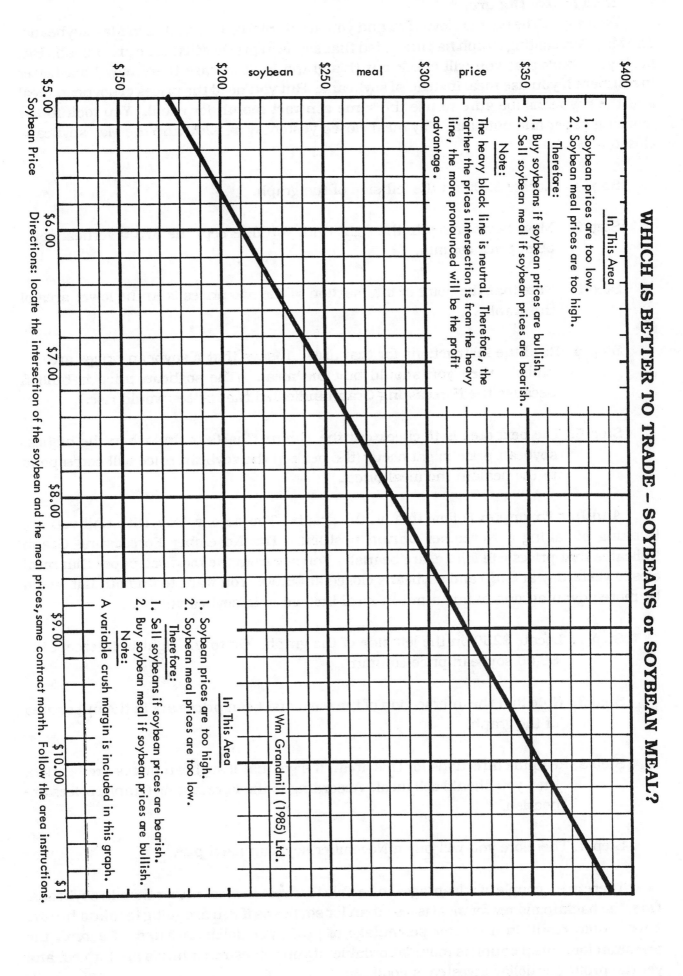

How to use the graph.

Example. The date is Nov. 15th and you are thinking of investing in May soybeans. The May Forecasting Graph has indicated that soybean prices will rise i.e are bullish. But first, you think that you will check out this graph, just in case there may be a better investment if you use meal instead of soybeans. But you need the prices of soybean meal and the soybeans (be sure to use the same contract month for each). You look in the morning paper and note that May meal closed yesterday at $200 and the May soybeans closed at $7.00 .

Step 1. Locate $200 on the left side of the graph.

Step 2. Move horizontally to the right until you intercept the $7.00 vertical soy bean price column.

Step 3. Note that the point of intersection of the two prices is in the lower area of the graph .

Step 4. Read the instructions for that area. It says that if soybean prices are bullish, then you should buy the meal. (The soybean price is bullish because the Forecasting Graph indicated that prices would rise.)

Step 5. The next step is to check out the Timing Charts to find when the highest soybean price might occur (the peak in the soybean price will correspond to the peak in the meal price).

Another Example: Follow this on the graph. The date is May 15th and you are thinking of taking a November **option** position. The November Forecasting Graph indicates that prices will fall i.e. are bearish. You see from the morning paper that meal closed yesterday at $250 and soybeans closed at $6.00. You want to find out if it would be more advantageous to buy a put in meal instead of in soybeans.

Step 1. Locate $250 on the left side of the graph. Go to the right to intercept the $6.00 soybean price column.

Step 2. Note that the intersection of the meal and bean prices are in the upper area of the graph.

Step 3. Read the directions for this area. It says that if soybean prices are bearish, then you should sell meal. According to the Forecasting Graph, prices are bearish.

Step 4. Therefore you will buy a November soybean meal **put.**

There are a couple of advantages to be able to invest in meal rather than in soybeans. **One,** the backup money for meal is less than for soybeans if you are going to take a future. This should result in a greater percentage of profit per dollar invested. **Second,** the premium for a meal option is more "affordable" if your investment funds are limited, and yet the profit per dollar invested is good .

THE JULY/NOV. SOYBEAN SPREAD

Here is one of the most popular spreads in the grain industry. Yet a trader who had taken this spread every year would likely have made money only about half the time.

It was decided to include a soybean spread in this book so the July/Nov. spread was selected. It was decided to research the spread by using the soybean price data of the past 15 years, with 3 objectives in mind: (1) what factors caused a person to lose money from the spread (2) what factors had to be present in the spread so that it became profitable (3) once the above factors had been identified, then the information had to be presented in an easy- to- use form .

After considerable research had been done, three factors stood out as being that ones which a trader should watch for.
1. **The size of the carryover %.** There was no doubt that the spread tactics from using a 10% carryover were very different from those when a 24% carryover was used.
2. **The size of the price difference** (July price minus the Nov. price) at the time that the spread was initiated. For example, if the price difference at the time the spread was taken was 80¢, then the results would be very different from a price difference of -10¢, for example.
3. **Timing.** In other words, is there a best time to take the spread? Tests were done on dates ranging from August to February. The time around Dec. 1st produced the best results i.e. fewer losses and larger profits.

Therefore, it was decided to make this an Automatic July/Nov. Spread by using the date of Dec. 1st as the time to take the spread.

A table was constructed based on taking the spread on Dec. 1st every time. Look at the spread table now. On the left side of the table you will see the price difference as of Dec. 1st (the July soybean price minus the November soybean price). Along the bottom of the table is the carryover % of the particular crop year in which Dec. 1st is situated.

Look within the table. The first thing that catches your eye is the string of "stay out" words. ' Stay out" means just that – to stay out of the spread – don't take it. This is the risky area where you are more likely to lose money than to gain it. Never take a spread here.

You also see number in the table, ranging from 1 to 5. Note that the l's are located near the "stay out" words. This is because a 1 is just slightly better than not taking a position at all – but it is risky. At the other extreme are the 5s. You will see that they are well away from the "stay out" words. A 5 represents the best opportunity to make a good profit. The 2,3,and 4 are gradations of increasingly better profit opportunities.

How to use the spread table. The date is Dec. lst. The July soybean price is $6.50 and the Nov. price is $6.00. The carryover is 16%.
Step 1. Calculate the spread difference (July – Nov.). $6.50 -$6.00=50¢

THE JULY/NOVEMBER SOYBEAN SPREAD – take on Dec 1st.

The size of the spread on Dec. 1st. (July soybean price – Nov. soybean price)

Key: "stay out" = a risky area   1 = weak potential profit   5 = excellent potential profit   TAKE THE SPREAD ON DEC. 1st

Spread \ Carryover	6%	8%	10%	12%	14%	16%	18%	20%	22%	24%	26%	28%
110¢	5	5	5	5	5	5	5	5	5	5	5	5
100	4	5	5	5	5	5	5	5	5	5	5	5
90¢	3	4	5	5	5	5	5	5	5	5	5	5
80¢	1	2	4	5	5	5	5	5	5	5	5	5
70¢	stay out	1	2	4	5	5	5	5	5	5	5	5
60¢	stay out	stay out	1	2	4	5	5	5	5	5	5	5
50¢	1	stay out	stay out	1	2	3	4	5	5	5	5	5
40¢	2	1	stay out	stay out	1	2	3	4	5	5	5	5
30¢	4	2	stay out	stay out	1	2	3	3	4	5	5	5
20¢	5	3	1	stay out	stay out	1	2	2	3	4	5	5
10¢	5	4	2	1	stay out	stay out	1	2	3	3	4	5
0¢	5	5	3	2	stay out	stay out	1	1	2	3	4	5
-10¢	5	5	5	3	1	stay out	stay out	1	1	2	3	4
-20¢	5	5	5	4	2	1	stay out	stay out	1	1	2	3
-30¢	5	5	5	5	3	2	1	stay out	stay out	stay out	1	1
-40¢	5	5	5	5	4	3	2	2	1	stay out	stay out	stay out

BUY JULY/SELL NOV. in this area

SELL JULY/BUY NOV. in this area

Wm Grandmill (1985) Ltd.

Soybean Carryover % on Dec. 1st. Take the spread on Dec. 1st. To find the spread difference: use the July price minus Nov. price When do peak profits occur? For carryover 5% to 11%, usually about April 15th. For carryovers of 12% or more, usually about May 1st.

Step 2. Turn to the spread table and locate 50¢ at the left side. Move horizontally to the right to intercept the 16% column. And you see a 4 which indicates a good profit potential.

Step 3. Note that the intersection was in the upper area which says "Sell July/Buy Nov. in this area". This is a worthwhile spread because the 4 represents a good profit. Don't miss this one! Phone your broker.

Step 4. The margin for a soybean spread is very small – likely about $300. But the spread can go against you temporarily so you should have some backup money in your account. The research showed that 9¢ ($450) would have been enough for any year of the 15 years which was researched.

What would have happened to the spread if it had been taken in each of the past 15 years? Research showed the following.

1. You would have "stayed out" of the spread in 5 of those 15 years because it was risky.
2. You would have used "Sell July/Buy Nov." in 8 of those 15 years.
3. You would have used "Buy July/Sell Nov." in 2 of those 15 years.
4. So you would have taken the spread in 10 of those 15 years.
5. **Profit?** Each of the 10 years in which the spread was taken earned a profit of 68¢ ($3400) before commissions were deducted.
6. The lower area of the table where you see "Buy July/Sell Nov." earned twice as much profit per spread as a spread in the upper area – but not many spreads occur in this area .
7. **When to get out.** Research indicated that if the carryover % was small, from 5% to 11%, then the average profit maximum occurred about April 15th. If the carryover % was 12% or large, then the average maximum profit occurred about May 1st.

Another Example. The date is Dec. 1st. The July soybean price is $8.00 and the Nov. price is $8.10 – which makes a price difference of -10¢ ($8.00 – $8.10 = -10¢). The carryover is 8%. What should you do?

Step 1. Locate -10¢ at the left side of the table and move to the right to intercept the 8% column.

Step 2. You see a 5 at the intersection which is located in the area which says "Buy July/Sell Nov.'

Step 3. This is an excellent opportunity for 2 reasons. First, it is a 5 which has the best profit. Second, the intersection is in the area which has twice the profit per spread, compared to a spread in the upper area.

U.S. SOYBEANS

	86/87	87/88	88/89	89/90*estimate	90/91	91/92	92/93	93/94	94/95
Beginning stocks (in million bushels)	536	436	302	155	—	—	—	—	—
Production	1940	1923	1539	1926	—	—	—	—	—
Total supply	2476	2359	1841	2081	—	—	—	—	—
Domestic use, crush	1283	1255	1156	1194	—	—	—	—	—
Exports	757	802	530	575	—	—	—	—	—
Total use	2040	2057	1686	1769	—	—	—	—	—
Carryover	436	302	155	312	—	—	—	—	—
Carryover % of total use	21%	15%	9%	18%	—	—	—	—	—

U.S., BRAZIL, ARGEN. combined supply

	86/87	87/88	88/89	89/90*est.	90/91	91/92	92/93	93/94	94/95
Beginning stocks (m.m.t.)	20.8	17.2	16.6	14.1	—	—	—	—	—
Production	77.5	80.5	70.9	83.4	—	—	—	—	—
Total supply	98.3	97.7	87.5	97.5	—	—	—	—	—
Domestic, crush	55.7	54.9	54.1	58.3	—	—	—	—	—
Exports	25.4	26.1	19.4	22.7	—	—	—	—	—
Total use	81.1	81.0	73.4	81.0	—	—	—	—	—
Carryover	17.2	16.6	14.1	16.5	—	—	—	—	—
Carryover % Of total use	21.2%	20.6%	19%	20%	—	—	—	—	—
Total supply / Last year's total use	135%	120%	108%	133%	—	—	—	—	—

1 metric ton = 36.74 bu.

PART IV

INVESTING IN CORN

INVESTING IN CORN

Somehow you must become as independent as possible when investing in grain. What you are really seeking is someone or something which will help you to reach the right trading decision – someone or something which can give you the information which you need in an unbiased manner – someone or something which does not pressure you to make a hasty decision. ***This book will do those things.***

What you want is a reliable method of determining the future corn price and its trend in the coming months. You know that the best price determinant for corn is corn's supply and demand . You know that when corn is scarce, prices will be high – and when corn is in a surplus situation, prices will be low. There is nothing more basic to corn prices than the supply and the demand for corn . The whole long term price structure is based on the amount of corn available for sale, and on the disposal of the corn. ***This book uses that basic premise to give you a method of estimating corn prices for months ahead.***

This book advocates using long term investing as the means to obtaining a good profit under stress free conditions. By investing for the long term, you are giving the corn fundamentals ample time to work . Most good investments require a long period of time. This book urges you to look upon an investment in grain with the same attitude which you would give to an investment in a good Blue Chip stock from the DJIA – that is, you would hold the stock for some months, you would have no fear of being put out of the market by a price reversal, and you know that a quality stock will be profitable in the long term. ***This book urges you to adopt the same outlook to an investment in corn, wheat, or soybeans.***

Grain commodities are about the only commodities whose prices react to fundamentals. Grain commodities are especially adaptable to long term trading because of their growing cycles which brings about seasonal price changes. Other commodities such as gold and foreign currencies are not seasonal and are not suitable for long term fundamental trading – technical trading is better. But because grains are seasonal and especially adaptable to long term trading, let's take advantage of that fact. ***This book will teach you a method of long term grain investment which is as safe as a Blue Chip stock and much more profitable.***

This book considers a ***stop price*** to be a very ***detrimental*** factor to the success of long term trading. You know the conventional wisdom, "When you take a grain position, place a stop price close to your entry price, and if prices go against you, you won't lose much because the stop price will be activated and you will be saved from further loss" . It gets activated alright, and it will keep being activated in future positions until all your money is gone. ***This book considers that a stop price does more harm than good in a long term position.*** A stop price is needed in a short term technical trade – but it has no place in a long term grain position which is based on grain fundamentals.

If you believe that your corn position is based on sound judgement, then you should be prepared to back up that corn position with enough money to see it through any temporary price reversal *or* you should use a corn option. This way, no stop price is needed. ***Backup capital or an option is a safer and more profitable way to invest in grain than by using a stop price.*** How much backup money is needed? How do you go about using an option? These will be explained in detail later.

HOW THE CORN SUPPLY AND DEMAND AFFECT PRICES

First we should have a definition of terms. The **corn supply** is made up by the size of the corn crop at harvest **plus** the corn carryover from the previous crop year. Add the two together and you get a number which is called the **Total Supply** of corn which is available for sale during the crop year. The **corn demand** is the amount of corn which is used domestically (in seed, feed, etc.) **plus** the amount of corn which is exported. Add the two together and you get a number which is called the **Total Use** of corn during the crop year. The **carryover** is the amount of corn which is unused or unsold at the end of the crop year.

The **carryover** is an important number because it tells you whether corn was in short supply or whether there was a surplus of corn during the crop year. A short supply or a surplus would cause corn prices to be high or low. ***This book contends that the size of the carryover can forecast what the future corn price will be in the months ahead.*** A detailed explanation later.

The Theory.

We know that when the corn supply is large, then corn prices are moderate to low. Also, when the corn supply is scarce, then corn prices will be high. That's basic. But between the two extremes of "surplus" and "scarcity" is a gradation of supply which will bring about a gradation of prices, ranging between "low" and "high". In other words, each level of the corn supply (from surplus to scarcity) will have its own price level (from low to high). All that is needed to be done, then, is to relate the size of the corn supply to its relative price. In other words, a carryover of X amount of bushels should cause a price of Y dollars. If we can do that, then we would be able to use the estimated carryover at harvest time to predict the corn price next May, for example, with reasonable accuracy. That's the theory.

But the above is easier said than done. In the first place, the size of the corn carry over can be misleading, especially to a novice trader . For example, if the corn carryover was given as 500 million bu., a novice trader would naturally consider it to be a huge amount of corn left over at the end of the crop year when in fact it is a small amount – the last time an amount this small occurred was in the crop year 75/76. Because the **number** of bushels in the carryover is misleading, a more exact method of expressing the carryover must be found. There is a more exact method. The more exact method uses %. It changes the carryover into %. This will be explained in detail later.

There Are Economic Limits To The Price Of Corn

This book contends that there are limits to the corn price. In other words there is a floor price below which corn prices will not fall, and there is presently a ceiling price above which corn prices will not penetrate.

The floor price is stable but the ceiling price will push upward gradually because of our inflation rate. For example, ten years from now the ceiling price will be higher than it is now because prices in general will be higher because of inflation.

As mentioned above, the corn carryover and the carryover % are good indicators of future corn prices. The carryover should also be an indicator of the floor and ceiling prices. Let's find out what the present floor and ceiling prices are by using the following line of reasoning. Consider this. If the corn carryover was estimated to be 0 bushels, then corn prices would soar sky high because it meant that every last kernel of corn was used and that there was none left over for emergency use or for new customers. But it will never happen ! It is impossible because the domestic and foreign buyers would stop buying corn when prices get too high. The result would be that some corn would be left unsold and the upward price trend would grind to a halt. The smallest carryover in recent history is 361 million bushels of corn, a carryover of 7%, in the crop year 74/75. The corn price rose to about $4.19, the customers stopped buying, and prices started down. That top price has never been penetrated since that time. A ceiling price was thus set at $4.19 because the customers refused to pay more. A good estimate of the ceiling price in the future would be $5 and it is unlikely that that price will be penetrated soon.

At the other extreme, let's say that the carryover was 7500 million bushels which is a full year's usage left over as surplus. That would be very bearish. Prices would fall precipitously, likely making a cycle low. But prices wouldn't likely stay there for more than three months because the farmers would refuse to sell their corn at such low prices – it would be below the cost of growing it. This is where the Government steps in with its various programs to help the farmer. The final result will be that corn will be taken off the market and likely the planted corn acreage will be cut back in the following year. The lowest price in the past 15 years was $1.44 – that's the present floor price.

You can see from the above that the floor and ceiling prices are caused by economic reasons – customers refusing to buy when prices are too high, and farmers refusing to sell when prices are too low. This book will use $1.40 per bu as the floor price for corn and it will never be penetrated. This book will use $5 as the ceiling price for the next few years. The future corn prices, then, will fluctuate between $1.40 and $5 for the forseeable future.

The Carryover As %

The carryover is a good indicator of future prices during the crop year. If an experienced trader saw that the carryover was 600 million bushels of corn, he would recognize that number as representing a fairly tight supply and he would conclude that corn prices would be above the average price in the months ahead. Therefore the carryover number is meaningful, but it can be made even better by changing the carryover to a percentage number – *by representing the carryover as a percentage of the Total Use.*

Below is the Supply and Demand table of the past few corn crop years.

Crop year	83/84	84/85	85/86	86/87	87/88	88/89	89/90*estimated
Beginning stocks	3120	723	1381	4040	4882	4260	1830
Production (mil.bu.)	4177	7678	8863	8252	7069	4921	7540
Total Supply	7297	8401	10244	12292	11951	9181	9370
Domestic use	4708	5182	5040	5906	5966	5510	5500
Exports	1866	1838	1164	1504	1725	1841	2000
Total Use	6574	7020	6204	7410	7691	7351	7500
Carryover	723	1381	4040	4882	4260	1830	1870
Carryover as % of the total use.	11%	20%	65%	66%	55%	25%	25%

Look at the corn Supply and Demand table. Note the carryover % on the bottom line. Look at the carryover % for the crop year 83/84. It is 11%. Here is how it was calculated: carryover ÷ total use x 100 = %: 723 ÷ 6574 x 100 = 11%. That small carryover % represents a tight corn supply. The highest December corn price that year was about $3.75 and it occurred about Sept. 1st. Look at the large carryover for the crop year 86/87 – it represents bearish prices ahead. December corn prices fell to $1.62 on October 16th that year. You can see now how you can use the size of the carryover in % to give you a preview of the price trend in the months ahead.

This book uses the carryover % as a price indicator. Thus, a 10% carryover indicates that the corn supply is tight and that corn prices will be high as a consequence and will likely come close to $4 per bushel. At the other extreme, a 60% carryover indicates that the corn supply for the crop year will be very large and that corn prices will fluctuate in the low price range. A 60% carryover would likely bring prices down to about $1.90.

Using the estimates above (a 10% carryover with a $4 price and a 60% carryover with a $1.90 price) and continuing with the same line of thought, then a gradation *of carryover percentages ranging between 10% and 60% should cause a gradation of corn prices ranging between $4 and $1.90.*

The premise here and in this book, is that if we know the size of the carryover %, then we can get a good estimate of the price of corn in the months ahead. This is the basis of the Forecasting Graphs which will be described in detail below.

THE FORECASTING GRAPHS

How They Were Made

The past 15 years of Supply and Demand numbers were used. The carryover % was correlated to the corn prices of each of the contract months for each of the 15 years, as well as the highest and the lowest prices in each of the contract months and years. The results were plotted on a graph and a price line was drawn. This price line represents the **average** corn price which was attained for each carryover %, according to the way it actually happened in the past 15 years. Each contract month was done separately. Therefore there is one Forecasting Graph for each of the contract months.

How accurate are the graphs? They are as accurate as an average can be. That means that because the average is derived from a composite of closely related numbers, it cannot be 100% accurate – it will be very close. Therefore, when you use the December Forecasting Graph, for example, you will get a good estimate of what the price of December corn will be on December 1st.

How To Use The Forecasting Graphs

The best time to use the graph is just after a USDA crop report has been issued.

It is important to have the latest information. It is easy to use the Forecasting Graphs. All that one has to do is to locate the carryover % of the pertinent crop year at the left side of the Forecasting Graph, move to the right to touch the price line, then straight down to the bottom line to get the estimated corn price.

Example. The date is July 15th, just after the July crop report. You are interested in taking a December corn position if the profit is worthwhile. The present price of December corn is $2.80. From the crop report data you calculate that the carryover % for the upcoming crop year (which begins on October 1st) will be 40%.

Method: (follow this on the December Forecasting Graph) Locate 40% at the left side of the graph. Move to the right to touch the price line. Go straight down to the bottom of the graph to read about $2.30 as the estimated price of Dec. corn on December 1st.

Analysis: The present price of Dec. corn is $2.80 and it is estimated to fall to $2.30 by December 1st. Therefore a price decline of 50¢ is expected. That means that you should **sell December corn** if you intend to use a future, or that you should **buy a December put** if you intend to use an option.

ESTIMATED SEPTEMBER CORN PRICE ON SEPT. 1st

Instructions: using the % carryover for the pertinent crop year, go horizontally to touch the price line, then go vertically to the price line at the bottom to get the estimated future price.

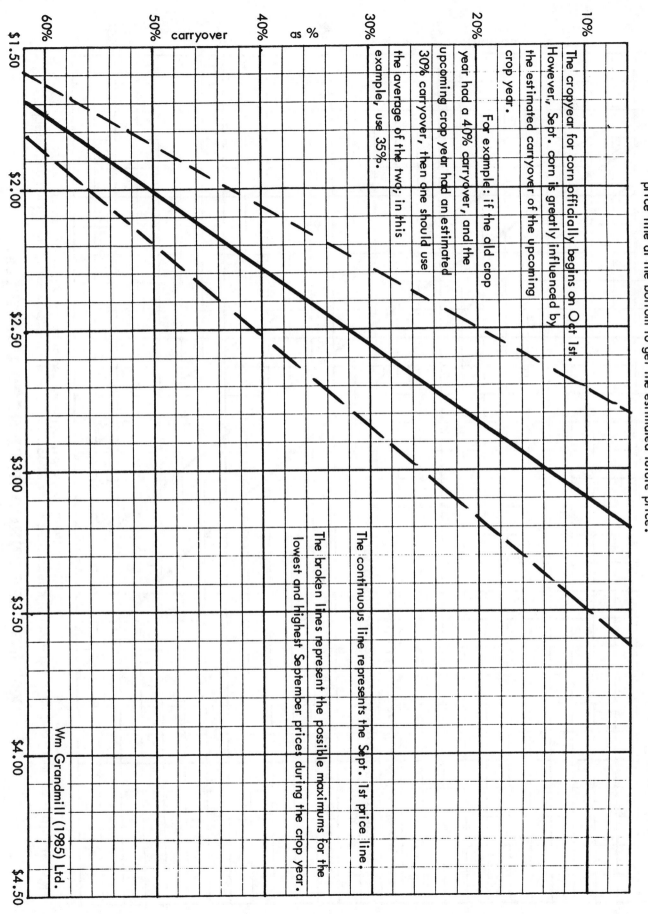

The cropyear for corn officially begins on Oct 1st. However, Sept. corn is greatly influenced by the estimated carryover of the upcoming crop year.

For example: if the old crop year had a 40% carryover, and the upcoming crop year had an estimated 30% carryover, then one should use the average of the two; in this example, use 35%.

The broken lines represent the possible maximums for the lowest and Highest September prices during the crop year.

The continuous line represents the Sept. 1st price line.

Wm Grandmill (1985) Ltd.

10%

20%

30%

40% carryover

as %

50%

60%

$1.50

$2.00

$2.50

$3.00

$3.50

$4.00

$4.50

166

ESTIMATED DECEMBER CORN PRICE ON DEC. 1st

Instructions: using the % carryover for the pertinent crop year, go horizontally to touch the price line, then go vertically to the price line at the bottom to get the estimated future price.

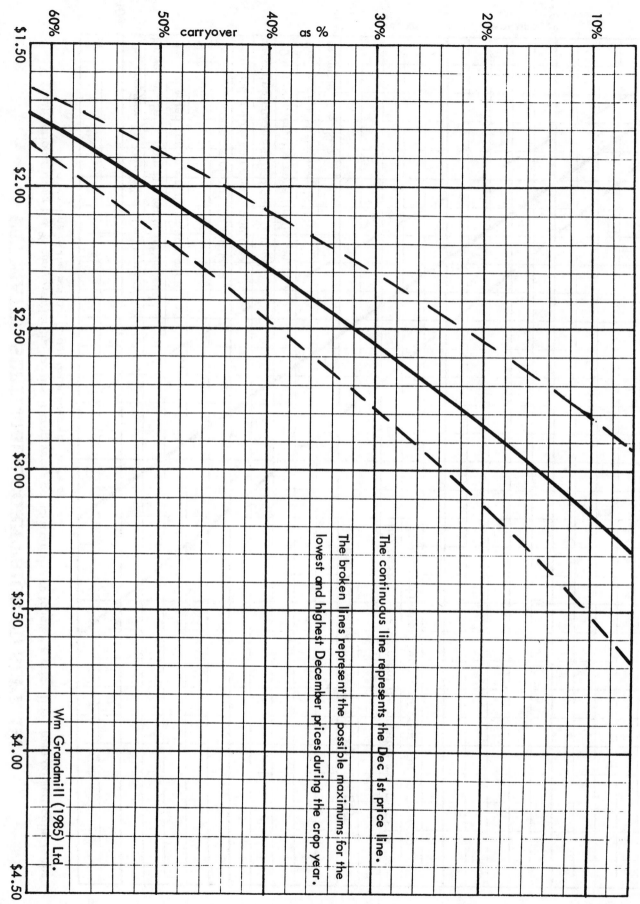

The continuous line represents the Dec 1st price line.

The broken lines represent the possible maximums for the lowest and highest December prices during the crop year.

Wm Grandmill (1985) Ltd.

167

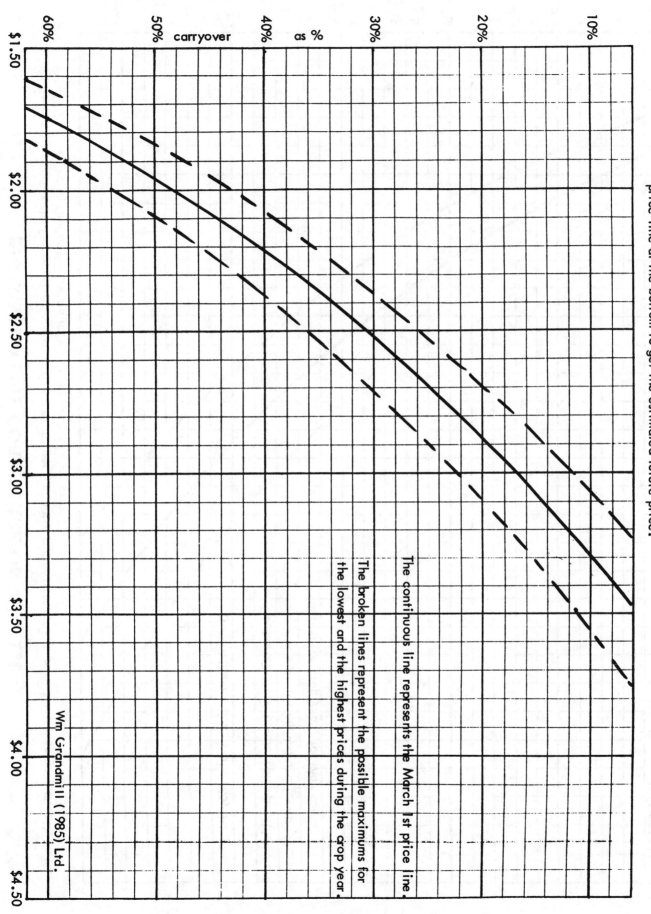

ESTIMATED MARCH CORN PRICE ON MARCH 1st

Instructions: using the % carryover for the pertinent crop year, go horizontally to touch the price line, then go vertically to the price line at the bottom to get the estimated future price.

The continuous line represents the March 1st price line.

The broken lines represent the possible maximums for the lowest and the highest prices during the crop year.

carryover as %

Wm Grandmill (1985) Ltd.

168

ESTIMATED MAY CORN PRICE ON MAY 1st

Instructions: using the % carryover for the pertinent crop year, go horizontally to touch the price line, then go vertically to the price line at the bottom to get the estimated future price.

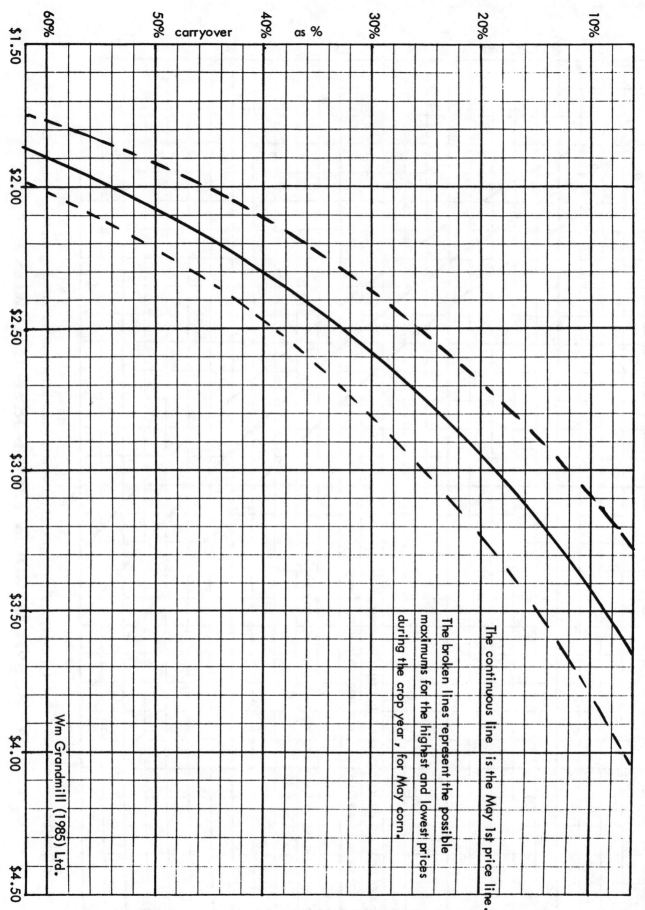

The continuous line is the May 1st price line.

The broken lines represent the possible maximums for the highest and lowest prices during the crop year, for May corn.

Wm Grandmill (1985) Ltd.

169

ESTIMATED JULY CORN PRICE ON JULY 1st

Instructions: using the % carryover for the pertinent crop year, go horizontally to touch the price line, then go vertically to the price line at the bottom to get the estimated future price.

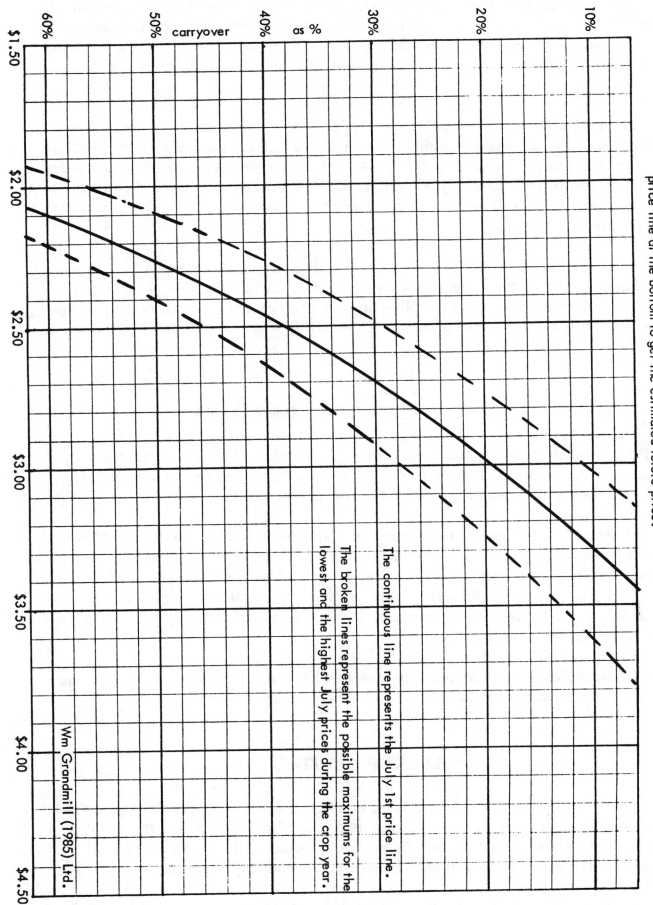

The continuous line represents the July 1st price line.

The broken lines represent the possible maximums for the lowest and the highest July prices during the crop year.

Wm Grandmill (1985) Ltd.

170

It is possible that the corn price might decline much faster than expected. It might reach the $2.30 price in September or October, for example. If it happens, take it! Take your profit and get out of your position early if you can. There is a monetary advantage to attaining your profit objective early – it frees your capital for another position.

A good rule to follow: Don't take a corn position unless the Forecasting Graphs indicate that you can make a profit of more than 12¢. Here's an example of what can happen sometimes – the present price of March corn is $3.00, the March Forecasting Graph indicates that the corn price will be $3.10 on March 1st. Should you take it? No, it is too close to call and too risky. The profit is not worthwhile. Try a wheat or soybean position instead.

This 12¢ rule was arrived at by research. The rule acts as a filter which filters out potentially losing trades. Past research has shown that about 20% of all corn positions will be affected by the 12¢ rule – and further research showed that if one had taken those "too close to call" positions, he would have lost money 2/3 of the time. It is a safety measure.

WHERE TO GET THE CORN DATA

USDA's monthly crop report – Get it from your broker. It is issued monthly, on a Friday usually, about the 11th or 12th of the month. It comes over the wire and will be in your broker's office within an hour after the market closes.

World Agriculture Supply and Demand Estimates – This monthly publication contains world and U.S. data on corn, wheat, and soybeans. It has the acreage, production, total use, carryover of all the grains. It's an excellent publication. The cost is $18 per year. To subscribe, write to: World Agriculture Supply and Demand Estimates, Superintendent of Documents, U.S. Government Printing Office, Washington, D C. 20402 – 9372

Electronic Access – The booklet above and other USDA reports can be accessed electronically on the day of release. For details phone (202) 447–5505.

BACKUP CAPITAL

One of the ways in which this book is different from other commodity books is this: this book suggests that you *do not use a stop price* with a corn, wheat or a soybean investment. Instead you should backup your grain position with sufficient capital so that you can ride out any trend reversal which goes against you.

How much capital is "sufficient capital"? You will be shown that in a moment. But first it is important that you understand fully what this book is about. This book is a radical departure from "commodity trading" books. This is an "investment" book. This is a book about "investing" in grain.

The definition of an investment is this: you pay a substantial amount of money for the investment, you wait a long time for your investment to mature, your profit is good but not spectacular, a 25% per year profit is a good investment.

A good Blue Chip stock is considered to be a good investment, one of the best in the country. You will pay about $4000 or more for 100 shares. You will wait for the shares to increase in value. You would be happy if the shares increased in value by 25% year after year. Your Blue Chip investment would be relatively safe – by that is meant that if there was another stock market crash like there was in October 1987, you would suffer a temporary decline in value but you would still be in the market, and it is likely that you will regain the loss, and more .

Here's the point. Use the same scenario as was used in the paragraph above. But substitute the words "Corn Investment" for the words "good Blue Chip stock". Now you can see what the idea is here. ***The corn is the investment.*** But there is a big difference now. Instead of earning 25% as you would have done in stocks, the corn investment will earn between about 80% to 120% per year. And it will be just as safe as a good stock, because in a worse case scenario like the crash of '87, you would have sufficient backup money to absorb a big price reversal, and to recover – corn prices always recover in time, always.

Many times you have seen corn prices fall below $2 only to recover to about $3.75 two or three years later – that's a move in value of about $7500, which would be at least a 100% profit on your corn investment per annum. Corn prices will always trend up and down. The best corn investment is made at just the right time to catch the trend. This book will teach you how to do just that .

The paragraph above shows you the difference between "trading in corn" and "investing in corn". They use completely different approaches. This book is about ***investing in corn*** and each investment is backed up with sufficient capital, just as in stocks. You don't have to buy the corn outright as you do in stocks – just sufficient capital to be sure that you are not put out of the market by a trend reversal.

The following graph will show you how much backup is needed in each situation. When we say that we earn 100% per year on our corn investment, we are talking about the amount of money used to back up the corn position. ***The backup money is the investment.***

Look at the backup graph. There are two heavy dark lines. The one at the left represents the lowest prices ever reached by corn in the past 15 years. The line on the right represents the highest prices ever reached by corn in the past 15 years.

An example is the best way to explain the graph.

Data .   Suppose that you were thinking of ***buying*** December corn. Let's say that the present price of Dec. corn on June 15th is $2.20. Let's also say that the carryover for the crop year in which Dec. is situated is 30%.

Method.   Locate 30% at the left side of the graph and move to the right. Locate $2.20 at the bottom of the graph and go directly up to intercept the 30% line.

AMOUNT OF BACKUP MONEY needed to trade corn safely

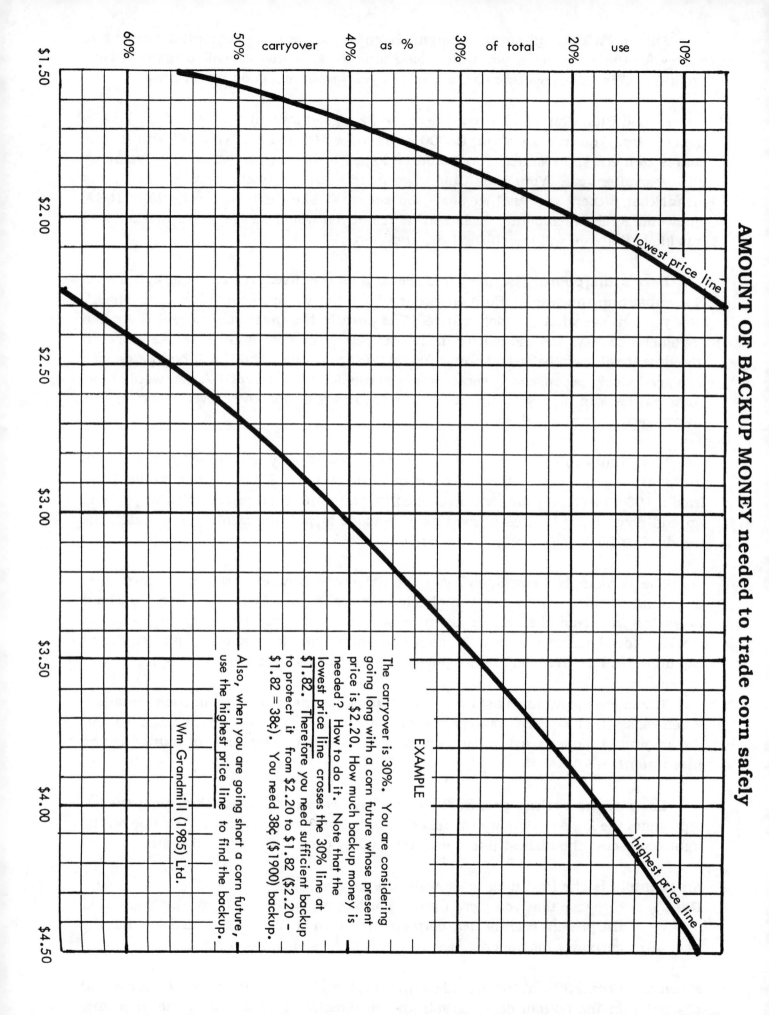

EXAMPLE

The carryover is 30%. You are considering going long with a corn future whose present price is $2.20. How much backup money is needed? How to do it. Note that the lowest price line crosses the 30% line at $1.82. Therefore you need sufficient backup to protect it from $2.20 to $1.82 ($2.20 - $1.82 = 38¢). You need 38¢ ($1900) backup.

Also, when you are going short a corn future, use the highest price line to find the backup.

Wm Grandmill (1985) Ltd.

173

Look at the heavy lowest price line and note that it crosses the 30% line at about $1.82. That point, $1.82, is the lowest ever price to which a 30% carryover should decline. That means that we should protect the long Dec. position all the way from its present price of $2.20 to the lowest ever price of $1.82. That means that 38¢ ($1900) is needed as backup money to protect the long Dec. future ($2 .20 – $1.82 = 38¢) .

Analysis. When you take the Dec. corn position with your broker, you will deposit into your account a margin of about $700 plus the backup money of $1900 for this example. Now you can relax and wait for the higher prices as forecast by the Dec. Forecasting Graph. The data of the past 15 years has shown that the corn price will never fall below $1.82 when the carryover is 30%. No stop price is needed.

Some people might say,"Wait a minute ! If the corn price has fallen to $1.82 once in the past 15 years, then it could possibly do it again! What about that? Isn't there a chance that I could be put out of the market before the prices rallied?" Not a chance ! For two good reasons. First, you have a margin of $700 which provides an additional protection of 14¢ which now takes the backup all the way down to $1.68. Second, our annual inflation rate gradually raises the corn price range upward, and that includes raising the bottom limit. There is now way that a 30% carryover will ever see a corn price fall to $1.82 again.

Another example. This time we will use the highest price line. The time is March and you are thinking of selling July corn because the July Forecasting Graph indicated that the price would be about an estimated $3 on July 1st. The present price of July corn is now $3.50 and the carryover is 20%. How much backup is needed to invest safely?

Method. Locate the junction of the 20% line and the $3.50 column. Note that the highest price line crosses the 20% line at about $3.87. Therefore 37¢ is needed as the backup ($3.87 – $3.50 = 37¢) .

How The Lowest and The Highest Price Lines Were Made.

(a) *The lowest price line.* All the lowest corn prices for every crop year, for every contract month, for every trading day back to 1973/74, were investigated. The object of the search was to find the lowest of all the low prices – that means not the lowest closing price but it means the lowest price during each day's trading. These lowest of all the low prices were correlated to the carry-over % and thus the lowest price line was made .

(b) *The highest price line.* A similar search was made for the highest of all the high prices. These were correlated to the carryover % to form the highest price line.

Note: You will see low and high price lines on each Forecasting Graph. Don't confuse those lines on the Forecasting Graph with the lowest and highest lines on the backup graph. They are very different. The lowest and highest lines on the Forecasting Graph represent the likely lowest and highest price during the crop year. Whereas the lowest and highest lines on the Backup Graph represent the lowest of the low prices and the highest of the high prices of the past 15 years .

CORN OPTIONS

Options can be used instead of backup money to finance your corn investment. In some cases, options are a preferable method of financing a corn position. Corn options are cheap compared to wheat and soybean options. An average 6 month corn option costs between about 10¢ and 15¢, whereas an average 6 month soybean option costs between about 20¢ and 40¢.

This book uses only the simplest type of option – a call and a put. Here is the procedure for using an option: (1) use the Forecasting Graph to find out whether the corn price is expected to rise or to fall (2) **buy a call** if you expect the price to rise (3) **buy a put** if you expect the price to fall.

That's all there is to it. As with futures, if prices should move rapidly and meet your price objective early, then take your profit by instructing your broker to take you out of the option position.

Even if you have never used options before, don't hesitate to do so now. They are cheap and convenient. **But there is a safety rule.** It is this: do not take an option position unless it is possible to make 100% profit or more.

Why this rule? Because, with the price of the option being so small, a shift in the price trend line could erase your profit edge quickly – but by aiming for at least a 100% profit, you can absorb a price trend change more easily.

To help you find the estimated profit, **use the handy Corn Option Graph.** Look at the Corn Option Graph. Note that the price of the option (the premium) is at the left side of the graph. The slanting lines give the various percentages of **net** profit (the commission costs and poor fills are taken into account).

Example.   Follow this example on the graph.

Data.   The date is June 15th, just after the June crop report. You wish to take a Dec. corn by using an option. You look in the morning paper and see that the present price of the corn is $3. You calculate the carryover from the crop report and you get a carryover of 32%. You consult the Dec. Forecasting Graph and you get the estimated Dec. corn price to be $2.50. So you are expecting a price decline of 50¢. That means that you should buy a Dec. put if you can earn at least 100% from it. The premium for a Dec. $3.00 put is 12¢, according to the quotes in the newspaper.

Method.   1. You are expecting a price decline of about 50¢, according to the Forecasting Graph.
2. Locate 50¢ at the bottom of the graph.
3. Move straight up to meet the 12¢ line, the option's premium.
4. Read the net profit % from the slanting lines, and you get about 300%.
5. If this was a real trade instead of an example, you should take it! It offers an excellent profit, considering it is only a 6 month investment.

CORN OPTION GRAPH

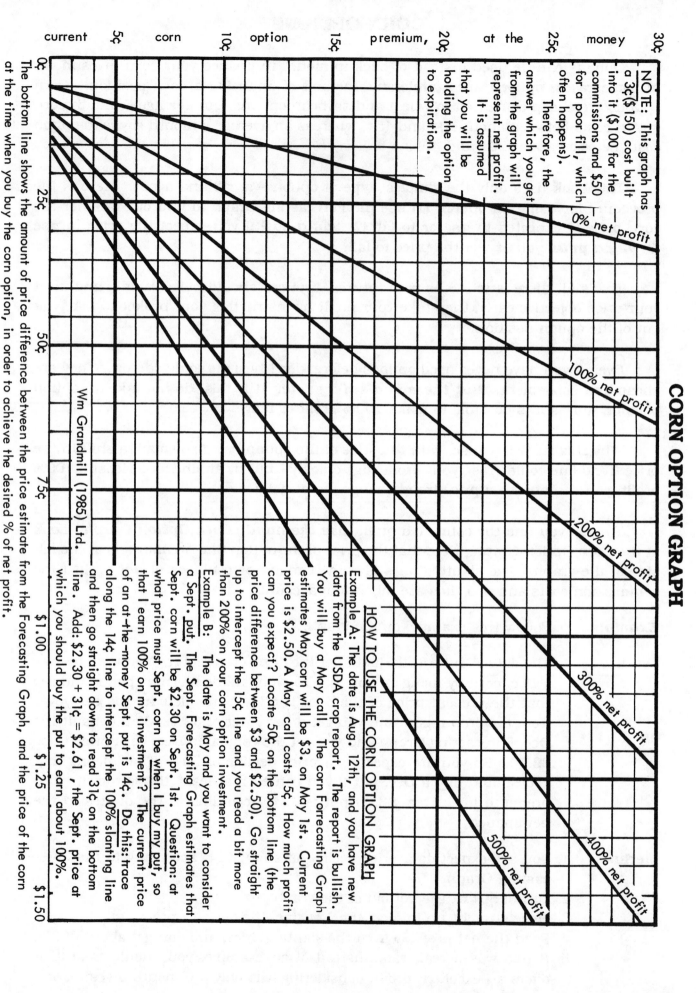

NOTE: This graph has a 3¢($150) cost built into it ($100 for the commissions and $50 for a poor fill, which often happens).

There, the answer which you get from the graph will represent net profit.

It is assumed that you will be holding the option to expiration.

Wm Grandmill (1985) Ltd.

(Left axis, top to bottom): current, 5¢, corn, 10¢, option, 15¢, premium, 20¢, at the, 25¢, money, 30¢

(Bottom axis): 0¢, 25¢, 50¢, 75¢, $1.00, $1.25, $1.50

(Slanting lines): 0% net profit, 100% net profit, 200% net profit, 300% net profit, 400% net profit, 500% net profit

HOW TO USE THE CORN OPTION GRAPH

Example A: The date is Aug. 12th, and you have new data from the USDA crop report. The report is bullish. You will buy a May call. The corn Forecasting Graph estimates May corn will be $3, on May 1st. Current price is $2.50. A May call costs 15¢. How much profit can you expect? Locate 50¢ on the bottom line (the price difference between $3 and $2.50). Go straight up to intercept the 15¢ line and you read a bit more than 200% on your corn option investment.

Example B: The date is May and you want to consider a Sept. put. The Sept. Forecasting Graph estimates that Sept. corn will be $2.30 on Sept. 1st. Question: at what price must Sept. corn be when I buy my put, so that I earn 100% on my investment? The current price of an at-the-money Sept. put is 14¢. Do this: trace along the 14¢ line to intercept the 100% slanting line and then go straight down to read 31¢ on the bottom line. Add: $2.30 + 31¢ = $2.61, the Sept. price at which you should buy the put to earn about 100%.

The bottom line shows the amount of price difference between the price estimate from the Forecasting Graph, and the price of the corn at the time when you buy the corn option, in order to achieve the desired % of net profit.

YEAR ROUND AUTOMATIC CORN INVESTMENT PLAN

Some people like to have help when making a decision. It can be stressful. Deciding **when** to take a future's position is one of those times. The questions going through a trader's mind are,"Should I buy the December corn now or should I wait for a better price? And when I liquidate the Dec. position, should I do it in October or November?" Decision time is often a time of stress for many people.

This chapter is for those investors who would like some help in making those crucial decisions of when to take a position and when to get out of it.This chapter is titled an **Automatic** investment plan because you would take only 2 corn positions per year, automatically on certain dates and exit from those positions automatically on certain dates. You can use either a future or an option – it's for you to decide. You will get details of each method later which will help you to decide which method of investment to use.

The automatic corn investment plan is initiated on June 15th. That's just after the June crop report from which you will calculate the latest carryover %. You will take a Dec. corn position on that date, if the profit is worthwhile. You will use the carryover % on the Dec. Forecasting Graph to find out whether you should buy Dec. corn or sell Dec. corn or whether to stay out of the market because the profit potential is too small. You will liquidate **the Dec. corn position on Oct. 15th.** This ends the first half of the Automatic Investment Plan .

The second half of the Year Round Automatic Corn Investment Plan is initiated on Nov. 15th. You will take a July corn position on that date. You will use the data from the November crop report to calculate the carryover %, and you will use that percentage on the July Forecasting Graph, to find out whether you should buy or sell July corn. **You will hold this position until July 1st** if you are using futures or until the last trading day in June if you are using options.

The dates of entry and exit for the corn positions were chosen only after testing and research. Many dates for initiating the two halves of the automatic plan were tested. The dates of June 15th and Nov. 15th were found to be the best ones – they produced more profit and required less backup money.

As for the dates for the liquidation of the corn positions, the dates of October 15th and July 1st were selected from the many dates tested as being the best ones. The object of the research here was to find the most **consistently** profitable dates which could be used year after year by those people who prefer a routine method of trading. It is time to examine each half of the investment plan in more detail.

THE FIRST HALF OF THE
AUTOMATIC CORN INVESTMENT PLAN

Buying or selling Dec. corn on June 15th and liquidating the position on Oct. 15th.

Example.   The date is June 14th and the USDA has just released the June crop report. From the information you calculate that the carryover will be 32% for the upcoming crop year which will begin on Oct. 1st. The present price of Dec. corn on June 15th is $2.90.

1. Use the 32% carryover on the December Forecasting Graph and you get $2.50 as the estimated price of Dec. corn on December 1st.

2. Because you are expecting a 40¢ price decline in Dec. corn, you will sell a Dec. future ***or*** you will buy a Dec. put after you have checked out whether you can earn at least 100% profit on the option graph.

3. You will exit from the position on October 15th – ***unless you have a good reason*** for not doing so. One plausible reason for staying with the position for a while longer would be if the crop report on October 12th showed new information such as a smaller than expected carryover if you were long the Dec. position, or a larger than expected carryover if you are short the Dec. position – then you should hold it until near December 1st because more profits are likely.

4. That's all there is to it.

What would have happened in the past 15 years if an investor had taken the Dec. corn position on June 15th and had exited on October 15th?

1. He would have ***bought*** Dec. corn (or bought a Dec. call if using an option) in 7 of those 15 years.

2. He would have ***sold*** Dec. corn (or bought a Dec. put if using an option) in 8 of those 15 years.

3. There was ***no year*** in which he was out of the market. (Remember the rule which says that there should be at least a potential 12¢ profit before you take the position.)

4. The average profit per position from ***using a Dec. future*** was 35¢ before commissions. ***The largest amount of backup money needed*** at any time in all of the 15 years was $2500.

5. The average profit per position ***from using an option*** was 45¢ before commissions . That excellent profit was only for the years in which one was in the market because one would have been out of the market for 8

of those 15 years because of the rule that one should earn at least 100% on an option, or stay out. By the way, a check was made on those 8 years in which one would not have taken an option position. **Results:** If an option position had been taken when the Option Graph indicated a less than 100% profit, the average of those 8 years showed a profit of only 3¢ – hardly more than enough to pay the commissions and definitely not worth the risk. Therefore, the 100% rule acts as a filter which filters out the uncertain corn option trades. If you can't take a corn option, check out the possibilities in a wheat or a soybean option.

When do the low and high Dec. corn prices occur during the first half of the Automatic Corn Investment Plan?

This is an **automatic** corn investment plan and you are advised to exit from the position on October 15th. But you have also been told to take your profits early if your price objective has been reached early. **But the question is,** When do the lowest and the highest December prices occur? When might it be possible to take one's profits early?" To help you to be prepared to act when the lowest or highest Dec. price might occur, a graph has been made showing when the lowest and highest Dec. corn prices actually occurred in the past 15 years.

Look at the graph now. Note the two streams – one for the lowest prices and one for the highest prices. About 90% of all the lowest prices in the past 15 years occurred between the two lines marked " lowest prices". Likewise, about 90% of all highest prices of the past 15 years fell between the two "highest price" lines. That's the way it happened in the past 15 years.

This graph will be a big help in timing the lows and highs of the Dec. corn contract. You should be able to estimate the time of most highs and lows to within 3 weeks or less. That's an advantage. Be prepared to get out of a Dec. position or to get into one when the time is right.

THE SECOND HALF OF THE
AUTOMATIC CORN INVESTMENT PLAN

Buying or selling July corn on November 15th and liquidating the position on July 1st.

You will be taking this July position right after the November crop report, about November 12th. This November crop report is an excellent one because it has a handle on the estimated crop production and carryover for both corn and soybeans. The carryover % which you get from this report will be very close to the final one, about a year away. Why is it the best report so far? The harvest is in full swing, weather scares are a thing of the past, the condition of the corn and soybean crops is known. The carryover % from this report sets the price pattern for the next 5 months.

WHEN DO THE LOWS AND HIGHS OCCUR for December corn?

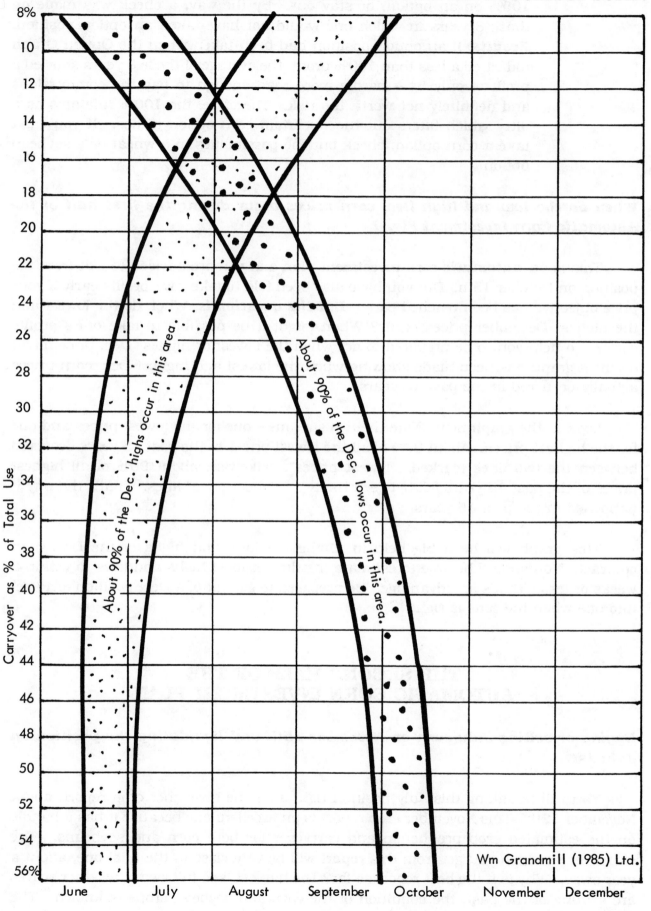

About 90% of the Dec. highs occur in this area.

About 90% of the Dec. lows occur in this area.

Carryover as % of Total Use

Wm Grandmill (1985) Ltd.

July 1st is the normal date to liquidate this position, but it could be sooner. Why? Because, if there is to be a drought or a dry spell in the summer, the first signs usually appear in June, or even in May if there was little or no snow or rain in the winter. Therefore, if you were **short** July corn and if there were signs of dryness or drought in May or June, then you had better get out of the short July corn position quickly because prices will rise. On the other hand, if you were **long** July corn and if there were signs of dryness, then you should stay in to July 1st because rising prices from a drought would work in your favor.

Therefore, because of the possibility of fluctuating corn prices in late May or June, *you should reanalyze the July contract by using the information in the May crop report.* Reanalyze the July corn by using the new carryover % for the upcoming crop year. It is realized that July is not in the new crop year which begins on October 1st. But, nevertheless, July prices will be affected to some degree if there is a significant change in the carryover %.

For example, suppose that you went short a July corn on November 15th when the carryover was 30%. Then on May 15th you calculated that the new carryover for the upcoming crop year would be 20% – that's bullish news, and July corn will respond partially by rising a bit in price rather than declining as you had expected on November 15th. Consequently you should liquidate the July short corn position on May 15th, as soon as you would have discovered the change in carryover %. A small change in the carryover %, such as 3% or 4% will have almost no effect on the July price if the carryover is large, like 30% or more. Make it a rule to always recheck the July price trend by calculating the new carryover % from the May crop report estimates by USDA.

An example of taking a July corn position on November 15th.

1. The date is November 13th and the USDA has just issued its latest crop report right after the commodity market closed for the day. You calculate that the carryover for corn is 30%. You are considering a July position. The present price of July corn is $2.20.

2. You consult the July Forecasting Graph and it estimates that the July corn price will be $2.70 on July 1st (follow this on the graph). Therefore you are expecting a price *rise* of 50¢ ($2.70 – $2.20 = 50¢).

3. You will buy July corn if you are using a future, and you will deposit sufficient backup money into your account.

4. If you intend to use an option, you will buy a July call after you have checked to see if it will earn at least 100 % profit. You may not be able to buy the July call until about November 21st because the July option may not appear on the board until then.

5. Right after the May crop report, calculate the carryover for the new upcoming crop year, and decide whether you should hold the July position or whether you should get out of it.

Using the corn data of the past 15 years, what would have happened if July position had been taken on November 15th every year.

1. You would **not** have taken a corn position in 2 of the 15 years because the potential profit was not larger than 12¢.

2. You would have **bought** July corn in 6 of those 15 years.

3. You would have **sold** July corn in 7 of those 15 years.

4. You would have **lost** money in 3 of those 13 years when you were in the market. The losses were –65¢, –32¢, –9¢.

5. The **average profit** for each of the 13 years when you were in the market was 23¢, before commissions.

6. The largest amount of backup capital needed at any time in those 13 years was 70¢.

What would have happened if a July option had been used in the past 15 years, taking the Option Position on November 15th.

1. The average premium used in this test was 16¢ and it was held until the last option trading day about June 20th.

2. You would **not** have taken an option position in 6 of those 15 years because the potential profit rate was less than 100%.

3. There were two years in which losses occurred. The losses were –16¢ (the cost of the option) and –6¢ (a partial loss).

4. The **average profit** for each of the 9 years in which an option position was taken was 25¢. That's a gross profit of 156% on your investment, in 6 months (25¢ ÷ the option premium of 16¢ x 100= 156%). That's a good profit.

5. It appears that it is much better to use an option rather than use a future, in the second half of the Year Round Investment Plan.

6. There is no timing chart for the 2nd half of the Investment Plan. The highs and the lows for July corn seemed to occur in every month – there was no pattern.

SUMMARY OF THE YEAR ROUND
AUTOMATIC CORN INVESTMENT PLAN

1. One can use either a Dec. future or a Dec. option position in the first half of the Automatic Corn Investment Plan. Use the Dec. Forecasting Graph for both the future and the option. Use the indicated amount of backup money if you are using a future. You do not need backup money when using an option.

2. Make use of the Timing Graph which gives an estimated time of when the Dec. low and high prices occur.

3. Use the two safety rules: (a) take the future's position only if there is a potential profit of more than 12¢, as indicated by the Forecasting Graphs (b) take an option position only if the Option Graph indicates that you can earn a 10% profit or more.

4. When investing in the second half of the year round plan, use only an option position because the future position requires too much backup and because the rate of profit return from using an option is much better than from using a future.

5. When the safety rules (the 12¢ rule and the option 100% rule) indicate that you should stay out of the market, check out the opportunities in wheat, soybeans, and soybean meal. Usually one of them offers a better rate of profit than the others.

GET A HEADSTART ON THE CORN MARKET

There is a monetary advantage in being among the first ones to know what is likely to happen to corn prices a few months down the road. The large grain companies and the large-scale professional grain traders know this and that is why their staffs and computers are trying to estimate the size of the new corn crop which will be harvested in the fall. They try to get a handle on the new crop in the spring, even before the corn is planted.

Some of the grain companies will have a private survey done to try to find out how many corn acres are likely to be planted in the spring, trying to beat the publication of the planting intentions done by the USDA so that they will have a headstart on the public.

But any survey that some companies may do pales by comparison to the extensive survey done by the USDA. Thousand of farmers are queried about their **planting intentions.** This information on the estimated number of acres which are to be planted in the spring, is released to the public likely in the April crop report. It is released usually on a Friday after the market has closed, likely about April 12th. The USDA is careful that everyone, you and the grain companies, get this vital information at the same time.

Once the report is released, the professional trader begins immediately to estimate the size of the upcoming corn crop. He will have an idea of the amount of soil moisture in the corn growing areas because he will likely have employed a private weather forecaster who will have a record of the rainfall and snow coverage during the winter. The private weather forecaster will also attempt to forecast the likely weather for the summer. From this information the professional trader will estimate the corn yield, and then estimate the size of the corn crop in the fall.

Now you can see what you are up against as you compete in the corn market. *The successful professional traders do their homework.*

But you **can** complete successfully. The contents of this chapter will put you in the forefront of forecasters. You can compete successfully by (l) using the new graphs in this chapter which have been constructed especially for this book (2) by investing for the long term (3) by using sufficient backup money with a future's position, or use an option.

THE CORN PRODUCTION GRAPH

Look at the Corn Production Graph. At the left side are the estimated **planted acres** (also called the **planting intentions**) . These first estimates are usually given in the April crop report, about April 12th. Remember, the real amount of planted acres won't be known until the following winter, after the crop is harvested, so everyone (you and the grain companies) has only the estimates to work with,so we must use those **estimated planted acres** as best we can.

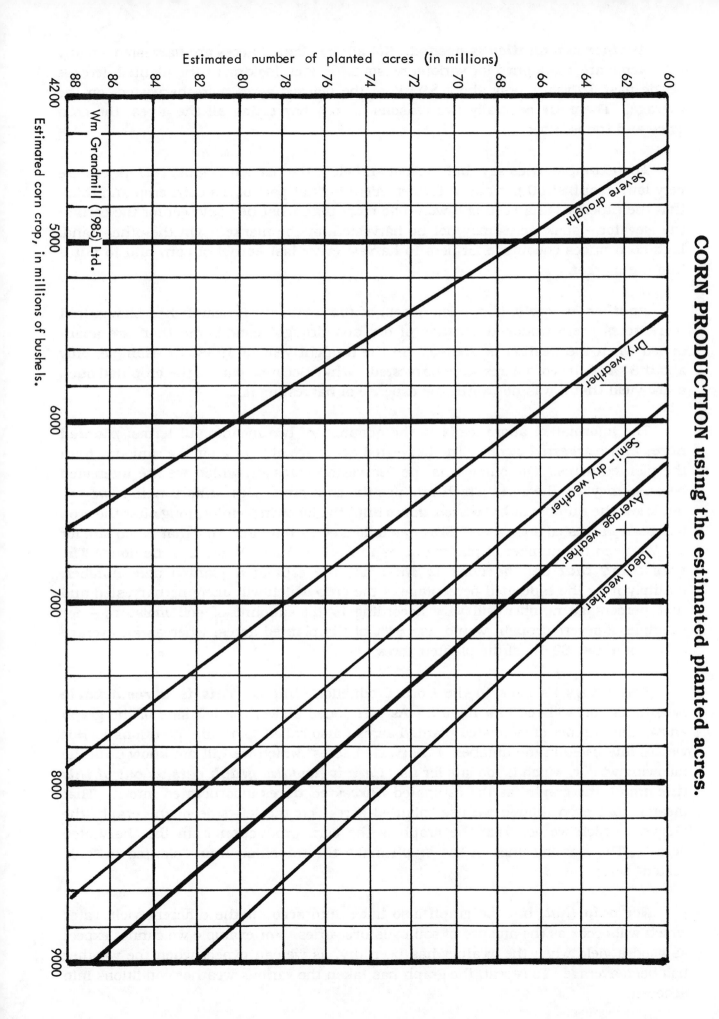

CORN PRODUCTION using the estimated planted acres.

Estimated number of planted acres (in millions)

Estimated corn crop, in millions of bushels.

Wm Grandmill (1985) Ltd.

Severe drought

Dry weather

Semi-dry weather

Average weather

Ideal weather

Another explanation is needed. Not all the planted acres are harvested – many corn acres are abandoned for various reasons. In fact, looking at the planted acreage of the past 15 years, only about 89.5% of the planted acres were harvested, on the average. There are generally two reasons for not harvesting all the acres: the corn price and the weather.

For example, Let's say that in August, before the harvest begins, corn prices are very low, about $1.80 per bu. · A farmer might look at part of his corn crop and think that the expense of harvesting it would be more than what he could get for the corn at the elevator – some acres may not be harvested for the market. On the other hand, high corn prices encourage farmers to harvest every last kernel of corn and to put it into the market.

Another example, about the effects of the weather. Research has shown that more acres are abandoned because of dry and drought conditions, than are abandoned when the weather is average. In the drought year of 1988, for example, only about 84% of the corn acres were harvested. Why? Because part of the crop had such a low yield that it was not worth the expense of harvesting it.

The information above leads to the adoption of two meaningful terms: ***planted acres*** and ***harvested acres.*** The harvested acres are always a smaller amount than the planted acres. Of course it is the "harvested acres" in which we are interested because they are the acres which produce the corn crop. But, unfortunately, we will not know the number of ***harvested acres*** until the following winter, long after the crop has been harvested and when USDA has tallied everything up. But that is too late for us! We need the number of planted acres in April or May. What is to be done? ***The only thing that can be done is this:*** use the estimated planted acre number, multiply it by the estimated percentage of the crop which will likely be harvested and that percentage number will vary according to the amount of soil moisture – for example, a severe drought would use 84% of the planted acres, whereas an average crop would use 89.5% of the planted acres.

This brings us back to the Corn Production Graph. ***This is a remarkable graph,*** as you will see in a minute. As mentioned above, the left side of the graph shows the number of estimated planted acres (also called "planting intentions"). But we are interested in the number of "harvested acres" which we will not know until the following winter, which is too late for us. ***Here is how the graph gets us out of this dilemma*** – the graph has the estimated ***harvested acres*** incorporated into it. That means, that even though we use "planted acres" on the left side of the graph, the answers which we get from the graph is the corn production from the "harvested acres". The slanting lines in the graph make the transition from "planted to "harvested" acres.

Not only that, but the graph also takes into account the different yield rates which will occur as the amount of soil moisture varies. For example we cannot expect as good a yield when the weather has been dry, as we can expect when the weather has been average. To repeat, the graph has taken the various weather conditions into account.

Look at the slanting weather lines in the graph. Each line: ideal, average, semi dry, dry, and drought represent what you believe was the weather condition since last summer (You are doing this weather recall in April). Every serious grain trader keeps an eye on the weather conditions in the grain growing areas. All you have to do is to think back to last fall and ask yourself,"Was there average rainfall or less than average or no rain at all last fall?" Then consider the winter,"Was there an average amount of rain or snow, less than average or no rain or snow at all?" Then consider the months of March and April for the amount of rain. Sum it all up and use the final result to select one of the weather lines on the graph as being representative of the amount of moisture since last summer.

Example. The date is April 12th and the latest USDA crop report has just been released. It estimates that the corn planting intentions are 70 million acres. You think back over the amount of rain since last summer and you conclude that you will use the "semi dry" weather line in the graph because the weather, in your opinion, was drier than average but it couldn't be called a real dry condition.

Method. Locate 70 million acres at the left side of the graph. Move to the right to touch the "semi dry" weather line. Go directly down to the bottom line of the graph to read about 6880 million bu. as the estimated size of the corn crop when it is harvested in the fall.

To help you to select the correct weather line, the following definitions are used to describe each weather line.

Ideal Weather. It is the best kind of growing weather that anyone could hope for – it couldn't be better. The previous fall had average or ideal conditions, the winter moisture and temperature was almost perfect, and there was just the right amount of rain and sunshine during March and April to the date of the crop report. An ideal year doesn't occur often, only about 10% of the time.

Average Weather. This is the most common type of weather and it occurs about 50% of the time. The corn crop thrives quite well with average weather. It means that there was average moisture last fall and last winter had average snow cover and rain, and the rainfall so far in the spring was about average.

Semi- dry Weather. This is a moisture condition about halfway between average and dry weather. Often there are times when one can't say outright that the soil is dry, and one can't say that it is average either – so this line will be the one to use.

Dry Weather. Dry weather and semi- dry weather occur about 25% of the time. The term "dry weather" in this book has the following meaning: the previous summer had below average rainfall, the previous fall had only about 50% or less than the average rainfall, the previous winter had little snow or rain, the months of March and April had almost no rain.

Drought. A drought occurs about 15% of the time – about 3 years out of 20. The previous summer was a dry summer, there was no rain in the fall, the winter had only about 10% of the usual winter snow or rain, no rain in March or April. If these moisture conditions occur, get ready for a dramatic rise in corn and soybean prices – the price rise will occur early, likely in May and June.

You don't always have to use one of the weather lines – you can use some place between two of them. For example, suppose that you considered the moisture conditions to be just a bit drier than average, just a bit. Then you could select a spot about halfway between "average" and "semi- dry". You should be as accurate as possible in your estimate of the weather conditions – and that means that you will likely be choosing a spot between two of the weather lines. Some people might prefer to subscribe to the services of a private weather forecaster to get this information.

WHAT TO DO NEXT

We now can get an estimate of the size of the corn crop coming up. But it is not the size of the corn crop that we are really interested in – what we want to know is how will this new corn crop size affect July and December prices – will they rise or will they fall as a result of one new crop size? That is our goal – to be able to forecast the July and December corn prices early in the year, in April. If there is to be a dramatic price rise or fall, we want to be among the first to know – among the first to get in at the beginning of a price move.

What is going to happen now is this: you are going to use the estimated corn production which you obtained from the Corn Production Graph on a new type of graph which will enable you to get an estimated July and December corn price. Turn now to the following graphs which use the corn production.

THE CORN PRICE GRAPHS WHICH USE $\dfrac{\text{the new total supply}}{\text{the previous year's total use}}$

This is a different kind of price graph than the Forecasting Graphs. These new graphs forecast prices, too, but they tackle the problem from a different angle. The Forecasting Graphs used the carryover %. These new graphs don't use the carryover at all.

Instead, these new graphs use *the total supply of corn* on hand, before any sales are made, as the means for finding the July and December prices. This is a completely different approach to price forecasting. We use the corn production number which was obtained from the Corn Production Graph.

But you might think,"Two different methods of finding the corn price? Won't that cause confusion?" No, it has the opposite effect. One method of pricing should support the other. Two methods of pricing are better than one.

There is an advantage to having two methods of finding the estimated corn price. It is like having two grain experts to help you, each of whom uses a different method of price analysis. Each is a specialist in his own system. If you were to ask each of those two experts for his estimated price for Dec. corn, don't expect to get exactly the same price from each. It won't happen because there are two different methods of analysis being used. Let's say that one gave an estimate of $2.60 and the other gave $2.78 as his estimate. Who are you going to believe? You can't say that one of them is right and the other is wrong because, in this example, both are experts in his own system. What should be done? The best solution is to use an average of the two estimated prices.

Here is the theory behind this method of finding the estimated corn price.

1. There are two key expressions here. One is the **new crop year's total supply.** The other is the **previous crop year's total use.**

2. **New crop year's total supply.** The words "Total Supply" means the total amount of corn which is available for sale in the crop year. The total supply is made from two separate amounts of corn – the corn crop at harvest **plus** the carryover from the previous crop year. These two amounts of corn when added together, are called the **Total Supply** which is the total amount of corn which is available for sale during the new crop year.

3. **Previous crop year's total use.** The words "Total Use" mean the total amount of corn which used domestically as feed, seed, etc. **plus** the exported corn. These two amounts of corn when added together, are called the **Total Use .**

4. The next step is to compare the new crop Total Supply with the previous year's Total Use. Just by looking at the two numbers, you can see if there will be enough new crop corn on hand to meet all the sales and corn use of the previous crop year. For example, if the new Total Supply was only 7000 million bushels, and the last year's Total Use was 7500 mil. bu., then it is obvious that there will not be enough corn to meet the estimated demand in the months ahead – therefore, corn prices will rise through the roof . **At the other extreme,** let's say that the new Total Supply was 15,000 mil. bu. and the previous year's Total Use was 7500 mil. bu. In this case we have twice as much corn on hand as will likely be used or sold and that's very bearish news. Corn prices will sharply decline in the months ahead.

5. The paragraph above illustrates the **Idea** behind this method of price analysis. In brief, will there be enough corn on hand for the upcoming crop year to satisfy the demand?

6. One of the best ways to compare the new Total Supply with the previous crop year's Total Use is to make a percentage from them. A % is a handy method of comparison. For example, a 100% figure would tell you that there was exactly enough corn on hand to satisfy the demand – that's bullish news. A 90%, for example, would indicate that there was only enough corn on hand to satisfy only 90% of the likely demand – that's very bullish news. A 150%, for example, would indicate that there was a surplus of corn, that there was 50% more corn than would likely be sold – that's bearish news.

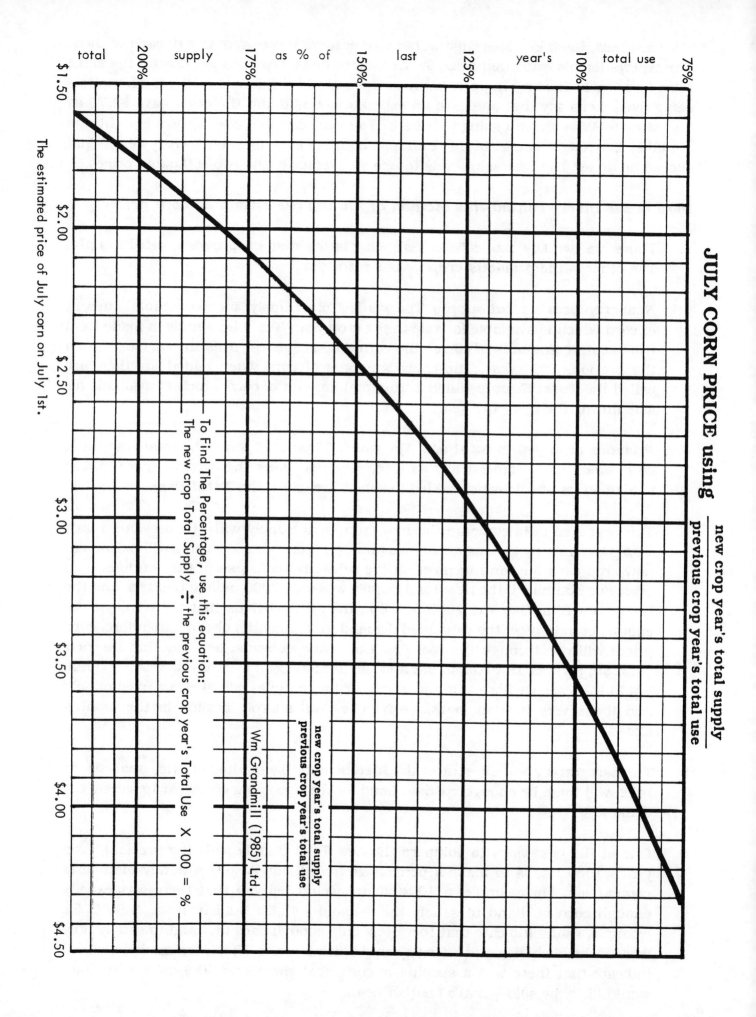

JULY CORN PRICE using
new crop year's total supply
previous crop year's total use

total supply as % of last year's total use

The estimated price of July corn on July 1st.

To Find The Percentage, use this equation:
The new crop Total Supply ÷ the previous crop year's Total Use × 100 = %

$$\frac{\text{new crop year's total supply}}{\text{previous crop year's total use}}$$

Wm Grandmill (1985) Ltd.

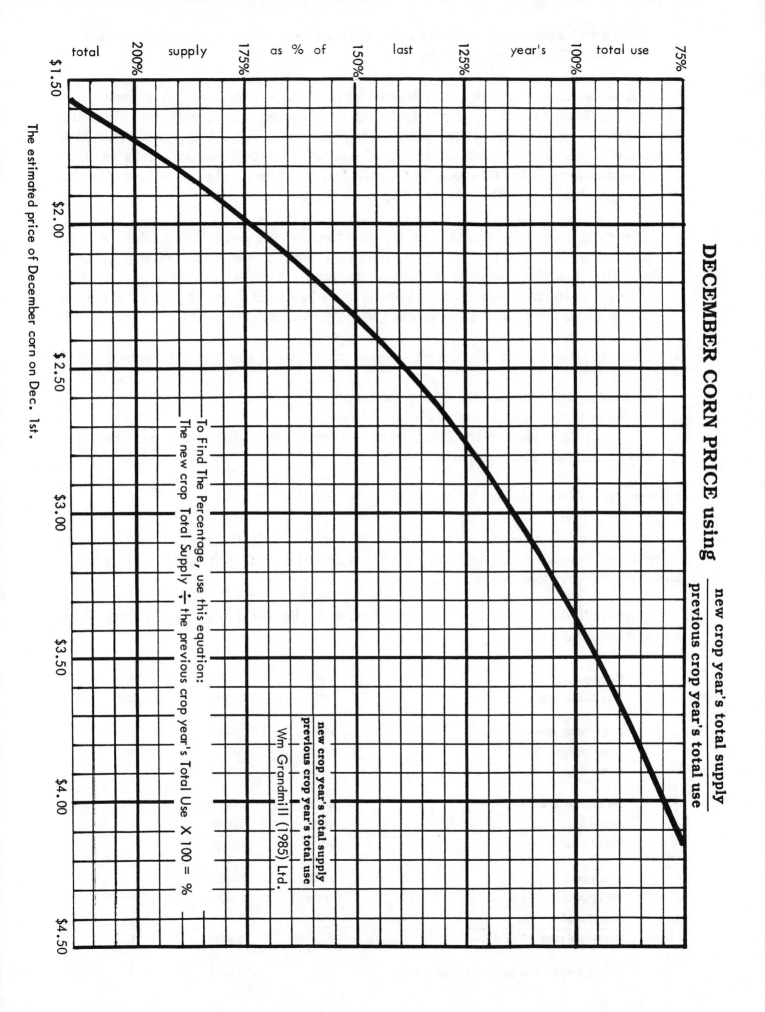

DECEMBER CORN PRICE using

new crop year's total supply
―――――――――――――――――――
previous crop year's total use

To Find The Percentage, use this equation:
The new crop Total Supply ÷ the previous crop year's Total Use X 100 = %

new crop year's total supply
―――――――――――――――――――
previous crop year's total use

Wm Grandmill (1985) Ltd.

The estimated price of December corn on Dec. 1st.

total use   75%   100%   year's   125%   last   150%   as % of   175%   supply   200%   total

$1.50 $2.00 $2.50 $3.00 $3.50 $4.00 $4.50

7. **Here's the equation for finding the percent:** new crop Total Supply ÷ previous crop year's Total Use x 100 = %

8. **Example.** Using the Corn Production Graph, let's say that we get an estimated crop of 7800 mil. bu. of corn. Let's say that the estimated carryover from the previous crop year was 1200 mil. bu. **Therefore, the Total Supply is 9000 mil. bu.** (7800 + 1200 = 9000). Looking at the previous crop year's data, let's say that the estimated **Total Use was 7500 mil. bu.** It's time to use the equation in the paragraph above: 9000 ÷ 7500 x 100 = 120%.

9. **The next step.** It is time to use the two new price forecasting graphs. Look at them now. Note the percentage numbers on the left side, the curved price line, and the corn prices on the bottom of the graph. One graph estimates the July corn price which is only about 3 months away (you will likely be using the graphs in April and May) . The other graph gives the estimated December corn price.

10. Let's find the estimated December corn price, using the 120% in paragraph 8 above.
    (a) Locate 120% at the left side of the graph.
    (b) Move to the right to touch the price line.
    (c) Go straight down to the bottom line to read about $2.85 as the estimated December corn price on December 1st.

It's Practice Time.

Below are the consecutive crop years X,Y, and Z with the supply and demand information for each crop year. Use the Corn Production Graph and the July price graph for the questions below.

Uses millions of acres and millions of bushels. Follow this on the graphs. Uses **average weather.**

Crop year	X	Y	Z
Planted acres	76	70	80
Beginning stocks	1320	2200	A
Corn production	7880	7250	B
Total Supply	9200	9450	C
Domestic use	5000	4950	
Exports	2000	1900	
Total Use	7000	6850	
Carryover	2200	2600	
Carryover % of use	31%	38%	
New Total Supply			
Previous year's Total Use		135%	D
July's estimated price from graph		$2.71	E

193

Look at the crop year Y in the supply and demand tables above. (a) Note that the Total Supply is 9450 million bushels. (b) Note that the previous crop year's Total Use was 7000 m.bu. (c) Therefore the % is: 9450 ÷ 7000 x 100= 135%. (d) Using 135% On the July price graph, we get about $2.71 as the estimated July corn price on July 1st.

Try these questions – use crop year Z in the table above.

(a) What number should be located in place A?
(b) Use the Production Graph to find the number for place B.
(c) What number should be in place C?
(d) What % should be in place D?
(e) What July price should be in place E?

Answers. (a) 2600 (b) about 8300 (c) about 10,900 (d) 159% (e) about $2.30

You now have the means to get into the corn market early. Check your calculations with each succeeding crop report because sometimes the USDA will alter the estimates.

BUYING OR SELLING A MARCH CORN FUTURE
ABOUT JAN. 2nd

Here is a small corn trade for those people who would like an automatic trade of short duration. It tested to be very profitable when checked by the corn data of the past 15 years.

This trade is based on pure corn fundamentals (but don't forget that corn prices are influenced a bit by the more overpowering soybeans) By the words "pure fundamentals" is meant (1) this trade is not affected by the weather (2) it functions completely on the carryover % during the short space of time (3) this trade will be too early to be affected by the planting intentions which are released in April (4) this 2 month period is one of the rare times when there are likely to be no disturbing outside influences.

Look at the March Corn Chart.

1. At the left side of the chart you will see the carryover %, in increments of 5%.

2. Along the bottom row you see the March corn price **on the day that you take the position.** (about Jan.2nd – right after the holiday of Jan. 1st).

3. In the body of the chart you see the words "buy" or "sell" or "neutral". The words "buy,sell" mean that you will buy or sell a March future position at those places.

   The word "neutral" means that there is neither a buy nor a sell opportunity there – it is too close to call. Do not take a position when the space is marked as neutral.

4. The farther that a buy or a sell signal is from the neutral area, the better the profit.

5. ***Example.*** The carryover is 20%. The price of March corn on Jan. 2nd is $3.50.

   Method.
   (a) Locate 20% at the left side of the chart.
   (b) Locate $3.50 at the bottom of the chart.
   (c) Move up from $3.50 to intercept the 20% row.
   (d) Read "Sell" at that juncture .
   (e) Sell a March corn future.

6. That was an easy example because it occurred along designated rows. But most often you will have to interpolate between two rows or columns.

BUYING and SELLING MARCH CORN on JAN 2nd

Carryover expressed as % of the total use	$1.50	$1.75	$2.00	$2.25	$2.50	$2.75	$3.00	$3.25	$3.50	$3.75	$4.00
5%	buy	buy	buy	buy	buy	buy	neutral	sell	sell	sell	sell
10%	buy	buy	buy	buy	buy	buy	neutral	sell	sell	sell	sell
15%	buy	buy	buy	buy	buy	buy	neutral	neutral	sell	sell	sell
20%	buy	buy	buy	buy	buy	neutral	neutral	sell	sell	sell	sell
25%	buy	buy	buy	buy	buy	neutral	neutral	sell	sell	sell	sell
30%	buy	buy	buy	buy	neutral	neutral	sell	sell	sell	sell	sell
35%	buy	buy	buy	buy	neutral	neutral	sell	sell	sell	sell	sell
40%	buy	buy	buy	neutral	neutral	sell	sell	sell	sell	sell	sell
45%	buy	buy	buy	neutral	neutral	sell	sell	sell	sell	sell	sell
50%	buy	buy	neutral	neutral	sell	sell	sell	sell	sell	sell	sell
55%	buy	buy	neutral	neutral	sell	sell	sell	sell	sell	sell	sell
60%	buy	neutral	neutral	sell	sell	sell	sell	sell	sell	sell	sell
65%	neutral	neutral	neutral	sell	sell	sell	sell	sell	sell	sell	sell
70%	neutral	neutral	sell	sell	sell	sell	sell	sell	sell	sell	sell
75%	neutral	neutral	sell	sell	sell	sell	sell	sell	sell	sell	sell

Wm Grandmill (1985) Ltd.

DIRECTIONS: The price of March corn on Jan. 2nd

(1) using the % carryover for the pertinent crop year, look to the right in the proper row (use the nearest row — for 33% use the 35% row). (2) Look at the price of March corn on Jan. 2nd, and move up vertically in the appropriate column (use the nearest price column — for a price of $2.90, use the $3.00 column). (3) At the juncture of (1) and (2) above, you will see whether you should buy or sell March corn — "neutral" means the prices are so similar it is not worth while doing it.

Here is a more difficult example. The carryover is 36% and the price of March corn on Jan. 2nd is $2.92.

Method.
(a) Change the % and price to the nearest designated row and column. In this example, use 35% and $3.00.
(b) At the juncture of 35% and $3.00 you see the word "sell".
(c) Don't expect a big profit here because it is next to a "neutral" area. Sell March corn.

7. ***What happened when this trade was tested with the past 15 years of corn data?***

    1. You would have been out of the market in 5 of the 15 years because you had settled on a "neutral" area.

    2. You would have **bought** March corn in 5 of the 10 years in which you were in the market.

    3. You would have **sold** March corn in 5 of the 10 years in which you were in the market.

    4. Each of the 10 years in which you were in the market earned an average gross profit of 22¢, in 2 months. A good profit.

    5. The maximum backup needed in all of the 10 years was only 7¢.

8. ***Do not use an option.***

    1. There are 2 strikes against an option in this trade.

        (a) The option cost will be about 7¢, which equals 1/3 of the profit.

        (b) You have the last trading day and the expiration day to contend with. That means that you would have to get out of the option soon after February 17th – and tests have shown that 1/3 of the gross profit can be made in the last 2 weeks of February – so you would lose another one third of the profit.

        (c) That leaves only a possible 1/3 of the profit, so it is not worth doing.

        (d) Use a March future with a 7¢ backup plus margin.

THE DECEMBER WHEAT/CORN SPREAD

A Few Facts About the Wheat/Corn Spread

Two spreads were researched (a) the Dec. w/c spread (b) the July w/c spread.

The theory behind the wheat/corn spread is sound. The theory behind the **December w/c spread** goes like this: the time is July and the winter wheat crop is mostly harvested and the wheat prices have likely touched bottom. The December wheat contract will likely stay flat for about another month, then start to rise to December. The corn does the opposite. The December corn price starts to decline usually, and reaches bottom in October and November usually. A perfect spread, theoretically, because wheat prices are rising and corn prices are falling from July to December. But it is not a perfect spread in real trading – rules must be followed .

The theory behind the **July w/c spread** is based on the belief that July wheat prices fall after Dec. 1st and bottom out in July, whereas July corn prices are believed to rise after Dec. 1st and peak in late June. This should make a profitable spread but real trading found it not to be very profitable.

The wheat/corn spread was thoroughly investigated from every angle, using the wheat and corn data of the past 15 years.

The research found that the **December w/c Spread** paid well if a few rules were followed. But the **July w/c spread** was unreliable no matter what tactics were used. Consequently the July w/c spread is not written up in this book – there is no point in putting your money in a spread which is not consistent. You should take a July w/c spread only if you have **strong evidence** that wheat prices are headed in one direction and corn prices are headed in the other direction.

But the December w/c spread was reasonably reliable and very profitable, when four spread rule were applied. (You will learn the 4 rules soon). When this spread was tested with the data of the past 15 years, here's what happened.

1. One year of the 15 years lost money – 14¢ was lost.

2. You would have stayed out of the spread in 2 of the 15 years because the potential profit was too small, and risky.

3. So you would have been taking a spread in 13 of the 15 years tested.

4. In 7 of those 13 years, you would have bought Dec. wheat/sold Dec. corn.

5. In 6 of those 13 years you would have sold Dec. wheat/ bought Dec. corn.

6. The average profit in each of the 13 years was 59¢, before commissions.

7. You need some backup money. Here's what happened in the 13 years of testing.
   (a) No backup at all was needed in 5 of the 13 years.
   (b) 10¢ backup was sufficient in 7 of the 13 years.
   (c) One year needed 24¢ as the maximum backup.

HOW TO TRADE THE DECEMBER WHEAT/CORN SPREAD

The December w/c spread is *taken about July 1st* and it can be held until December 1st but the peak profit of the spread might occur earlier, usually in late October or in November. (See the timing charts for both wheat and corn) There is a monetary advantage to taking your profit early if you can.

Wheat is the dominant grain of the spread for about 75% of the spreads – it usually sets the trend of the spread. Corn is the dominant grain of the spread during a drought or a dry spell – this is because wheat is usually being harvested just as a drought gets underway, whereas the corn crop is at a critical stage in its development and is seriously affected by drought and dry weather at this time.

How to trade the spread – follow these steps.

1. On July 1st note the present size of the Dec. w/c spread by doing this: *the Dec. wheat price – the Dec. corn price = the present size of the w/c spread.*

2. (a) Use the December Forecasting Graph to get the estimated price of Dec. wheat on December 1st.

   (b) Use the December corn Forecasting Graph to get the estimated price of Dec. corn on December 1st.

   (c) Do this to find the estimated size of the w/c spread on December 1st: *estimated price of Dec. wheat on December 1st minus the estimated price of Dec. corn on December 1st = the estimated size of the w/c spread on December 1st.*

3. Compare the *present spread* taken on July 1st, with the *estimated spread* of December 1st. Is the estimated spread of December 1st larger or smaller (wider or narrower) than the present spread of July 1st? This is important.

4. When you checked out the Dec. wheat on the December Forecasting Graph, did the estimated wheat price *rise* or *fall,* from July 1st to December 1st? This is important.

5. The two factors above (in paragraphs 3 and 4) are the keys to success for this spread. They are so important that you should read them again.

6. **Follow these rules.**

(a) **This is a strong indicator of a profit.**

(1) If the Dec. wheat price (as indicated by the Dec. Forecasting Graph) is estimated to **rise** to December 1st from the date when you took the spread about July 1st......

(2) **And** if the estimated w/c spread on December 1st is **larger** than the spread was when you originally took it about July 1st.....

(3) **Then buy Dec. wheat / sell Dec. corn.**

(4) The larger the estimated w/c December 1st spread is, compared to the size of the w/c spread about July 1st, then the larger will be the profit.

(b) **This is a strong indicator of a profit.**

(1) If the December Forecasting Graph shows an estimated **wheat price decline** from July 1st to December 1st......

(2) **And** if the estimated w/c spread on December 1st is **smaller** than the spread on July 1 st .....

(3) **Then sell Dec. wheat/buy Dec. corn.**

(4) The smaller the Dec. w/c spread is estimated to be on December 1st, as compared to the w/c spread on July 1st, then the greater the profit.

(c) **This is a weaker indicator of a profit,** but still worthwhile

(1) If the Dec. wheat Forecasting Graph indicates that the Dec. wheat will be **higher** in price on December 1st than it was on July 1st....

(2) **And** if the estimated Dec. w/c spread on December 1st is **smaller** than the spread was on July 1st **by at least 20¢......**

(3) **Then sell Dec. wheat/buy Dec. corn.**

(4) The 20¢ is a safety feature. This is a weaker spread situation than in (a) and (b) above – and if the spreads of July and December are nearly similar in size, then it is too risky to take.

(d) **_This is a weaker indicator of a profit_**, but still worthwhile.

    (1) If the Dec. wheat Forecasting Graph indicates that the Dec. wheat price will be **_lower_** on December 1st than it was on July 1st.....

    (2) **_And_** if the estimated Dec w/c spread on December 1st is **_larger_** than the w/c spread was on July 1st, **_by at least 20¢_**....

    (3) **_Then buy Dec. wheat/ sell Dec. corn._**

    (4) The 20¢ is a safety feature which should filter out any "too close to call" spreads.

7. **_More words of advice._**

This is an easy- to- do, very profitable spread. The investment is small .

This book suggests that you use a backup of 10¢ ($500) for all the Dec. w/c spreads. Only once in 15 years was more than 10¢ required as backup capital, and your broker will phone you for more money if that rare event occurs.

Another important observation was made as the Dec. w/c spread was being tested with 15 years of data. The observation was this: the size of the spread changes slowly and there are only minor fluctuations in the spread size. And sometimes your spread which already has a profit, will slowly start to go against you by decreasing in size. When this happens, liquidate the spread at the break even point because, in the past, if a spread started to lose money after being on the profit side, it never recovered and it always finished as a loser.

U.S. CORN	86/87	87/88	88/89	89/90* estimate	90/91	91/92	92/93	93/94	94/95
Beginning stocks	4040	4882	4260	1830	—	—	—	—	—
Production (mil.bu.)	8252	7069	4921	7540	—	—	—	—	—
Total Supply	12292	11951	9181	9370	—	—	—	—	—
Domestic use (feed,seed)	5906	5966	5510	5500	—	—	—	—	—
Total Use	7410	7691	7351	7500	—	—	—	—	—
Exports	1504	1725	1841	2000	—	—	—	—	—
Carryover	4882	4260	1830	1870	—	—	—	—	—
Carryover as % total use	66%	55%	25%	25%	—	—	—	—	—
Total Supply / Previous year's Total use	198%	161%	119%	127%	—	—	—	—	—

CHRONOLOGICAL ORDER

The investments which have been written up in the text are presented here in chronological order so that you will have an easy reference to their times of occurrence.

Date for taking position	Grain	Type of position	Type of graph or chart	Graph page	Liquidation date
Jan 2	corn	future	chart	196	March 1
Apr 15	wheat	future option	planted acres forecasting	51	July 1 Dec 1
Apr 15	soybeans	future option	planted acres forecasting	144	Nov 1
Apr 15	corn	future option	planted acres forecasting	186	July 1 Oct 15
May 15	soybeans	option	forecasting	108	Nov 1
May 15	soybeans	option	US, Brazil supply/use	139	Nov 1
June 15	soybeans	option	chart % change	151	Nov 1
June 15	corn	future option	forecasting	167	Oct 15
July 1	wheat/ corn	spread with futures	forecasting	199	Dec 1
July 15	wheat	future option	forecasting	35	Dec 1
Nov 15	soybeans	future	forecasting	111	May 1
Nov 15	corn	future option	forecasting	170	July 1
Dec 1	wheat	future	forecasting	36	July 1
Dec 1	soybeans Jul/Nov	spread	chart	157	July 1

THE CREAM OF THE CROP

La Crème de la Crème

A select group of investments is assembled here. They were selected as being superior to the other investments in this book. Here is how the selection was made.

Each investment was rated according to its profitability, in relation to each of the following: The maximum amount of backup needed to invest safely, the number of times that one was out of the market because the investment did not meet the rules of safety, the number of losses in the testing period of the past 15 years of data.

Each of the investments was given an A or a B rating, based on the criteria mentioned in the paragraph above. The following list represents the investments which earned an A rating.

But don't think that the B rated investments aren't worth doing! Sometimes a B rating will outperform an A investment. All the investments mentioned in the book are worthwhile. It's just that some are more worthwhile than others.

Important Note. There will be times when one or more of the elite investments will not be taken because it did not pass the standards for a safe investment. Looking back over the past 15 years of data, it shows that, on the average, each of the investments below would not have been taken because of the safety rules, in 4 years out of the 15 years tested. But even taking into account the times when one would be out of the market, this select group earned between 200% and 300% on the investment, as a whole, based on the prices of the past 15 years.

Date for taking the position	Grain	Type of position	* Estimated Profit	Maximum Backup or premium	Liquidation date
Jan 2	corn	future	22¢	$350	March 1
May 15	soybeans	option	72¢	40¢	Nov 1
June 15	corn	option	45¢	20¢	Oct 15
July 1	wheat/corn	spread	59¢	$500	Dec 1
Nov 15	soybeans	future	114¢	$3250	May 1
Dec 1	wheat	future	45¢	$1200	July 1
Dec 1	soybeans Jul/Nov	spread	68¢	$450	July 1

*This is the estimated average profit for each time that one was in the market.
On the average, one would have been out of the market in 4 of the 15 years.

204

To receive a FREE copy of our most recent
catalogue of investment books, please write to:

WINDSOR BOOKS
P.O. Box 280
Brightwaters, N.Y. 11718